Exemplary Teachers of Students in Poverty

Education and poverty exist in a highly contested relationship even in the developed world. On the one hand, educational outcomes seem solidly attached to socio-economic status (SES), and on the other, education is often cited as a way out of poverty. Success at de-coupling poverty from educational outcomes varies across the developed world. The issues connecting education and poverty are complex: the successful engagement of students from poor backgrounds involves a mix of public policy on poverty, public policy on education, and teacher action. This book focuses on a number of exemplary teachers who demonstrate a set of common pedagogical qualities, assisting them to work productively with persistent classroom challenges in low SES classrooms.

Exemplary Teachers of Students in Poverty shares successful classroom practice from schools serving diverse and disadvantaged communities, and stresses that opportunities in school can influence educational engagement and encourage students to achieve. The text locates itself in international debates about education and poverty, and reports on the *Teachers for a Fair Go* project – an Australian research project into the work of a number of teachers who were successful at engaging students from poor backgrounds. Issues covered in the book include:

- teaching in low SES communities;
- what exemplary teachers of students in low SES communities do;
- specific pedagogical approaches in literacy, ICT, creativity and culturally responsive practices;
- students' voices;
- the professional qualities of these exemplary teachers.

This book will greatly benefit researchers, teacher educators and trainee teachers, allowing them to gain a much deeper understanding of the issues, constraints and perspectives in teaching contexts across low SES communities.

Geoff Munns is a researcher at the University of Western Sydney, Australia, and leader of the *Fair Go Program*, actively working to make schools and classrooms more productive for students in poverty.

Wayne Sawyer is Director of Research in the School of Education at the University of Western Sydney, Australia, and a member of the Centre for Educational Research.

Bronwyn Cole is an Associate Pro Vice-Chancellor in Education at the University of Western Sydney, Australia, and a founding member of the *Fair Go Program*.

Exemplary Teachers of Students in Poverty

The Fair Go Team

Edited by Geoff Munns,
Wayne Sawyer and Bronwyn Cole

LONDON AND NEW YORK

First published 2013
by Routledge
2 Park Square, Milton Park, Abingdon, Oxon OX14 4RN

Simultaneously published in the USA and Canada
by Routledge
711 Third Avenue, New York, NY 10017

Routledge is an imprint of the Taylor & Francis Group, an informa business

British Library Cataloguing in Publication Data
A catalogue record for this book is available from the British Library

Library of Congress Cataloging in Publication Data
Exemplary teachers of students in poverty / edited by Geoff Munns, Wayne
Sawyer, Bronwyn Cole.
p. cm.
1. Children with social disabilities–Education. 2. Poor–Education.
3. Educational equalization. I. Munns, Geoff. II. Sawyer, Wayne. III. Cole,
Bronwyn.
LC4065.E94 2013
379.2'6–dc23
2012028245

ISBN: 978-0-415-53156-6 (hbk)
ISBN: 978-0-415-53157-3 (pbk)
ISBN: 978-0-203-07640-8 (ebk)

Typeset in Galliard
by FiSH Books Ltd, Enfield

MIX
Paper from
responsible sources
FSC® C004839
www.fsc.org

Printed and bound in Great Britain by
TJ International Ltd, Padstow, Cornwall

Contents

Contributors

Leonie Arthur is a Senior Lecturer in Early Childhood education and is Director of Academic Program: Early Childhood Education at the University of Western Sydney. Leonie has published widely in the areas of Early Childhood curriculum and young children's literacy learning. Publications include book chapters and journal articles on parents' perspectives on literacy learning, critical literacy and effective literacy learning environments.

Jon Callow is an experienced educator and teacher, having worked in primary schools, universities and in professional development for teachers. He currently teaches at the University of Sydney, in the areas of English and multiliteracies and he has worked alongside teachers in their classrooms, both in Australia and the United States. His research interests include visual literacy, children's literature, social justice and pedagogy, using digital media and promoting exemplary classroom literacy practices.

Bronwyn Cole has held a number of administrative positions at the University of Western Sydney. She is currently Associate Pro-Vice Chancellor (Education): Arts. She lectures, researches and writes about K-6 curriculum and pedagogy, particularly in the area of Social Sciences education, teacher pedagogy and student engagement.

Shirley Gilbert is a Gunditjmara woman. She has had a 20-year association with a broad range of NSW Aboriginal educational settings and organisations. She has worked on a number of key Indigenous consultations concerning both education and health preparing contributions and research for reports to government. She currently works in the School of Education at the University of Western Sydney in secondary teacher education with particular responsibility for Social Science areas, including Aboriginal Education.

Caroline Hatton currently works as Research Assistant and Project Officer for a number of university projects relating to pedagogy, pre-service teaching, assessment of teaching standards and development of cultural awareness and competency. She was a research assistant on the *Teachers for* *a Fair Go* project. Caroline remains interested in contributing to opportunities for teachers to engage in reflective practice and gain experiences that enrich teacher capability and commitment.

Margery Hertzberg is a Lecturer in the University of Western Sydney's School of Education. She lectures in ESL, Drama and Literacy across preservice and postgraduate programs. Her key research interest is in the area of educational drama and literacy. She is interested in how educational drama methodology enhances children's language and literacy development – particularly children learning English as an additional language.

Mary Mooney works at the University of Western Sydney in a range of areas in the field of education such as drama education, critical and creative pedagogy, effective teaching and positive behaviour for learning. She is Deputy Dean of the School of Education. Mary is interested in theoretical framings around the cultural practices of young people ranging from investigations into creative, digital and performative youth arts.

Geoff Munns principally researches into ways to improve social and academic outcomes for educationally disadvantaged students, including those from Indigenous backgrounds. Before working at the University of Western Sydney, Geoff had 25 years experience in schools serving poor communities as a classroom teacher, school executive and Principal. As a university researcher he has continued this strongly focused commitment to making schools and classrooms more productive for poor students.

Phil Nanlohy worked as a classroom teacher in inner city schools and as an advisor within the NSW Department of Education and Training for 15 years. For the last 20 years he has worked as a lecturer in the Primary Teacher Education program at the University of Western Sydney. He has worked across a number of content areas most recently with an emphasis on pedagogy and the use of information technologies within learning. His key areas of research are ICT and student engagement in low SES schools

Joanne Orlando lectures at the University of Western Sydney. She examines contemporary life through the lens of Information and Communication Technologies (ICTs) to understand how ICTs contribute to our actions, our knowledge and our identity. In particular, her research focuses on how ICTs sit alongside and against established social, cultural and pedagogical practices of teaching and learning.

Leonie Pares was a secondary English teacher in high school and English/Communications teacher in adult settings and has been a tutor in Education at the University of Western Sydney. Leonie was a research assistant on the *Teachers for a Fair Go* project.

Anne Power teaches Music Education in the School of Education at the University of Western Sydney. Anne is known for leadership in the field of professional practice. She has an extensive music teaching and research background.

Wayne Sawyer was joint Chief Investigator with Geoff Munns on the *Teachers for a Fair Go* project. His funded research project history has been largely in the field of effective teaching. Before joining the University of Western Sydney, he was a Head of English in Sydney's Western suburbs, an area of significant social disadvantage and where all of the metropolitan case studies in the *Teachers for a Fair Go* project are set. As well as effective teaching and pedagogy in low SES schools, he researches in the areas of secondary English curriculum, curriculum history and literacy policy.

Les Vozzo is a Senior Lecturer in the Badanami Centre for Indigenous Education at the University of Western Sydney where he has taught various undergraduate and graduate programs in teacher education for the past 15 years. Research interests include teacher professional learning, portfolio construction, science education and Indigenous education.

Katina Zammit is a Lecturer in English in the School of Education, at the University of Western Sydney, specialising in degrees in primary teaching. Katina has an extensive career in education, as a primary school teacher, a literacy consultant in Metropolitan East Disadvantaged Schools Program, as an adviser on state and national projects, and as an academic. Her research focuses on i) *the use of semiotics*, such as systemic functional theory (SFT) to inform praxis and the understanding of texts in context ii) *curriculum development* in schools and higher education focusing on the integration of information and communication technology and iii) *literacy pedagogy*, with a focus on multiliteracies/new literacies and the engagement of students.

Foreword

Professor Bob Lingard

This is an important book, indeed a much needed book at this time, with its focus on research-based pedagogies that make a difference in schools serving disadvantaged communities. Indeed, this is an especially important book at a moment when education policy has become central to economic policy with its focus on human capital and productivity in the context of a global economy, and growing inequality within and between nations. Contemporary schooling policies tend to neglect this context of growing inequality and neglect research findings of the kind reported in *Exemplary Teachers of Students in Poverty*, despite pervasive talk of the need for evidence-based (surely evidence-informed) policy. In a sense, for politicians the production of education policy has become too important to be controlled and framed by educators and educational researchers. Worse than this, many contemporary education policies, while arguing the centrality of teachers, also display a distrust of them and their professionalism. *Exemplary Teachers of Students in Poverty*, while specifically Australian in location, carries many transferable lessons for teachers and policy makers alike, especially for teachers working in schools serving poor communities and for policy makers concerned to ensure socially just schooling. This book provides a plenitude of resources of hope that schools might be sites of opportunity and meaningful education for all students towards more democratic and equal futures.

The contextual and policy realities alluded to above are experienced in vastly different ways in nations across the globe. The austerity policies in the UK and Europe have different impacts upon poor communities and the schools and teachers that serve them, than does the Australian context of comparative economic wellbeing. Nonetheless, inequality is also growing in Australia and is in some ways hidden by the growing economy, yet exacerbated by its patchwork character, whereby the resource rich parts of the nation are growing and other regions are in economic decline. Yet despite these differences, there is a hegemonic education policy discourse that circulates globally and that helps frame vernacular expressions of schooling policies within different nations. The OECD's Programme for International Student Assessment (PISA) and the International Association for the Evaluation of Educational Achievement's (IEA) Trends in International Maths and Science

Study (TIMSS) and Progress in Reading Literacy Study (PIRLS) have become important international comparative tests of the performance of schools and national schooling systems, and they are helping to construct a global education policy field and to circulate globalized education policy discourses. Related here has been the global reach of what Sahlberg (2011) has called GERM, the Global Education Reform Movement, manifest mainly in Anglo-American nations, but having effects elsewhere as well.

Sahlberg (2011: 103) lists the following as key elements of GERM: test-based accountability, prescribed curriculum, a focus on literacy and numeracy, encouragement of standardized teaching and learning and the borrowing of market-oriented reform ideas, for example, new managerialism, school choice and competition between schools. Accountability at a distance, based on high stakes testing, has become the norm with a focus on improving test scores and the shaming of poorly performing schools, most often those serving the most disadvantaged students. When consideration is given to context in that framework, it is about value-added effects of the school and teachers' work, which in a somewhat fatalistic fashion simply accepts that young people from poor families will not do well at school or at least will not do as well as their more affluent peers. GERM also impacts most negatively on schools and the work of teachers in disadvantaged communities. Writing about the USA, Linda Darling-Hammond (2010) has argued persuasively that the nation's future will be determined by what happens to the most disadvantaged through schooling. *Exemplary Teachers of Students in Poverty* shares that commitment for economic and, more importantly, ethical and moral reasons and suggests a way forward. The various chapters also assume a trust and respect for teachers, a feature that Sahlberg sees as a central productive feature of Finnish schooling, which he contrasts positively with the negative effects of GERM and its distrust of teachers.

International data and national performance data are together used to steer education policy in reductive ways through teaching to the test, teaching by numbers, scripted pedagogies, defensive teaching and the like. Any focus on disadvantaged students from poor communities and their schools is framed by this test driven accountability and likely to limit the intellectual demands made on students, exacerbating inequality in and through schooling. At a broader level there is an audit culture and the phenomenon of policy as numbers (Lingard 2011). Numbers reflect a limited and limiting political moment. There has been a weakening of political commitments and aspirations for a better, more democratic, more equal and fairer society since a global version of neo-liberal capitalism won the Cold War and continues to hold sway. At one level, politics has been reduced to the managing of the mundane everyday, leading to incremental reforms and a weakening of resources of hope for a better society.

Within this policy framework and socio-political reality, there has also been a policy disposition to decontextualize schools and to focus on teachers and their pedagogical practices as the way to better learning outcomes for students living in poverty. This stance places a very heavy burden on teachers, who simultaneously are being positioned by test-based accountabilities and a culture of performativity, a situation which scarifies their souls, as they feel they are inhibited from authentic practice, including pedagogies and assessment (Ball 2003). Teacher standards, performance pay, and new hiring and firing practices are all part of this decontextualized focus on teachers. Even the reading of performance data is done in this decontextualized way (see Condron 2011). Thus there has been a focus on Finland as a high performing nation on PISA, yet in attempts to borrow or learn from Finland, there has been no recognition that this is a comparatively equal society, one with a low Gini Coefficient of Inequality. Wilkinson and Pickett (2009) have clearly shown how more equal societies have better and more equal schooling outcomes, better health outcomes and better social policy outcomes. Redistributive policies are necessary to open up opportunities for poor communities and for schools serving those communities.

The sales success of John Hattie's (2009) *Visible Learning* is significant here. Hattie provides a most useful and comprehensive meta-analysis of the research on which in-school factors, largely teacher practices, have the greatest impact upon student learning. However, we should note that Hattie acknowledges that other contextual factors also affect student learning outcomes, including poverty; he simply notes that he is not dealing with those factors. However, he also acknowledges that these contextual factors might have greater effects than in-school factors. Yet his book has been read as furthering a policy stance that all that matters is teacher quality, often confused with the more important issue of teacher pedagogical practices, and that any focus on context and the need for broader redistributive policies is often deemed to be a 'cop-out' by teachers! While Hattie notes the significance of good pedagogies, he does not elaborate what these might be. *Exemplary Teachers of Students in Poverty* focuses on pedagogies that make a difference for schools in disadvantaged communities. Herein lies its important contribution.

Exemplary Teachers of Students in Poverty provides real resources for hope for teachers and schools located in poor communities in this socio-political context and at this current policy conjuncture, this neo-liberal policy moment. It is research-based and as such demonstrates the importance of educational research for improving educational policy and practice at a time when there have been attempts to reduce the definition of research topics in education as well as to narrow methodologies and theoretical frameworks. It exemplifies an ethical and committed practice of researching *with* schools, systems and teachers. This is real evidence to inform policy and practice. The book addresses the severe gap in educational outcomes created by poverty. It does so through focusing on exemplary teachers currently working in schools in communities made disadvantaged in New South Wales, Australia. While documenting a research-based model of a 'fair go' (a vernacular Australian aphorism) pedagogy, the book also acknowledges the pressing need for policies of redistribution and recognition: unlikely policy responses in the current neo-liberal era. However, it needs to be noted that the Rudd and Gillard federal Labor governments in Australia (2007–present) established a National Partnership Low Socio-economic School Communities program, which has redistributed substantial monies into schools serving poor communities (\$860 per student, each year for three years). Yet accountabilities in that redistributive program are linked to improved outcomes on high stakes testing, potentially reducing the width of pedagogies and curriculum open to such students.

The *Fair Go* pedagogies described in this fascinating book are empirically derived from the research reported throughout, but also grow out of earlier research literature. These are pedagogies that also recognize context and the significance of *Fair Go* teachers' scaffolding to a community, as well as the funds of knowledge that exist in all communities as a basis for scaffolding and effective teaching practices. Thus, unlike the contemporary de-contextualized political and policy focus on teachers and their pedagogies, *Fair Go* pedagogies involve the contextualization of their practices. These are highly cognitive, highly affective and highly operative practices that work on deep engagement and the building of caring and robust relationships between teachers and students. All of these exemplary teachers stress learning rather than behaviour control, focus on intellectual demand, create inclusive learning environments and predicate their pedagogies on the assumption that everyone can learn. Engagement is also seen to be a central first step in *Fair Go* pedagogies; this is a specific feature of effective pedagogies for students living in poverty. At the same time, *Fair Go* teachers continually reflect upon their practices and are supported by colleagues and through collaboration with leadership teams focused on leading learning. The research upon which this book is based was also done with these teachers as collaborators, as part of their own reflexive practice and development. This research *modus operandi* recognizes and operationalizes the recognition that teaching should be both research-informed and research-informing (Lingard and Renshaw 2010)

The Fair Go Team at the University of Western Sydney should be heartily congratulated on this research and its dissemination in *Exemplary Teachers of Students in Poverty*. It is also significant that the University of Western Sydney has made a concerted effort for the higher education of students from low SES backgrounds. While the cogent, research-based arguments presented throughout this book recognize the 'thisness' of each school and the specificity of their contexts, which *Fair Go* pedagogies take account of, there are insights for teachers everywhere. There are also important insights for policy makers who believe in the democratic and socially just potential of schooling for all. Such teachers and policy makers need to recontextualize the arguments and evidence in this book to develop *Fair Go* pedagogies in their own locations. This book acknowledges that schools cannot compensate for society. Yet, it also demonstrates that schools and exemplary teachers can make a difference. *Fair Go* pedagogies provide an approach to maximise teacher effects in schools serving poor communities. This book should be read by teachers, teacher educators, policy makers and politicians as the basis for sensible rather than 'cruel' optimism (Berlant 2011) regarding the possibilities of schooling for all students, especially those from disadvantaged backgrounds.

Professor Bob Lingard
School of Education and Institute for Social Science Research,
The University of Queensland

Acknowledgements

The Australian Research Council, under its Linkages program, funded the research reported in this book. The research reflects the continuation of a long-standing collaborative partnership between Priority Schools Programs and Equity Coordination (New South Wales Department of Education and Communities) and the Fair Go Team (School of Education, University of Western Sydney). Special thanks are due to the Priority Schools and Equity Coordination team: Kerry Johnson, Tracey Kick, Rani Lewis-Jones, Chris Murray, Mary-Lou O'Brien and Therese Weir. They are also due to the project manager Mona Shrestha, and our three outstanding team co-researchers, Caroline Hatton, Lynne Munsie and Leonie Pares. The Fair Go Team is indebted to the Principals and the students in the research schools, who gave their whole-hearted cooperation during the research. This research would not have been possible without the dedication and enthusiasm for making a difference that each of the co-researching teachers brought to their classroom pedagogies, and their willingness to share their practices and ideas with the wider educational community. We thank: Tammy Anderson, Susan Barrett, Josephine McKell (nee Camilleri), Mark Campbell, Rebecca Chandler, Georgia Constanti, Donna Deehan, Jo Fairclough, Kim Fraser, Ehab Gerges, Daniel Henman, Harmonie Husband, Kaili Iles, Vanessa Mah Chut, Chantal Mamo, Eve Mayes, Diane McCue, Nancy Morvillo, Jennifer Neradovsky, Margaret (Missy) Nicholls, Jodie Peart, Kate Pidgeon, Andrew Pryce, Bronwen Smith, Dan Sprange, Sonia Squires, Nicole Wade, Sarah Webb (nee Houghton). Finally, the team expresses its sincere gratitude to Professor Susan Groundwater-Smith (University of Sydney) for her critical friendship, insights and feedback. She helped us to 'go well'.

1   A fair go in education

Joanne Orlando and Wayne Sawyer

The West Wing: public policy and education

In the episode 'Full disclosure' of the US television series *The West Wing*, the mayor of Washington D.C. tells Democrat President Jed Bartlet that he (the mayor) has run out of options to improve schools in his district and wants to introduce a system of school vouchers,[1] which Republicans in Congress have offered to fund. Bartlet tells the mayor that giving out vouchers for enrolling students in private schools sends the message they have given up on public schools and that that could mean the end of such schools. The mayor reminds Bartlet that he (the mayor) is probably the only person in the room who actually went to public school, but, he (only partly) jokes, that was at a time before guns appeared in schools. Bartlet sees the Republican offer as politically motivated – a way of dividing the Democrats. The mayor acknowledges this, but replies that he doesn't know how to refuse the money since the Congressional money could actually help students and that the move would be popular with public school students who aspired to college. Bartlet asks his young, black, personal aide, Charlie Young, where he (Young) went to school. Young names a public school. The mayor, however, asks Young where he *wanted* to go to school. Young names a parochial school and explains that almost everyone there went to college, but that it was a school his family could not afford. Young affirms that he would have gladly accepted vouchers. Bartlet reluctantly agrees to the scheme and asks the mayor for assistance in convincing the rest of the Democrats.

The scenario highlights many of the issues public policy in education faces in many countries. The most obvious is the shortfall in educational outcomes created by poverty. Coupled with this can be a day-to-day grimness in many schools in poor communities even in relatively wealthy nations. A key issue is the political football that education becomes – especially education in low socio-economic areas – when parties exploit the state of schools as an opportunity for political one-upmanship. Competition between schools and positioning educational advantage as a matter of 'choice' begs the serious question of why all schools are not resourced – in the broadest sense of that term – so that all students could realistically choose to go to college. Why is it that the poorest communities – who can least afford to lose the opportunities presented by education – are, in many systems, allowed to be the poorest served? Why should the advantages facilitated by a good education be the subject of market forces? Bartlet questions whether taxpayer dollars should be directed to educational institutions which put themselves outside the 'public' sphere. He champions the importance of public education based on the moral imperative that the right to a good education ought not to be a matter of one's parents' financial status. He sees himself holding a long-term, principled view but the mayor faces the pragmatic reality that money is being made available that could advantage poor students immediately. That vouchers can make choice real for poor parents creates a conflict for the mayor. Bartlet's instincts rub up against Washington parents' immediate needs for their children. The mayor's gently delivered barb that he is the only one in the room who actually attended a public school also highlights the removal of political leaders from the personal experiences that create tensions around such issues of principle.

As it often is, *The West Wing* treatment of these issues was prescient. *The Washington Times* reports that when President Obama appeared on *The Today Show* in 2010, he was asked by a Florida teacher whether he thought his own daughters 'would get the same high-quality, rigorous education in a D.C. public school as compared to the very elite private academy they attend.' The real life President answered, 'No' and conceded that 'connections' and postal addresses can sometimes drive the range of options available as 'choice' (see *The Washington Times* 2011b). *The Washington Times* also reports that some months afterward, a black single mother in Ohio was jailed for 10 days for falsifying records by using her father's address to enrol her children in a school district away from her own public housing area. Undoubtedly, part of this mother's thinking was that in 2009, seventh-graders in her local school district scored 16 points below the state average in mathematics on standardized tests, 15 points below the state average in writing and 17 points below in reading. In the school district she desired for her children, seventh graders scored 16 points above the state average in mathematics, 14 points above the state average in writing and 13 points above in reading. A not irrelevant ingredient to this story was the fact that the mother was herself a student teacher and that, as a result of her conviction, would be unable to pursue her chosen career in Ohio. The case became a cause celebre for proponents of choice and competition between schools and for advocates of school vouchers (see, for example, *The Washington Times* 2011a, 2011b, 2011c).

This book is directly concerned with issues of equity for students who are from low socio-economic backgrounds, such as those highlighted in the *West Wing* scenario. It details a research project carried out in Australia among teachers of students from such backgrounds. It presents teachers who are highly effective in engaging students from low socio-economic communities with their education and it centres that effectiveness in their pedagogies. The book presents the teachers, the contexts in which they teach and, above all, their classroom practices. It argues that these teachers make a difference to their students' engagement with education because of these practices. However, we do not want to present a naïve view of the world in which educational success can somehow be removed from the socio-economic circumstances in which students find themselves. Therefore, in this chapter, before outlining the case for the book, its assumptions, and the research on which it is based, we want to pick up on some of the issues raised by the *West Wing* scenario and contextualize the work within larger international issues of the relationship between socio-economic status (SES) and educational success.

SES and student outcomes: an international comparison

The Programme for International Student Assessment (PISA) presents one kind of picture of how nations fare in relation to each other in terms of student achievement, socio-economic status and equity outcomes. PISA is subscribed to by the 34 OECD member countries and (in 2009) 41 partner countries/economies and uses an index of economic, social and cultural status (ESCS[2]) to draw correlations between aspects of advantage or disadvantage and academic achievement across its member countries. In reading, for example, across OECD countries in 2009, a student from a more socio-economically advantaged background outperformed a student from an average background by 38 score points, or about one year's worth of education. On average across OECD countries, a 14 per cent difference in student reading performance is associated with differences in students' socio-economic background. In Hungary, Peru, Bulgaria and Uruguay, more than 20 per cent of the difference in student performance is associated with differences in background (OECD 2010a: 14). Other results that can be related to relative disadvantage include:

- students from single-parent families scoring five points lower than students from other types of families – a particularly large gap of 23 points being evident in the United States (OECD 2010a: 46);
- students in city schools outperforming students in rural schools by 40 points, or the equivalent of one year of education (OECD 2010a: 49).

Internationally, then, does SES = educational destiny?

These results seem to simply confirm a kind of social determinism around educational disadvantage. The PISA 2009 report stated that 'the socio-economic background of students and schools does appear to have a powerful influence on performance' (OECD 2010a: 13). The moderation of the language here masks what is usually a taken-for-granted area of educational research. And yet, with equity gaps an almost universal 'given', what would seem to be of most interest are those systems in which equity gaps are significantly less than in other systems. Canada, Finland, Japan, Korea and the partner economies Hong Kong-China and Shanghai-China all perform well above the OECD mean performance in reading and students tend to perform well regardless of their own background or the school they attend (OECD 2010a: 13). In Finland, Japan, Turkey, Canada, Portugal and Singapore, between 39 per cent and 48 per cent of disadvantaged students are what PISA refers to as 'resilient' (they come from the bottom quarter of the distribution of socio-economic background in their country and score in the top quarter among students from all countries with a similar socio-economic background). In Korea and Macao-China 50 per cent and 56 per cent of disadvantaged students respectively can be considered 'resilient', and this percentage is 72 per cent and 76 per cent in Hong Kong-China and Shanghai-China, respectively (OECD 2010a: 13). In Belgium, Finland, Germany, Greece, Iceland, Ireland, Israel, the Netherlands, Poland, Sweden, the United Kingdom and the United States, the phenomenon of rural/city difference is not observed (OECD 2010a: 14). In Austria, Slovenia, Portugal and Switzerland, about 15 per cent of students live in single-parent households and there is no marked difference in their performance compared with students from other family structures – while in Estonia, students from single-parent families actually perform better than students from other family structures after accounting for socio-economic background (OECD 2010a: 46).

What happens in countries that run against the SES trends?

A feature of countries that run against the equity gap trend is the comprehensive nature of their education system and equitable access to high quality education. The school systems that are more likely to perform above average in PISA and show below average socio-economic inequalities (OECD 2010b: 13) are school systems in which all students, regardless of their background, are offered similar opportunities to learn. That is, socio-economically advantaged and disadvantaged students attend the same schools and students rarely repeat grades or are transferred out of schools because of behavioural problems, low academic achievement or special learning needs. Among the school systems with above-average performance and below-average socio-economic inequalities, none show high levels of student differentiation. However, among the school systems with high average performance but comparatively large socio-economic inequalities, Belgium, the Netherlands and Switzerland routinely select and sort students into schools, programs or grades. This suggests that the level of differentiation is not closely related to average performance, but does relate to socio-economic inequalities in education (OECD 2010b: 27).

A second feature of schooling systems that demonstrate both high performance and equity from PISA 2009 is related to high levels of school autonomy in formulating curricula and using assessments with low levels of school competition. The results from PISA 2009 show that school systems that grant individual schools authority to make decisions about curricula and assessments, while limiting school competition, are more likely to be performing above the OECD average and show below-average socio-economic inequalities. Many school systems with high average performance but comparatively large socio-economic inequalities tend to allow higher levels of school competition (OECD 2010b: 27). Perry (2008) discusses similar trends in earlier versions of PISA such as: the relation between school selectivity and social inequality; the relation between differentiated curriculum and socio-economic inequality, and increases in mean school SES being associated with consistent increases in academic achievement. Perry concludes that 'results from PISA suggest that educational inequality can best be tackled by making schools more similar to each other in terms of curriculum, resources, and students' (2008: 83).

What is 'fair' in education?

These results make one consider what is a fair education system and why this concept seems to be compromised in various approaches to education around the world. The research project which is detailed in this book focuses on the concept of a 'fair go' in education. One of the things we ask in this book is how can we position a 'fair go' as a central concern in education and what makes a 'fair-er go' in schools for low SES students.

A 'fair go'

A 'fair go' is an Australian idiom referring to equity. Appeals for a fair go are appeals to give someone 'a chance', an opportunity. The online dictionary *msn Encarta* gives two related definitions: 'a reasonable chance' and 'an appeal for just treatment' (*msn Encarta* 2009). 'Go' as a noun itself sometimes picks up the meaning of 'chance', 'opportunity', which is related to its meaning as turn-taking and hence, perhaps inherently, to even-handedness. There may even, then, be a sense in which a 'fair go' is sometimes a tautology – in Australia, to 'give someone a go' can itself refer to giving them a fair chance.

In Australian English, the coincidence of appeals to moderation and justice in the phrase 'fair go' are perhaps telling. To seek a 'fair go' is to seek equity, but also to make in effect a modest claim. 'Fairness' has its origins in 'even-handedness' (itself an idea derived from the notion of 'morally pure', which one can see, in turn, as connecting to the early sense of 'fairness' as 'physically unblemished'). There is, then, an understatedness about seeking a 'fair go' in the world, a diffidence about the demands the phrase makes. The Bastille might be stormed in the name of *egalite*, but possibly not for a 'fair go'.

It is hardly news that in an age in which the grand narrative is the market, 'a fair go' can often run a poor second place. In 1995, the United Nations World Summit for Social Development adopted the Copenhagen Declaration, a significant statement committing governments to a number of social goals. To implement these goals, Denmark organized the Copenhagen Seminars for Social Progress. The Copenhagen Seminars argued that 'there is no example in human history of a laissez faire political philosophy bringing more equality and more fraternity' (Baudot 2001: 52). Because many governments feel duty-bound to favour market conditions above regulation, the Copenhagen Seminars were moved to argue that fundamentally

> there appears to be in the world in general ... a weakening of the principle and objective of equality... the reduction of inequalities (is) no longer (a) major objective ... of most governments.
>
> (Baudot 2001: 18, 64)

A 'fair go' and education

This 'neoliberal social imaginary' (Rizvi and Lingard 2010) which characterizes contemporary globalization clearly also characterizes education policy in its wake. One clear consequence of this in English-speaking countries such as England, the USA and Australia has been the increasing marketization of education in the name of consumer choice (for the US, see Ravitch 2010). It is as if putting in place 'choice' is, of itself, the central public service that governments can perform. If particular groups in society, such as the poor, suffer disproportionately in marketized education regimes, it is simply because of making the wrong choices by keeping their children within 'underperforming' schools (Apple 2001: 60). In such a scenario, governments act as if choice is equally available to all, whereas in education, marketization has largely benefited those who are already advantaged (Rizvi and Lingard 2010: 41; Ball 2002). On the other hand, Perry argues that PISA shows that 'Promoting parental school choice within a comprehensive, undiversified system may actually lessen educational inequality by reducing school segregation by SES' (2008: 83). In the context of Perry's whole analysis, the qualifying phrase 'within a comprehensive, undiversified system' is absolutely central to this conclusion because

> PISA suggests that educational inequality can best be tackled by making schools more similar to each other in terms of curriculum, resources, and students. Specific measures include reducing curricular differentiation between and within schools, reducing institutional diversification, reducing the ability of schools to select students, promoting inclusive (non-segregated) schooling, and providing an equitable distribution of resources.
>
> (Perry 2008: 83)

It is easy to simply conceptualize the role of government in the neoliberal economy as 'getting out of the way' of the market. In fact, capital needs governments to create optimal market conditions in its favour. Moreover, and paradoxically, the operation of the market in education depends for its success on the growth of the 'audit state' (Power 1997). Those countries such as England, the USA and Australia, which have elected to increasingly marketize education, have at the same time used extensive auditing regimes in the name of both operationalizing 'choice' and making teachers account-able. These regimes include extensive high-stakes testing and the creation of public league tables of schools' results – league tables that usually reveal much more about the socio-economic status of a school's community than about the quality of its teaching.

High-stakes testing and league tables may be set in place to serve the cause of choice, but in themselves do nothing to close the equity gap in a country such as Australia, which, in reading literacy, is regarded as 'high quality–low equity' in the terminology of PISA (see, for example, Council for the Australian Federation 2007: 12). When *The Washington Post* used the case of the Ohio mother cited earlier in this chapter to argue for school vouchers and 'to bring competition to the system' so that parents have 'the chance to move their children to the school of their choice', their argument was based on the fact that American students were 'behind' a series of nations which included Canada, Estonia and Finland (*The Washington Times* 2011a). These three countries (along with Iceland, Japan and Norway), in fact, are charac-terized by PISA as offering 'limited school choice to parents and students', while performing 'above average' and showing 'below-average socio-economic inequalities' (OECD 2010b: 27).

Australia likes to pride itself on being the land of the 'fair go', but policy discourse around social equity can often be effectively closed off simply by accusing those who open such a debate of the 'politics of envy'. In Australia, the hold of the 'neoliberal social imaginary' has, along with many other countries, shifted the 'view of education from being a benefit to the whole community to providing a positional advantage for individuals' (Bonnor and Caro 2007: 31). Bonnor and Caro (2007) detail the effect on public educa-tion of shifts in national government spending in a number of years up to their time of writing. Erebus International shows that by 2005, the effect of the overall mix of policies driving the marketization of education in general in Australia had been 'greater socio-economic segregation...in which the average socio-economic status of advantaged schools (was) increasing' (Erebus International 2005: 13; see also Bonnor and Caro 2007: 116). It is a situation which has led to the 'transfer of the effects of socio-economic status from the individual level to the school level' (Erebus International 2005: 13). Thus, Australia has moved towards increasing school segregation by SES. To be fair, we should note that the current national government has distributed extensive funding to schools in low-SES communities to be continued until 2015 and, at the time of writing, national and state governments in Australia are debating a major revision of school funding which may further support such schools. Nevertheless, Australian education is increasingly segregated by SES and marketized, with the accompanying drivers of high stakes testing and publication of schools' results.

The schools we represent in this book sit in communities that are in the lowest socio-economic strata of the state of New South Wales (NSW) in Australia (see Vinson 2007: 71–74). They experience from the inside the reality that 'concentration of disadvantage rather than disadvantage *per se* is the significant driver of educational under-performance' (Erebus International 2005: 15). The educational effects of poverty are exacerbated when everyone around you is also poor, such concentration being generally a strong predictor of average school performance (Holmes-Smith 2006). This is part of the background against which the teachers in this book are working.

As we have seen, success at de-coupling SES from educational outcomes varies across the OECD, with some countries better at it than others. There are education systems around the world in which the educational equity gap is smaller than in other places, and this is achieved with no loss of 'excellence'. The strategies used by these countries give a strong sense that any determinism of low SES can be ameliorated with concerted action. That action has to begin with government policy. However, while this book does not shy away from the complexity of the structural factors that influence educational outcomes for low SES students, it does take seriously the notion that teachers also make a difference for those students.

Work by Newmann and Associates (1996), Hill and Rowe (1996), Creemers (1996), Darling-Hammond (2000), and Hattie (2003) has highlighted the importance of classroom teaching on student academic performance in general. Teachers have also been shown to make a difference specifically for students who live in poverty (Haberman 1995; Hayes *et al.* 2006). Addressing the equity gap in education requires a mix that includes public policy on poverty, public policy on educational equity and teacher action in the classroom. This book recognizes the complexity of that mix, but focuses on one key area within it: the area of teacher action.

The project: *Teachers for a Fair Go*

This book, then, reports on a research project carried out in NSW, Australia, which set out with four aims:

1   To research and develop criteria to identify teachers who were making a positive impact on the engagement with schooling of students from low SES backgrounds across early (pre-school to Year 4), middle (Years 5 to 8) and later (Years 9 to 12) stages of schooling, and in a variety of rural and urban contexts.

2   To use these commonly agreed on criteria to select 30 teachers (15 rural and 15 urban) who were considered to be 'exemplary' teachers at

engaging students from low SES backgrounds with their education (the project aimed to identify 'exemplary' teachers across a range of contexts, rather than claiming these were the 30 'best' teachers of such students).

3   To undertake intensive case study research into the classroom pedagogies of these teachers, exploring the causal impact of their work on the engagement and social and academic outcomes of their students. The selection of the teachers acknowledged that there are different ways towards engagement and toward equitable social and academic outcomes and that these are highly dependent on context. The aim was to capture both the fine distinctions between, and the commonalities among, these exemplary teachers.

4   To explore the personal and professional journey that had brought each of them to their (current) pedagogical position.

One of the unique aspects of the project was the role of teachers as researchers of their own and others' practice. This aspect of the methodology is elaborated in Chapter 2.

The project was entitled *Teachers for a Fair Go* and, as these aims show, the key concept with which it began was that of student engagement. High levels of high quality engagement are at the core of educational success. The adjectives in that last sentence are important. Worthwhile educational outcomes probably depend most fundamentally on students being engaged by their education, but that engagement cannot simply be about compliantly operating on low-cognition tasks. The engagement we were interested in was engagement that was deep and committed and grappling with tasks and ideas that made commitment worthwhile. A discussion of this approach to engagement is contained in Chapter 2, in which we discuss the theoretical framing of the project.

The project was funded by the Australian Research Council under its Linkages scheme, which funds research with industry partners. The 'industry partner' for *Teachers for a Fair Go* was the Priority Schools Program (PSP) of the (then) New South Wales Department of Education and Training (NSWDET). The PSP gains its very raison d'etre in setting out to narrow the equity gap for public school students in the poorest communities of NSW. To this end the program allocates considerable resources and energies to the professional development of teachers in the (then) 574 Priority Schools across the state (411 rural and 163 urban). The PSP is committed to addressing the educational effects of entrenched poverty through its work in schools and the Program's administrators see classroom pedagogy as fundamental to their work: students from low SES backgrounds might need smaller classes and other forms of support, but they certainly need, and deserve, good teachers. The PSP motto is 'Fair go, Fair share, Fair say, Fair content'. Teachers on the project all worked in Priority Schools. As will be seen, they themselves were advocates for a 'fair go', committed to creating opportunities for students from low SES backgrounds and particularly to addressing any entrenched cycle of low expectations.

There is diversity in low SES communities and their schools and the teachers we discuss here worked in diverse contexts. If life can sometimes be difficult in these schools, it is so in different ways and these differences are discussed in detail in Chapter 3. The schools in the project embodied many tensions and dilemmas. However, we believe that our research shows that it is possible to 'disturb and disrupt' current understandings of what schooling for low SES students is about. We show that these students' 'funds of knowledge' can be recognized and respected. This is not a book designed to romanticize poverty, but to acknowledge the ways in which it is possible for school communities to resist simple stereotypes.

Exemplary teaching: professional practice

We think of pedagogy as professional practice. There is a substantial body of literature characterizing effective practice. Some research focuses on the technical aspects of teaching, commonly associating effective practice with classroom climate, teaching strategies and attitudes towards students (Martin 2002; Rowe 2003; Ayres *et al.* 2004; Sawyer *et al.* 2007). Key factors include: knowledge of content; the ability to make relevant content selections, and knowledge and practice of pedagogies that motivate, engage and commit students to learning (Alton-Lee 2003; Fair Go Project Team 2006; Fouts 2003; Hayes *et al.* 2006; Newmann and Associates 1996; OECD 2005; Rowan *et al.* 2004). Zammit *et al.* (2007) show that teaching influences student learning in positive ways when it is flexible, creative and adaptable, and employs a range of practices and resources that take into account different student needs and expectations and contexts of schooling. Teachers' personal qualities, relational qualities and their professional learning form a further domain of influence (Darling-Hammond 2000; OECD 2005; Hargreaves 2000). Exemplary practice has also been theorized in terms of how responsive a teacher is to the context in which they teach: high quality teaching is marked by serious interaction with the contextual and professional factors that influence student and school outcomes (ACDE 2004; Blackmore 2004; Law 2003; Luke 2004).

In a broader sense, Kemmis (2009) closely examines the ways in which practice can be characterized as: performance; behaviour; patterns of social interaction; intentional actions, and language, discourses and traditions. What we hope to demonstrate in this book is that these teachers 'cut through' the low expectations and constrained curriculum that are so often related to young people from low SES communities, to develop a different set of practices. Their practice, developed in the course of teaching young people 'well', (Kemmis 2009) is a morally committed response to challenging circumstances. Throughout, therefore, we try to foreground the practice behaviours of the teachers.

As we outlined above in stating the aims of the project, our central focus here is on student engagement. The operation of pedagogical expertise, responsiveness to context and commitment to student engagement is manifested in exemplary practice. In a challenging low SES environment, being an 'exemplary teacher' involves a far greater array of factors than level of teacher qualifications, years of experience or academic ability (OECD 2005) – important as these undoubtedly are (Darling-Hammond, 2000, 2010). Haberman argued in his classic text, *Star Teachers of Children in Poverty* (1995), that teachers who are successful with students from poor backgrounds possess particular characteristics, such as tolerance, optimism, good communication skills and openness to ideas. This study builds on the work of Haberman by looking to those professional practices which teachers draw on and develop to facilitate successful engagement in low SES contexts. We ask what important pedagogical practices are used by teachers that produce engagement with education for students in low SES settings.

Over thirty years ago, Lortie (1975) argued that teachers' work was not transparent – that there was so much going on behind the desk that was never seen. Similarly, Bransford *et al.* (2007) draw a parallel between teachers and orchestra conductors in that one only ever observes a conductor conducting, which is the end product of much prior planning, creativity and knowledge vital to the music being produced. By undertaking contextualized investigations of their pedagogies, and probing influences on their professional growth, this project sought to gain insights into the complexity of how teachers can achieve more socially just outcomes from schooling. Importantly, the study provides evidence that student engagement is not just a result of happenstance.

Just as low SES contexts are diverse, so, too, are exemplary practices in those contexts. Effective teachers understand the wide diversity of lived experiences across and within low SES communities and they develop different practices as locally produced solutions to the unique challenges of their context. Nevertheless, this research shows that there are important shared pedagogical themes among this group of exemplary teachers, and reflecting on these offers an opportunity to further consider what might make the educational difference for students from low SES backgrounds.

It is not our intention to discuss in any great detail in this chapter the pedagogy of these teachers. That is done in the rest of the book. However, a few introductory themes are worth touching on:

- The teachers' pedagogy centered on learning, not behaviour control, and this was a message that their students received. How this was achieved, of course, is the subject of later discussion. These teachers manage to convey an expectation to students that learning is important and that neglecting learning is an opportunity lost. They stimulated and sustained ongoing classroom conversations about learning and how to learn.
- Rather than limiting the content with which the students worked, these teachers focused on high cognition tasks. Public testing results in low

SES locations often lead to limiting the content with which low SES students work – more practising of the test, in order to improve test results (see, for example, Luke 2010).

- The teachers established an inclusive learning environment that communicated the idea that everyone could achieve. This runs against the trend of disengaging messages which students from low SES communities are historically more likely to receive from their schooling (Munns, Lawson *et al.* 2006)
- The teachers carried out continuous and systematic reflection on their own practice.

The teachers were selected because they were bringing important ideas to what it means to be a good teacher. The reflection of experienced teachers can often be informal and intuitive (Smith *et al.* 2009), however the teachers in this project consciously developed their teaching in ways responsive to their students' needs. They reflected on and frequently problematized their own teaching, gathering relevant data (such as relevant literature, the work of other educators, their tacit and formal knowledge of low SES discourses) and tested this against their vision of learning. Reflection was not a separate aspect of their teaching but was constant and embedded and facilitated the 'reframing' (Schon 1983) of practice. The process of reflection can be understood as an ethical enquiry into the professional dilemmas they, as practitioners, were seeking to improve in their practice (Kemmis 2009; Dahlberg and Moss 2005). The teachers also therefore trusted themselves as agents of change. They were articulate about their work and this deliberateness is a recurring theme throughout the book.

We do not want to romanticize these teachers or their students. Rather we want to put the strong emphasis on *practice* as manifested in their classrooms. The classrooms we describe may often seem like idealized sites far removed from the kinds of challenging circumstances we describe in Chapter 3. Some readers may be tempted to reject the practices we outline as emanating from classrooms that bear no resemblance to those in which they themselves work. However, we want to remind readers here – as we will throughout the book – that these classrooms were in some of the poorest communities in Australia. Life can often be very tough in these communities and, indeed, as we have said, can be difficult in these schools. If the classrooms we describe do not seem to fit the stereotypes of such communities and schools, that has much to do with the conditions created by teacher practice as we describe it here. That these teachers were highly successful in engaging their students came after much intellectual work on making connections between their students, the curriculum and their own pedagogy. This also meant that the teachers had thought carefully about preventing the behaviours that might interfere with learning before these behaviours manifested. Our key message is that this prevention did not entail a 'lesser' busywork curriculum for their students. In fact, as we show, the reverse was true.

Challenge

Finally, these teachers have a strong sense of advocacy for their students. The notion of 'challenging' need not always simply mean 'difficult'. 'Challenge' carries with it the sense of 'a call to engage'. The teachers in this project were working with those issues which teachers in many low SES areas face, and which we have been referring to as 'challenging'. However, they saw these challenges as a call to engage, viewing challenge as an invitation to develop their skills, knowledge and practices. They appeared to enjoy the challenge and satisfaction of getting at the heart of a problem and solving it. We saw them as 'creative', using that word consciously to describe an intellectual, deliberative process, not a moment of genius. The call to engage was also set to their students – challenge being presented as crucial to learning. They saw their own work in terms of intellectual, creative and deliberate action and set out to facilitate that mindset in their students. Crucially, what will become evident in this book is the sense the teachers had of working with their students in a 'long project'. They were not expecting quick outcomes or simple solutions, since good pedagogy attached to developing relationships takes time and the acceptance of this commitment was reflected in their attitude to challenge.

Notes

1   Vouchers are a system whereby funding follows students rather than going directly to schools. The key plank in the system is parental choice of school. Schools which are well subscribed become well funded. Schools with fewer students opting in lose commensurate funding. Vouchers work differently in different countries, but in the US are mainly framed as opportunities for students from low SES backgrounds to attend private schools.

2   ESCS is derived from the indices of: highest occupational status of parents; highest educational level of parents in years of education and home possessions (the latter itself derived from a further set of indices, including measures such as number of books in the home).

2   Student engagement

The research methodology and the theory

Geoff Munns and Wayne Sawyer

The *Fair Go Program*

The project *Teachers for a Fair Go* set out to pay close attention to exemplary teaching practice in low SES school communities. What successful teachers in such schools do in their classrooms is an important story that needs to be told in a thorough and comprehensive way. In fact, *Teachers for a Fair Go* sits within a larger program of research that we have come to call the *Fair Go Program* (*FGP*). The *Fair Go Program* of research has investigated the relationship between teachers' pedagogies and student engagement for over ten years. The stories about teaching reported in this book reflect this research concentration on the practices of teachers identified for their engaging pedagogies, and who have committed themselves to improved social and academic outcomes for students who live in poverty. There are three sections in this chapter. The first is a description of the research processes used in the collection and analysis of data in *Teachers for a Fair Go*. The second is the story of the historical development of theory on student engagement and the framework that was used in the collection and analysis of data in the *Teachers for a Fair Go* project. The third section describes how this theoretical framing was used in *Teachers for a Fair Go*.

Conducting the research in *Teachers for a Fair Go*

As outlined in the previous chapter, the *Teachers for a Fair Go* project set out to find 30 teachers in Priority Schools across NSW, Australia, who were highly successful in engaging their students. These teachers were to represent classrooms from the early (pre-school to Year 4), middle (Years 5 to 8) and later (Years 9 to 12) stages of schooling, with equal representation from rural and urban schools. The research was not attempting to find the thirty 'best' teachers of students in poverty in NSW, but rather a selection of highly accomplished engaging teachers across a range of contexts.

Selecting the teachers

In order to research and develop criteria to identify teachers, data was used from state and national testing results, using the notion of 'value-added' (the schools making the most difference in students' literacy and numeracy scores and in high school subject results). Early conclusions were that this was not going to yield results. Even if we could identify schools (or subject faculties) from this data, identifying the teachers responsible for the results would not necessarily be possible from the available data. The decision was made to adopt a process of nomination. Nomination had the added advantage of allowing nominators to define in their own terms what successful engagement meant. In effect, the project was allowing the criteria to develop themselves, as previous experience had suggested that 'local knowledge was good knowledge' and that people 'on the ground' would recognize strong engagement when they saw it. This turned out to be a correct assumption. Aware of the dangers of nomination, a number of constraints were built in that also acted as data triangulation. Nominations came from Principals, local (regional) educational consultants and professional associations. A number of teachers nominated themselves. Nominators had to supply reasons for their nominations and two referees had to be prepared to speak up on behalf of nominees. These were 'vetted' to achieve the desired range of contexts and then teachers were invited to join the project. The 'invitation' asked them to complete a piece of writing in which they discussed their approaches to student engagement. The writing was to explicitly address: attitudes to their present teaching context; approaches to classroom engagement; evidence of successful engagement; and perceived professional standing and reputation among their peers. From these pieces of writing, we arranged an interview with the nominee, again canvassing their approaches to student engagement. Interviews again further addressed the written application questions as well as information about their professional development. Interviews were conducted by two people – an academic researcher and a member of a reference group that had been set up for the project. Referees were then contacted for verification of claims made at interview and in the written application process. At each stage of this quite detailed process, teachers were selected or rejected until a final group of 28 teachers was chosen.

Case studies

Case studies involved week-long observations of the teachers in their classrooms, followed by daily interviews with them to explore and validate the data. Interviews with their students were also conducted. Teachers were asked to teach as 'business as usual', but were also asked to nominate in advance a 'highlight lesson'. This latter was filmed in some cases. In addition, photos were taken of the classroom. Students were involved in this task. These photographs became research artefacts, along with the usual documentation

– programs, units of work, and lesson plans. For reasons to do with child protection legislation in NSW, no filming was made available to anyone other than those involved in the research and was only available for the time of the analysis, and photographs showing students were not made public.

The academics and research assistants were each assigned to only one group ('early years', 'middle years', 'later years'), but the whole team participated in the first case study as a pilot. Two researchers – an academic and a research assistant – conducted subsequent case studies. The research assistant remained as a constant for each group ensuring the conduct of the case studies was consistent. The two researchers on each case had defined roles in the observation. The research assistant was to carry out observations based on the MeE Framework (described in detail from page 25) and the academic researcher was to take notes on everything observed, 'unhindered' by the theoretical framing. In this way we hoped to allow the framework to have a role in driving the research and, at the same time, to test its robustness as an explanatory framework. On the other hand, we did not want to be constrained by the framework to miss other possible explanations of these teachers' work. We felt that having the two researchers focus on different areas would achieve all of these aims.

Teachers-as-researchers

Why would teachers subject themselves to the process of nomination and to the case study process we have described? One reason was the way the research framed them. From the outset teachers were to be co-researchers on the project. The research was aware of not too glibly positioning teachers-as-researchers (see Doecke *et al.* 2007). On the other hand, there was a firm belief that promoting and giving room for a sophisticated 'researchly disposition' (Lingard and Renshaw 2010) among teachers is in itself a major contribution to professional practice. We did not want this to be tokenistic and, from the first, the teachers were aware that joining the project meant a commitment to research. The research commitment that teachers undertook in joining the project was to:

- write about their practice on engagement (as part of the application/selection process);
- agree to be the subject of a case study, but also to:
    - be a co-author of the case study itself;
    - read and respond to the case studies of other teachers on a project intranet;
    - take part in an intensive cross-case analysis over six days at the conclusion of all the case studies.

In order to be co-authors of their case studies, teachers were asked to meet with us at the end of every day of the case study week. We presented them with what we thought we had observed, talked this through and made any adjustments following discussion and explanation. At the last meeting of the week, we discussed and agreed on the 'big themes' of the case study. The research assistants had a week to write up the case study which was done to a common pro-forma. This report was subsequently negotiated with the teacher, and all co-authored case study reports were placed on the research project intranet for the other teachers to read.

Cross-case analysis

At the conclusion of all of the case studies, all of the teachers, academic researchers, research assistants and an external 'critical friend' assembled for six days to interrogate the data and develop cross-case analyses. During these days the specific focus was on identifying:

- and conceptualizing the characteristics of the contexts in which the teachers worked. The challenges of the contexts were identified and there was discussion of how these were being met. These challenges were not identified as 'common';
- the key features of high cognitive, high affective and high operative pedagogy (see definitions of engagement following) within the stage ('early', 'middle', 'later') groups;
- the ways in which high expectations were being realized among the students (how do the teachers have students themselves 'buy into' high expectations?);
- the key features of the 'insider classroom' (see outer circle of Figure 2.1 on page 22 for elements of the insider classroom);
- how teachers provided individual support for students within the stage groups;
- the role of leadership within the schools (some of the teachers were Principals or subject heads);
- specific work among Indigenous students;
- approaches to creativity;
- uses of ICT and multiliteracies;
- individual professional journeys of teachers.

Along with the case study reports, the cross-case analyses underpin the findings and stories in this book. In this way, while the teachers have not directly contributed to the writing of this book, their ideas and understanding of what works in classrooms for low SES students are strongly represented throughout. The teachers are not anonymous in this book, as their position as co-researchers meant they needed to know each other and to read each other's cases. Anonymity would have prevented this.

Thus far we have described processes of identification and the case study methodologies used in the research. The next section provides an overview of the theoretical framework developed over a number of previous research phases. This framework was a key instrument in the conduct, case analysis and cross-case analysis of *Teachers for a Fair Go*.

Student engagement and the *Fair Go Program*

Beginnings

In the early 2000s a research partnership was formed between a team of researchers from the University of Western Sydney (UWS) and the then NSW Department of Education and Training's Priority Schools Programs (PSP). The aims were at the same time open-ended and ambitious:

> What does good teaching look like in the schools serving the poorest and most diverse communities?

> What kind of teaching practices will bring about improved social and academic outcomes for students who live in poverty?

The *Fair Go* research program (*FGP*) took its name from a PSP equity principle that was based on the Australian idiomatic expression discussed in Chapter 1. It is commonly understood as a call for just treatment and a value that speaks of equality for all, regardless of social and cultural background. In this respect the name matched its aims. We were interested in finding and analyzing the work of teachers whose pedagogies gave students a fair chance at educational success, regardless of their backgrounds or personal circumstances.

The research soon found itself in the housing estates and the poor suburbs close to the university. For both UWS and PSP this was a logical first step. The university is strongly committed to serving the people of Greater Western Sydney, one of the most socially and culturally diverse areas of Australia, and home to more than two million people (over 10 per cent of the total population of the country). For the Priority Schools Programs, the region had the largest number of schools receiving their support.

Drawing initially on Newmann and Associates' (1996) ideas about 'authentic instruction' and the Queensland School Reform Longitudinal Study's (see Hayes *et al.* 2006) research into 'productive pedagogies', *FGP*'s first steps were 'research conversations'. Researchers visited and observed schools and classrooms recognized for the quality of teaching and student achievement of outcomes. Conversations with the school leaders and teachers followed about what pedagogies helped students to be more successful learners. These happened at the schools and in seminars at the university. From the outset *FGP* saw itself as a research partnership closely linked with the teaching profession.

Student engagement as a focus

School visits, classroom observations and research conversations almost inevitably brought the project to the issue of student engagement. Both theoretically and practically this was a logical and important development. The schools being visited for the research worked daily with large numbers of students for whom school and classroom relationships were complex and difficult. Research into schools in poor areas has consistently shown that there are enduring tensions between student resistance and teachers' classroom practices (McFadden and Munns 2002). Studies have continually shown that even when (and often, especially when) teachers' pedagogies are well intended and theoretically sound there is no guarantee that the students with whom we are concerned will accept and comply with them. Furthermore, the teachers were building classroom relationships with groups of students who have historically not had the same emotional attachment and commitment to education as students from more privileged backgrounds. In short, as a group, these are the students who have generally not gone the same educational distances physically (retention to higher levels), academically (results leading to further studies and/or opportunity) or emotionally (seeing schools as places that work for them). The *FGP* research had earlier rejected a focus on student behaviour, even though classroom management was a pressing professional issue for many of the teachers. Rather, it wanted to explore classroom pedagogies that inspired active, enthusiastic and involved student learning, as opposed to tasks designed to control students. As one of the Principals at a seminar put it: 'in task', rather than 'on task'. Discussions then began to explore wider ideas about ways to encourage students to develop longer-term feelings that school was a place that 'worked' for them. Ideas of small 'e' engagement and big 'E' engagement began to emerge. Small 'e' engagement was defined as substantive involvement in classroom learning experiences. This was distinct from procedural engagement where students were merely complying with teachers' instructions without necessarily psychologically 'investing in' the tasks. Big 'E' engagement was the more enduring relationship with education and school, a sense that education was a resource that students could use productively in their present and future lives, and that school was a place that worked educationally, socially and culturally for them. Both these levels of engagement became key centralizing concepts for the co-researching next phase of the project.

Researching student engagement

Partnerships were formed between UWS researchers, PSP consultants and teachers from ten primary schools in Sydney's Greater West. These partnerships were to undertake action research, co-researching projects implementing and evaluating classroom changes designed to increase levels of student engagement. The UWS team and the teachers co-planned and co-taught in these collaborative research partnerships. The developing concepts around student engagement were connected with ideas about quality teaching from the Newmann and Associates and 'Productive Pedagogies' research. The coalition of these concepts provided a research position that suggested improved student engagement and enhanced outcomes are strongly influenced by pedagogies of high intellectual quality, where students are active and involved in learning experiences that connect to their daily lives. This was a primary theoretical framing. For a more detailed description of the theoretical framing for the project, see Munns (2007).

The Fair Go Program's *student engagement framework*

There were ten action research projects in this phase of the evolution of the *FGP* and these were conducted over a three-year period. At the end of the research period, the UWS team was involved in intensive workshops where data were shared and cross-case analyses were undertaken. What emerged was that across all projects there were signs that the changes to the teachers' pedagogies were encouraging greater levels of student engagement as defined by:

- greater focus by students on learning experiences;
- students wanting to remain longer on their learning experience and share these experiences outside the classroom with friends and parents;
- learning being sustained over longer periods and operating at higher levels;
- greater frequency of student-to-student interaction;
- greater risk-taking;
- improvement in the quality of work;
- improvements in attendance;
- fewer discipline issues;
- major improvements in retention rates, with groups of previously disengaged and poorly attending students achieving close to state average attendance rates.

(see Munns *et al.* 2008)

The team returned to the earlier ideas about small 'e' engagement to analyze common themes across each of the projects and this led to both a definition and a new framework around student engagement, as viewed from a pedagogical standpoint. Carefully planned learning experiences sat at the heart of this new emerging framework. Data commonly showed that there was a balanced interplay between high cognitive, high affective and high operative experiences. Put simply, the analysis showed that a key component of encouraging student engagement through classroom practices was through the teacher providing regular and consciously crafted opportunities for students to think hard (high cognitive), feel good (high affective) and work towards being more productive learners (high operative). The *FGP* incorporated this as both a central pedagogical focus and a definition of student engagement. This reflected and contextually reshaped the research literature. A review of research into student engagement at that time described its multifaceted nature, incorporating cognitive, emotional and behavioural elements. The conclusion from this review was that the term *engagement* should only be used when all three of these components are strongly interplaying (Fredricks *et al.* 2004). The *FGP* research had confirmed this view, though the data highlighted some subtle but critical differences. The cognitive and emotional aspects of engagement were accepted by the *FGP*, though 'affective' was considered to offer a clearer pedagogical focus for teachers than 'emotional'. Changing 'behavioural' to 'operative' recognized not only the rejection of compliance discussed above, but also a central research argument that for low SES students to be beneficially engaged, they need to be highly effective, active and self-regulated learners. The term 'operative' again provided a stronger pedagogical and outcome focus for both teachers and students.

The data had also shown that engagement was as much in the 'playing out' as in the task design, and so another level of analysis of classroom processes suggested that four interrelated components were being employed by teachers to develop an 'insider classroom' (see outer circle of Figure 2.1). An insider classroom helped learners to become part of the learning community, to become recognized as valuable members of the community and play meaningful roles for the benefit of all learners. The learning experiences and the insider classroom processes became the first part of the *FGP*'s student engagement framework (Figure 2.1). This constituted the substantive small 'e' engagement that the project had wondered about in its earlier investigative phase. As described thus far, the framework was reached through an extensive review of literature, and then inductively from the research, with both the literature review and the action research occurring simultaneously and iteratively.

The next step of the analysis was to consider the relationship between small 'e' engagement and big 'E' engagement. Again this process involved both research data and links with research literature.

'The future in the present'

As stated above, the program from the outset was not interested in researching ways to manage or control student behaviour. It was always more interested in teachers' pedagogies and the impact these had on substantive classroom engagement on both short- and long-term educational bases. That is, it saw the importance of students from low SES backgrounds not only being substantively engaged in their current classroom experiences ('e'), but also developing enduring and rewarding relationships with the larger project

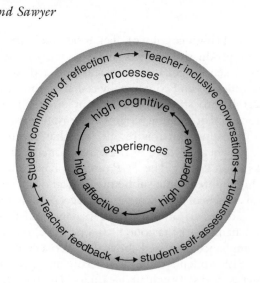

Figure 2.1 The *Fair Go* project engagement framework – small 'e' engagement

of education generally ('E'). Connecting these two levels of engagement was the next research step, and the next piece of the engagement framework. This utilized two seminal ideas. First, concepts from Willis's (1977) research into student resistance were taken up. Second, Bernstein's (1996) notion of classrooms as message systems was incorporated.

Willis (1977) conceptualized 'the future in the present' as a way of understanding how daily classroom experiences impacted on students' long-term views about education. The concept captures the sense that future opportunity can be either denied or realized within present day learning activities in classrooms. In Willis's research, low SES students resisted their teachers' efforts because they believed these would make little difference to their future lives. Their freely chosen actions to reject the offer of academic success helped cement their future unequal position in society. They made 'a free choice to be unfree' (Munns and McFadden, 2000: 61). The *FGP* reasoned that resistance and engagement operated towards opposite ends of the spectrum of responses to education. At the points surrounding student engagement, the project then hypothesized that the kinds of engaging experiences that formed and informed the research could encourage students to develop a stronger sense that school 'worked' for them. That is, if this level of small 'e' engagement became the central focus of the teachers' pedagogies, then a consciousness surrounding big 'E' engagement could be developing at the same time. In this way there was not a continuum between 'e' and 'E', but rather they were happening at the same time (Figure 2.2). Again, these ideas were tested against project research data.

Figure 2.2 Links between 'e' and 'E' – 'the future in the present'

At this point it should be noted that the *FGP* was not naïve about the theoretical standpoint of resistance theory. Aware that there has long been an argument in the sociology of education that what happens in schools and classrooms cannot compensate for the structural inequities of society (Bernstein 1996), the project nonetheless was prepared to adopt research stances that challenged a determinism that saw few real opportunities for success for educationally disadvantaged students. Indeed, the next step in the development of the student engagement framework had a particular equity focus on the workings of small 'e' and big 'E' engagement. This brought the project to the notion of classrooms as message systems.

Engaging messages

Bernstein (1996) argued that classrooms, through pedagogy, curriculum and assessment, deliver powerful messages to students about who they are now, and who they might become in the future. The *FGP*'s definition of substantive student engagement showed that this was as much about student thought as student action. Central here was the dynamic interplaying of classroom pedagogies and students' consciousness. The idea of the classroom as a network of message systems provided a way of understanding the processes of student engagement. Again, data analysis linked with theoretical framing helped the project connect these ideas. Working within the concept of classroom messages, the analysis of data revealed that the classroom experiences could be categorized under five 'discourses of power' – knowledge, ability, control, place and voice. Research literature reveals that across these discourses many students from low SES backgrounds have historically received disengaging messages. Educators familiar with these kinds of contexts can confirm this, knowing that many students develop a view that their learning is disconnected from their lives, that they are lacking in ability, that they have no voice and are not valued as individuals or learners. Their options are to accept, comply with, or struggle over classroom pedagogical spaces. These are the very conditions of disengagement that the project had set out to challenge.

The *FGP*'s alternative pedagogy of high cognitive, high affective and high operative classroom experiences working in tandem with insider classroom processes, was believed to offer opportunities for teachers to build classrooms in which students are challenged and motivated, and are given opportunities to become more successful learners. The suggestion was that these students can feel valued within an atmosphere of sharing and reflection, where their voices as learners are encouraged and respected. These ideas were supported through research data from the action research project. The engaging messages are outlined in Table 2.1.

Table 2.1 Discourses of power and engaging messages for low SES students

knowledge	'We can see the connection and the meaning' – reflectively constructed access to contextualized and powerful knowledge
ability	'I am capable' – feelings of being able to achieve and a spiral of high expectations and aspirations
control	'We do this together' – sharing of classroom time and space: interdependence, mutuality and power *with*
place	'It's great to be a kid from . . .' – being valued as an individual and learner and feelings of belonging and ownership over learning
voice	'We share' – enjoying an environment of discussion and reflection about learning with students and teachers playing reciprocal meaningful roles

The student engagement framework to this point had a distinct pedagogical focus, and was as much interested in teachers' pedagogies as it was in the responses of students. That is, the responsibility for student engagement centred on the careful and theoretically informed planning of classroom experiences and processes. This constituted a pedagogy designed for the whole classroom and all learners. The framework and the research projects illustrating the research program to that stage in its evolution were published in 2006 by the NSW Department of Education and Training (see Fair Go Project Team 2006).

Support for individual learners

Action research in partnership with teachers continued, using the theoretical framing in a number of projects in schools in Greater Western Sydney. These projects confirmed that the framework worked for the majority of learners and provided a strong basis for teacher planning around student engagement (see Munns *et al.* 2008). However, it also became apparent in the majority of classes that there were significant numbers of learners who needed individual support and extra encouragement to embrace the learning experiences. This was hardly surprising given the well-documented history of challenging classrooms in schools serving the poorest of communities (see Furlong 1985, 1991). The final piece of the student engagement framework emerged from the view that the *Fair Go* research needed to offer a more complete picture of the complexity of student relationships with education, schools and classrooms. To this point the *FGP* theory had taken up ideas from research into pedagogy and from the sociology of education. What was missing was an understanding of the complexity of the individual. More than a decade earlier Furlong (1991) had pointed to the weaknesses of adopting either a psychological or a sociological viewpoint on student disaffection. In short, Furlong argued that psychologists hardly ever get to the dimensions of social power affecting students' responses. On the other hand, he suggested that sociologists invariably suffer from a denial that there are important psychological questions to pose and answer in any social exploration of the relationship between students and education, 'particularly at an emotional level' (Furlong 1991: 295). The *FGP* turned to research in the psychology of education to complement the pedagogical/sociological focus and finalize the framework.

The motivation and engagement framework (MeE)

A collaboration was formed between the *Fair Go Program* and Andrew Martin (then UWS, and currently University of Sydney). Martin's research in the psychology of education had led to his widely published 'Motivation and Engagement Wheel' (Martin 2007, 2009). This model drew on an extensive literature into the motivation of students. It showed that there were specific factors that comprised adaptive motivation: self-efficacy, mastery orientation, valuing of school, persistence, planning, and task management. By *adaptive* it is meant that these are the thoughts and actions that 'motivated' students commonly display. The collaboration resulted in the psychological and pedagogical ideas coming together. The adaptive motivational factors were added to the *FGP* pedagogical framework and the result was the MeE Framework (Figure 2.3). This final frame is an integrative two-sided framework that the project believed had the potential to offer clearer insights into the individual (psychological) and classroom (pedagogical) connections for school students. As both an analytical and planning tool, the

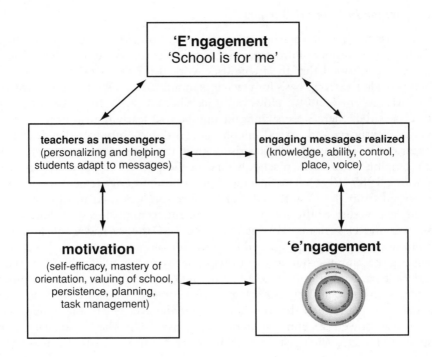

Figure 2.3 The MeE Framework

MeE Framework highlights ways that teachers can strengthen student motivation and engagement and improve student outcomes.

While the intent of the MeE Framework is to view the complexity of classroom relationships from a 'both sides' perspective, the diagrammatic representation highlights its interactive nature. Put another way, the kinds of engaging pedagogies captured in the 'e'ngagement perspective are highly supportive of the individual support factors that teachers can encourage. Furthermore, the engaging messages are more likely to be realized when teachers offer individual adaptive support for students.

The MeE Framework in action

The MeE Framework was first deployed as an analytical and evaluative tool in a report to the Australian Government into the motivation and engagement of boys at all ages of schooling (Munns, Arthur *et al.* 2006). It was also used in student engagement action research projects (with primary and secondary school students) commissioned by the NSW government (Cole *et al.* 2010). Since its inception it has been used in the professional development of teachers and in action research projects in NSW Department of Education schools across all school years. Quantitative research (Munns and Martin, under review) into the MeE Framework used confirmatory factor analysis and structural equation modelling across a data set of more than 3000 Australian secondary school students and found:

- motivation (M) and 'e'ngagement ('e') are significantly correlated
- motivation (M) and 'E'ngagement ('E') are significantly correlated
- 'e'ngagement ('e') and 'E'ngagement ('E') are significantly correlated
- motivation (M) and 'e'ngagement ('e') positively predict 'E'ngagement ('E').

Qualitative and quantitative research and a wide take-up by teachers in their everyday professional work justified its use as a key theoretical and research tool for the *TFG* study of exemplary teachers reported in this book.

The MeE Framework was used to design a data gathering tool consisting of four integrated components:

- classroom planning guide – ('e') classroom pedagogies
- classroom planning guide – ('e') insider classroom processes
- observation and reflection guide – message systems
- observation and reflection guide (M) – individual support strategies.

This data gathering tool was used by all researchers (teachers, academics, research assistants) during the case study week.

The MeE framework in the case studies for *Teachers for a Fair Go*

Classroom planning guide

The classroom pedagogies and the 'insider classroom' processes were the subject of the 'Classroom planning guide'. It was used in the following ways. First, teachers were asked to plan lessons around these pedagogical features. Second, the guide was the subject of end-of-day interviews in preparation for the next day, or used as a way of focusing a discussion of the day's work. Third, the experiences and the processes were the subject of specific observation by research assistants.

The first part of the planning guide corresponded with the inner circle of the *Fair Go Program* student engagement framework. Its focus was the nature of classroom experiences in relation to the definition of engagement – high cognitive, high affective and high operative (see Table 2.2).

The second part of the planning guide corresponded with the outer circle of the *Fair Go Program* student engagement framework. The focus was on insider classroom processes that helped learners become part of the learning community (see Table 2.3).

Table 2.2 Classroom planning guide – learning experiences

The Learning Experiences (inner circle of 'e')		Teacher planning or Observation data
High cognitive	• reflective involvement in deep understanding and expertise • students are involved in elements of the dimension of intellectual quality (deep knowledge, deep understanding, problematic knowledge, higher-order thinking, metalanguage, substantive conversation – Hayes *et al.* 2006)	
High affective	• deeply valuing • teacher and students negotiate learning situations that they both enjoy	
High operative	• actively participating in experiences working towards students becoming more effective learners • students are involved in learning experiences that are helping them to become more competent and empowered learners	

Observation and reflection guide

The 'Observation and reflection guide' was designed to gather data about the classroom message systems and individual support strategies. It was again used by the research assistants for classroom observations.

The first part had a focus on the ways that teachers' pedagogies delivered engaging messages to the students (see Table 2.4).

The second part looked at the ways teachers supported individual students towards adaptive motivation strategies – the 'M' part of the MeE Framework (see Table 2.5).

As well as the end-of-day meetings in which all researchers discussed and validated data gathered, one 'formal' interview was conducted with teachers and with student focus groups. These formal interviews were also centred largely on the message systems, and with capturing the teacher's professional journey.

Table 2.3 Classroom planning guide – insider classroom processes

The Insider Classroom (outer circle of 'e')		Teacher planning or Observation data
Student self-assessment	• continuous opportunities for students to think about and express ideas about the processes of their learning • focus on cognitive, affective and operative aspects of learning and towards deeper levels of reflection • movement away from teacher as sole judge and towards students taking more responsibility for evaluation of learning	
Student community of reflection	• conscious environment of cooperative sharing of ideas and processes about learning • focus on substantive conversations encouraging student control and voice • movement away from compliance as a way of students responding to task completion and evaluation and towards shared ownership over all aspects of the learning experiences	
Teacher inclusive conversations	• emphasis on sharing power with students; visibility that encourages sharing of classroom culture; promotion of thinking and opportunities for students to interact and share processes of learning • focus on learning not behaviour • movement towards conversations about learning (shared, mutual, reciprocal)	
Teacher feedback	• awareness of power of written, oral and symbolic feedback on students' self-concept as learners • focus on staged process: 1 the task (talking explicitly about achievement and what students have done that is right or wrong) 2 processes (helping students acquire processes and better ways of doing tasks) 3 self-regulation (encouraging effort and confidence and helping students to stay committed to the learning experiences) • movement away from generalized and unrelated feedback towards feedback tied to investing more effort, more attention, or more confidence into the task being undertaken	

Table 2.4 Observation and reflection guide – message systems

Messages	What it means to students	Data about students – signs they are receiving engaging messages	What it can look like	Data about teachers' pedagogy (learning experiences + insider classroom) – examples of engaging messages
Knowledge reflectively constructed access to contextualized and powerful knowledge	'we can see the connection and the meaning'		• students' local knowledge and experiences are used and valued as a contribution to everyone's knowledge and learning • frequent and serious conversations to show how learning has real life and immediate application	
Ability feelings of being able to achieve and a spiral of high expectations and aspirations	'I am capable'		• tasks are positive and allow all students to demonstrate what they know and can do but also challenge them to learn more • students are encouraged and helped to see the connections between working well, thinking hard and feeling good	
Control sharing of classroom time and space: interdependence, mutuality and 'power with'	'we can do this together'		• struggles over student behaviour are let go by teachers – they can't be won • students get chances to think about, discuss and look after their own behaviour	

Table 2.4 continued

Messages	What it means to students	Data about students – signs they are receiving engaging messages	What it can look like	Data about teachers' pedagogy (learning experiences + insider classroom) – examples of engaging messages
Place valued as individual and learner and feelings of belonging and ownership over learning	'it's great to be a kid from'		• within the full range of learning activities students are helped to make constructive connections with their own real world • continuous and positive affirmation about the importance of all learners within their own community	
Voice environment of discussion and reflection about learning with students and teachers playing reciprocal, meaningful roles	'we share'		• students are given lots of time, opportunities and tools to reflect on, assess and drive classroom learning • classroom talk becomes more like a series of conversations between students, their teacher and each other	

Conclusion

This chapter has located the pedagogical stories of the exemplary teachers within a long-standing research program with its centre as engagement for students in poverty. Details of the case study methodology and data analysis were followed by a description of the evolution of the MeE Framework that was employed as the key research instrument in the collection, analysis and description of the data. While much of this chapter has been a narrative about the theory and research of the wider *Fair Go Program*, the rest of this book reports on the latest project, *Teachers for a Fair Go*.

Table 2.5 Observation and reflection guide – ('M') individual support strategies

Adaptive motivation strategies	*Observation data*
What support is available for individuals to develop a belief and confidence in one's own ability to succeed at school, overcome challenges and perform at their best?	
What kinds of individual encouragement are available to focus on learning, solving problems and developing skills?	
How are individuals helped to see that school is useful, important and relevant?	
How is there individual help for students to overcome anxiety, take risks (not avoid failure) and have more control over their learning?	
Is there pedagogy that promotes effort and persistence?	
Where can there be teaching and learning fostering key self-regulatory processes such as planning, monitoring, and study management?	
How can there be practices that help students manage or minimize maladaptive behavioural dimensions such as self-handicapping and avoidance?	

3 Teaching in low socio-economic status communities

Geoff Munns, Caroline Hatton and Shirley Gilbert

Introduction

Heartening the way so many of our inner-city schools deal with diversity. They are not perfect of course, but think of the way so many schools have absorbed migrant children, many of whom arrive with no English. Consider the way they have absorbed the citizenship curriculum and the focus on not just Christianity but the whole gamut of the world religions. That doesn't mean it's easy. And it's not just the obvious stuff, involving the core beliefs and the core curriculum that causes problems. Sometimes it's the niggling stuff that comes out of nowhere. Who knew that, as apparently happened in London the other day, parents might raise religious objections to music lessons? Who knew that a Muslim girl's headscarf, while symbolizing belief, can also be a neat way of disguising the fact that she's listening to her iPod during lessons? So many challenges, but also so many rewards. Whatever the complexities, the best part is the kids.

(Hugh Muir, *The Guardian*, 14 July, 2010)

There are few places where the complexities and challenges of diverse societies play out as vigorously as the schools serving the poorest of communities. This extract from a London newspaper article captures something of the tapestry of many inner-city schools, where woven together are culture and language, old worlds and new times. The writer of the article is thinking about schools in poor and diverse communities in England's major cities, but his descriptions and sentiments could equally apply to many teaching contexts in the western suburbs of Sydney. Change the cultural mix and the specific details, and the issues might well relate to urban schools in North America or Europe. Here then is a critical aspect of the teachers' stories that constitute the *Teachers for a Fair Go* (*TFG*) research. There are teachers in schools throughout the developed world who daily respond to a great variety of similar challenges as they seek to engage poor and diverse students in their learning. A consideration of the commonalities and differences in their responses across international contexts is vital to the wider pedagogical project, and is a fundamental purpose for this book. Importantly also, and on the other hand, there is an astonishing range of teaching experiences across low SES communities and this is strongly reinforced in the research. Put simply, not all teachers in low SES schools are dealing with the same issues, and this means their creative contextual responses need to reflect their own personal, professional and pedagogical narratives. This chapter works across these two ideas: common themes and diversity of teaching experiences. As the different teaching and community contexts of these exemplary teachers are introduced, there is an invitation for readers to consider the ways the teachers' journeys and pedagogies shed light on their own school and class-room challenges, and this consideration works through both likeness and distinction.

The contexts

As outlined in Chapter 1, all the research contexts in the book are govern-ment schools and part of the Priority Schools Programs of the (then) NSW Department of Education and Training. Priority Schools are those serving the poorest 18 per cent of communities in the state and they receive targeted support to improve teaching and learning with the aim of reducing the equity gap of school outcomes between advantaged and disadvantaged students. In addition, there are Priority Action Schools that are in the 70 most needy communities in NSW. Teachers in the research are working in pre-schools (under 5 years), primary schools (5–12 years) and secondary schools (12–18 years). Schools vary in size and in some smaller contexts there are central schools catering for all school ages.

The community, teaching and learning contexts of the teachers are organ-ized here into eight interrelated themes. These themes are not intended to be seen as exclusive to particular schools, but rather reflective of the complexity of the low SES teaching experience. That is, they should be read as intersecting categories that play out variously across the diverse contexts of the research, and arguably across different low SES community and language groups through the developed world. The research is well aware of the dangers of adopting a deficit view of students, their learning conditions, their families or their communities. Indeed, this book is based on the assumption that student background and educational responses need not be the ultimate determinants of engagement with education. On the other hand, it is vital to understand and appreciate the real teaching and learning challenges many teachers and students tackle in these kinds of contexts. The research also acknowledges that not all classrooms in this research (nor in low SES communities) operate at the extremes of these challenges. There are classrooms where students are academically able, keen to be involved and not strongly pressured by the conditions of their existence. For many of these students, there are tensions surrounding their interactions with fellow students for whom learning and growing up is a difficult and demanding process. That these tensions are mediated by the classroom practices of teachers is a key story emerging from the research.

Teachers across this research are working with the following kinds of students.

1 **Students whose oppositional behaviour places significant physical, emotional and pedagogical pressure on the classroom** This is a critical and persistent issue across many low SES contexts and certainly a central issue for large numbers of the research teachers. Long depicted in films such as *Blackboard Jungle* (1955), *To Sir With Love* (1967), *Dangerous Minds* (1995) and *The Class* (2008), it is often also the focus of media and political attention. Research literature on student behaviour has been extensive across sociological, psychological and pedagogical traditions and across international boundaries. Consider, for example, resistance theory (Willis 1977), research into student motivation (Martin 2009) and strategies for classroom management (Rogers 2006). The importance of classrooms encouraging high levels of student engagement in challenging contexts cannot be overstated. At this point it is also important to reinforce that overt and disruptive student resistance does not characterize all low SES contexts. Indeed there are schools in this research where compliance by students is the defining classroom feature and the task is to convince students that active, authentic and collaborative learning is productive for school success.

2 **Students from impoverished housing estates** In the Australian context these estates are often less culturally diverse than the kinds of inner-urban communities described in the opening of this chapter. There are generally large numbers of single-parent families (often female headed), high levels of unemployment (particularly among youth), violence, drug and alcohol problems, and attendant surveillance by police and security. Many of the estates are geographically separated from more affluent areas. Not surprisingly, students living in these estates are invariably lacking in learner self-concept and their parents are generally not optimistic that schools will deliver a better educational outcome than they received themselves. 'Housing estates' in the United Kingdom, 'projects' in the USA and Canada, and European examples like France's *'habitation à loyer modéré'* display very similar community and learner characteristics.

3 **Students from inner-urban multicultural communities** Many schools serving poor students are located in the kinds of communities described in the opening section of this chapter. Featured in this research are ghetto communities of mainly Middle Eastern and South East Asian people that are found throughout the western suburbs of Sydney. Among the hardships for many of these people are uneasy relationships with mainstream society and frequent negative media attention. How productive relationships are developed between these communities and their schools is a central aspect of the stories of the *TFG* research.

4   **Students who need support in achieving outcomes in literacy and numeracy and across all curriculum areas** Many teachers working in schools serving poor communities across the developed world daily support large numbers of students who struggle to attain adequate academic standards in literacy and numeracy. This struggle has a flow-on impact on student achievement across the whole curriculum. And so it is for teachers in this research. It is a vital part of their work and strongly interplays with the other contextual themes discussed here. These teachers do not need the results of large-scale high stakes standardized tests (for example the National Assessment Program in Literacy and Numeracy in Australia) and published 'league tables' to understand that their students require dedicated and informed teaching at individual and whole class levels to meet expected academic outcomes. These test results often seem to condemn their intentions and efforts in a reductive process that turns complex and valuable gains across social and academic outcomes into narrow snapshots of progress.

5   **Students with high English as Additional Language (EAL[1]) needs and/or students from refugee backgrounds** The urban schools featured in the research strongly reflect Australia's multicultural society. Successive waves of immigration and refugees have created many of the kinds of vibrant diverse communities described above. It is not uncommon for some schools in Sydney's western suburbs to have more than 40 language groups represented. Other schools have strong concentrations of particular language speakers (for example Arabic, Vietnamese, Mandarin). In this respect the project for teachers is not dissimilar to those in London's Brick Lane, in Berlin's Kreuzberg or in South Central Los Angeles. Teaching and student acquisition of English competence invariably intersect with community issues in the wider relationships schools have with their neighbourhoods. Add the arrival of children of refugees fleeing conflict and persecution from Africa, the Middle East or Central Asia, who need particular support as they deal with trauma, dislocation and adjustment to different schooling experiences, and there is a picture of the critical part played by many of these teachers within the multilayered fabric of society.

6   **Students of Indigenous backgrounds** Indigenous students in Australia attend school in a great variety of contexts. Many live in the poorer suburbs of cities and public housing estates where they are a minority in the school. Other students are in larger groups in regional centres or more remote communities where they make up almost the total school population. This research reports on schools that represent each of these situations. While difficult and dangerous to generalize across schooling experiences and educational outcomes for Indigenous students worldwide, recurring themes in the international literature (see, for example, Sarra 2003; Berger *et al.* 2006; Craven 2011) of low academic standards, learning problems associated with traversing cultural borders and school

alienation are encountered and addressed in the teachers' stories represented in this book.

7 **Students from all cultural backgrounds who live in remote contexts** The research was undertaken with some teachers who worked in remote locations. This is not unusual in a country like Australia with a relatively small population and a large land mass with wide open spaces. Remote schools in the research are typically small and cater for students from pre-school through to senior secondary years, often in multi-grade classrooms, and mainly catering for majority Indigenous student populations. Over the last decade in Australia severe droughts and a rural recession have compounded the existing difficulties associated with living very long distances from services and transport. Teaching in these isolated communities presents unique challenges and asks for a particular professional and personal commitment.

8 **Students with special needs** Across all research contexts, and in one particular research school, teachers are supporting students with a variety of special physical, emotional and learning needs. Given these are public schools, they accept all students regardless of their backgrounds or physical and learning requirements, and this responsibility underlines the important role they play in contemporary societies.

In summary, the contextual themes and locations that form the backdrop to the pedagogies of the *Teachers for a Fair Go* research are strongly representative of the kinds of teaching and learning environments found in low SES communities in the developed world. This chapter now turns to an introduction of the personal, professional and pedagogical challenges found within these environments, and the kinds of responses offered from this exemplary group of teachers.

The teaching challenge

The *Fair Go* teachers are 'up for the challenge'. The research showed that, across the whole group, challenge is viewed as a positive. Indeed challenge is seen as the catalyst for the pedagogies that they develop and refine in their classrooms. As outlined in Chapter 1, 'challenge' in the sense of the 'call to engage' has a particular meaning for these teachers. In addition, one of the chief ways that these teachers are distinctive is in their ability to see the positive in what some other teachers might see as 'too difficult', and this ability helps them to shift their classrooms into spaces that offer hope for their learners and their communities. It is acknowledged from the outset that challenge is strongly context dependent and varies significantly across the schools represented in the research. Nonetheless, there are a number of common challenges that frame the collective work of the *Fair Go* teachers, and that help us understand the complexity of the teaching endeavour, and appreciate its impact on the social and academic outcomes of the students.

The system

The pressures of being accountable to the system are significant and a constant challenge facing these teachers. When accountability is strongly aligned with high stakes one-off national tests and school results published in 'league tables', the strain is compounded. Student performance in national testing in the research schools often places the schools under the media spotlight and makes for even more difficult situations in terms of student confidence in learning and community belief in school and classroom performance. During the research period the school of one of the teachers was listed last in the state of NSW in a league table splashed across the front page of a leading major city newspaper. While this is an extreme example, the system's demand to justify classroom approaches with narrow test data is acutely felt by all the teachers. This is not to say that they are not strongly committed to improving academic outcomes. They are. But a consideration of the range of contexts presented earlier will show that results in literacy and numeracy are achieved against considerable odds. We are also reminded when we visit these schools that some of the teachers' most important work: for example, critical gains in student engagement and in developing the values of a cohesive learning community, cannot be measured in tests. The universally felt challenge is to hold onto the kinds of authentic, engaging pedagogies described in detail later in this book, and resist practice in which the curriculum is constricted and rehearsing for tests is commonplace. The situation also highlights injustices and inconsistencies in educational and political systems. Injustice plays out when the most disadvantaged schools are 'exposed' through test results. Inconsistencies are evident when 'quality teaching' is espoused on the one hand, and restrictive assessment policies are promoted on the other. There is another side to this challenge. In some of the contexts the community view is that test results will be achieved through compliance, rote-learning and long hours spent after school in coaching colleges. Another layer of work is needed in these schools to help students and their parents see that different approaches to learning can be more productive for long-term social and academic outcomes.

The community

The majority of teachers in the research enter their school communities as 'outsiders' and quickly need to establish themselves as 'insiders' (see Chapter 6). Becoming an insider requires the teachers to negotiate recognized ways of knowing as a result of their personal commitment to their students as learners. Such ways of knowing include particular insights, empathy and understanding about the parents and extended familial relationships of the communities. Relationships between the schools, the teachers and the local community are strongly impacted by systemic, media and local pressures. The research confirmed that there is a wide spectrum of community feeling with respect to one's own position in society.

It is not uncommon for people living in housing estates and in Indigenous communities to have a view that they are 'up against' the system, and the school is a vital part of this same system. Testing regimes discussed above invariably reinforce this idea. As one teacher put it, 'They see the school on [the website] and it destroys their positive perceptions.' These are often areas of inter-generational poverty and durable disadvantages (Vinson 2007) implicated in a persistent lack of success at school.

Other places are characterized by transience and high mobility among student populations. Breaking cycles of low expectations is imperative work in these contexts. Elsewhere, more recently arrived migrants and refugees have high expectations that schools will deliver success for their children and assessment results often don't seem to deliver, and this affects school relationships. A complicating factor is the role of some sections of the media that are quick to condemn groups of people through stereotyping which is, in turn, picked up and echoed by many outside a community. A pressing challenge for these teachers is how to build positive relationships across the whole community. A teacher explains:

> ...the hardest battle is not to conform to stereotypes, despite disadvantages from refugee status, single incomes and poverty...show confidence that any student who wants to learn and to be literate...can have a different future.

This is particularly important when the prime focus of the teachers is on learning goals and how these can be achieved. The key to this focus is breaking down barriers between school and community. Teachers talk of 'taking the school out into the community, bringing the community into the school.' Authentic teaching processes are constantly employed as central to the curriculum.

The school

There is a wide variety of professional experience among the *Fair Go* teachers. There are Principals, Deputy Principals, long-serving classroom teachers and others in the early years of their career (many schools serving low SES communities across the developed world have inexperienced teachers). Quite understandably, this means there are different challenges to be faced across the research group. Notwithstanding these differences, most of the teachers see various levels and sites of negativity in school culture as a significant professional challenge. For school leaders, this quite often means taking all staff members on a journey away from degrees of low level controlling pedagogies towards highly engaging classroom practices. This is summed up below by one of the Principals.

> Shifting teacher expectations to be more accountable. Professional learning must be reflected in classroom practice. This may be a huge and

possibly unachievable cultural change within [the system] but necessary for our underachieving students.

Another Principal argues for emotional intelligence, 'to ensure a quality learning environment where every member feels valued, a sense of community and successes are promoted and celebrated.' For newer teachers this sometimes entails holding on to beliefs about what counts in their teaching in the face of conservative pressures to conform and be valued according to criteria (for example quietness and compliance) that are outside the learning needs of students. The importance of the whole school focusing on learning is argued for here by a *Fair Go* teacher:

> ...the focus in all classrooms should be learning – learning of the students, teachers' learning, learning in and about the community. The focus is learning – not teachers but 'expert learners'! This magnifies itself in collegial discussion, open classrooms, discussion amongst the whole learning community.

Leadership is a decisive factor in the development of the engaging pedagogies that are the focus of this book. Effective leaders are involved in shaping school culture so that the concentration on learning is maintained at a whole staff level. Their support for teachers to take risks and challenge themselves pedagogically is also essential. The majority of teachers in the research report that they are able to develop their teaching practices because they are encouraged and backed by their school leaders. There is a real sense that, in the research, both those professionals in leadership positions and the teachers they support are pedagogical leaders in their schools. Further challenges to the *Fair Go* teachers' pedagogies at the school level are about the relationships of different stages of school experience to each other and are also about grouping and streaming of students. The impacts of the former are felt in the tensions students invariably meet as they negotiate changes to different teachers and transitions to other schools with different approaches to teaching and learning. Within the latter there are perceived effects on student self-concept and engagement as they move between groups or are assigned to lower achieving sets of students. At both points the challenge for teachers is the maintenance of strong learning conditions as a prime professional focus, while at the same time helping their students cope with their current and future educational standing. This brings the discussion to the classroom itself, and the positive challenges that help transform the *Fair Go* teachers' pedagogies.

The classroom

It should already be evident that the overwhelming research evidence from this group of exemplary teachers is that the challenges they face are mediated through their classroom teaching. In interviews they talk of developing optimum learning conditions and making the curriculum work for their students. This is far from a straightforward task. In these kinds of contexts it is not unusual for teachers to daily meet many of the student learning conditions outlined above in this chapter. To recapitulate across the research, there are students whose responses (either resistant or compliant) exert pressure on the classroom. Others need support in developing English literacy. In many classrooms there are wide ranges in academic standards requiring differentiation and individualising of the curriculum. Large numbers of students require informed and sensitive assistance to develop purposeful and enduring relationships with education. What sets teachers like these apart is that responses to these challenges are primarily targeted at their own pedagogy, rather than dwelling on supposed student inadequacies. Similarly, Haberman (2005) draws an analogy between his 'star' teachers of students in poverty and dentists who do not throw up their hands and give up when they see a patient with work to be done on their teeth. They accept the task, draw on their professional knowledge and go about getting the job done. Importantly, interviews also revealed that many *Fair Go* teachers see their classrooms as 'long projects'. This means they put in place ambitious plans for their students and their learning, rather than looking for 'quick fixes' along the lines of a compromised curriculum with a focus on controlling behaviour. As one teacher puts it, '[It] is a long term project but the rewards are extraordinary.' The long-term project involves building classrooms where learning is the focus over behaviour, and often requiring a shift from a welfare community mindset (primarily focused on looking after students' wellbeing), to a learning community mindset (building student wellbeing through a serious concentration on learning). Often this requires teaching 'through' negative behaviours and not expending emotional energy on disruptions. Pedagogical processes of building confidence, raising expectations, encouraging students to resist negative peer pressure and inviting shared ownership of the classroom are paramount: 'You find the slightest thing to help them believe in themselves as learners.' Delicate messages about place come into play when this belief is to be built. A curricular and pedagogical challenge is to help students appreciate their own place and their own community while at the same time opening up the possibilities of a wider world. Teachers in the project recognize that students need to be resilient and equipped to face future barriers: 'Preparing students for a world they don't necessarily live in every day.'

Beyond the classroom

While the classroom and teacher pedagogy are the critical places where these teachers respond to challenges in order to benefit their students socially and academically, many also saw their roles extending well beyond the school fences. Commitment to a community, sometimes over extended periods of time, becomes a crucial decision for many of these teachers who become involved in the daily social and business life of their suburb or town. A teacher expands on this: 'The community needs to see teachers beyond their professional role and to have opportunities to have social interactions. The community needs to know you care.' Sometimes these communities are in remote locations and this calls for a greater level of dedication. However, strong messages emerge from student data that school and classroom emotional stability is bound to the level of commitment teachers bring to their school, and to them as individual learners. Consider this comment from a teacher: 'Students appreciate you as a staff member because you are not leaving them, going anywhere.' For students from diverse cultural backgrounds (including Indigenous students), it is not only the teachers' focus on social and emotional stability that they bring to their classroom practices. It is also the crucial roles they embrace with regard to cultural respect and the valuing of informed and respectful cultural exchanges at both personal and pedagogical levels.

Finally, the most transparently accepted challenge of these *Fair Go* teachers is their enormous capacity to care. Care extends from the classroom through to the community, from students as individual learners, to the whole learning community. Developing a sense of safety by providing a classroom space that 'works' for these students is a consistent message from the research. Challenges for these teachers are calls to engage.

> Once you get over the hurdles, you start to see results of quality teaching, building up relationships, loving the class, making learning enjoyable, challenging, always reflecting...Building a dream, keep a goal, something you want. Where do you want to be? What do you want to do? At the start of the year not one student could answer these questions. Now, so many kids have aspirations. Part of it is having these conversations about life.

To this point in the chapter we have explored the contexts and discussed the kinds of challenges that these exemplary teachers embrace as they attempt to make 'the' difference for their students. The final section highlights some of the ways that the teachers respond to these challenges as a preface to a more detailed discussion of classroom pedagogies in the chapters that follow in this book.

Responding to contextual challenges

Thus far we have established that there are intersections of multiple and diverse themes about student conditions in the research contexts. As with previous sections in this chapter, the discussion of responses to challenges is presented as a summary of the common ways that different teachers construct their professional and pedagogical narratives within their particular contexts.

Professional and passionate

The *Fair Go* teachers respond positively to the challenges of their contexts by developing and acting upon clear and passionate educational philosophies and ideals. These teachers discussed in interviews how their contexts developed and refined their attitudes and ideals. These are initiated in their own learning experiences and teaching practices as well as those of their role models. Their school contexts forge these attitudes, by requiring teachers to experiment with and adapt teaching pedagogies and practices as they seek to address what are often the high learning needs of students. A contributing factor to the teachers' reflecting exemplary practice is their commitment to ongoing professional learning that is personal, purposeful and related to themselves, their colleagues and the wider profession. Willing to explore ways to minimise their students' educational disadvantage, these teachers show capacity to initiate, collaborate and be involved in research about what counts in classrooms for enhanced student outcomes.

Developing literacy

A central curriculum challenge in all research contexts is to support students in the development of their English literacy. The generalised response of the teachers is to make the curriculum work for the students by individualizing and differentiating teaching. In schools with high Indigenous communities, these teachers recognize the motivational power of connecting with the natural environment and local area. In multicultural and urban contexts, many students are still working towards proficiency in the English needed for academic success across the curriculum. Excursions into the local community, and visual and multimodal literacy and the use of technology are utilized to respond to the challenge of improving students' literacy. When distance enforces isolation on school contexts, teachers harness the capacity of technology to connect classrooms, provide images and link learners with resources to understand the wider world. In some of the contexts, family mobility, extended travel overseas to countries of origin, school refusal or absences due to behaviour sanctions, influence teachers to cater for interrupted schooling. Self-direction is promoted for all students and teacher preparation includes work units that students could pursue while travelling overseas or between schools. Despite the range of physical environments and locations encountered in this research, a common response in the pedagogy of all teachers is the promotion of critical thinking and the application of high intellectual quality.

Innovation and creativity

Innovation, flexibility and willingness to be part of educational changes aimed at addressing intersecting contextual issues underpin the attitudes of the teachers engaged in this research. Many learners are dealing with attendant social conditions of living in poverty: family difficulties, enforced mobility, limited experiences outside their local community, the pressures of the 'system'. Teachers respond with a range of approaches depending on the particular conditions of their community contexts. Many imbue their teaching with creativity, a sense of surprise that fosters curiosity. Other teachers use the stability of routines in learning to allow students to feel in control of processes and see a daily progress in their skills. Isolation, whether due to distance, cultural and language barriers or social distress, leads to teaching practices that develop collaboration and a sense of belonging to a learning community. If a pedagogical model or integration of technology offers a means of success to learners or a shift of responsibility for learning to the learner, these teachers show willingness to trial, experiment and share control of the learning process. No one approach or resource proves a magic formula. However, the teachers express their own enjoyment in building teaching repertoires, driven by local contextual needs and tenacity when confronted with challenge.

Support for learning

The *Fair Go* teachers reject stereotypes. They emphasize the need to engage with learners as individuals, not just with pedagogy but also in terms of relationships and interactions. Teachers care for and commit to their learners in ways that go beyond just nurturing. To reduce the struggle for education experienced by learners across all case studies, teachers anticipate and inconspicuously supply fundamental resources for learning: pens, books and learning tools when needed. Any restriction of choice imposed on students by limitations of context is addressed by teachers seeking opportunities for student choice in the exercise of their learning voice as well as in their ownership of teaching processes and products. While teachers are advocates and agents of educational growth, they encourage learner autonomy and structure their classroom as a shared space in which students can access learning, develop learner identities and self-efficacy. By connecting learning with other contexts, these exemplary teachers position their students to believe in future successful life choices, in different contexts not limited by the constraints of poverty.

Safety

A theme that emerges from all the school research contexts concerns concepts of safety. Feeling safe, being safe to learn and going to a place of safety are concerns that become more than semantics. They are complicated by differing expectations held by teachers, school cultures, students and parents. In Indigenous school contexts, parental experiences convince some parents that school is not necessarily a safe cultural or learning place for their children. In some urban contexts, parents are seemingly unaware of, or unable to protect their children from, the potential dangers that students who resist school could encounter when truanting. Some parents appear to hold a perception that it is a safe and worthwhile alternative for girls to remain at home on some days to assist with childminding. Hence, there seems to be an acceptance from some parents about school refusal and absenteeism. The *Fair Go* teachers work hard to combat and change attitudes within their communities towards positivity, optimism about learning and safe life choices. Notably, they also address the concept of safety through their pedagogy. Teaching and learning strategies try out new ideas, technologies or groupings. These communicate the message to learners that it is safe to experiment, take risks and learn from mistakes. By addressing behavioural issues through engaging pedagogy and making conscious choices about managing the classroom emotional spaces, teachers respond to challenges and seize opportunities to show students it is safe for them to learn.

Connecting with place

Associated with the concept of safety is the development of feelings of belonging and taking pride in the community, the school and the classroom. All the *Fair Go* teachers, in all the research contexts, foster this development. By conceiving of place as a learning entity, as well as a geographical area, teachers enable students to redefine themselves and expand their opportunities of acceptance. Extending the concept of the learning place allows learners to go beyond their immediate realities and challenges of context. Place encompasses their learner identity, family and community, local environment, and at times a global society. This proves very significant in the case study located at a school for students with intellectual disabilities, where socio-economic disadvantage is compounded by the extra impediment to belonging that separates these students from their mainstream peers.

Positive community relationships

While recognizing the complications of challenges and barriers that exist in their students' communities, these teachers do not blame the learners. Teachers aspire to be positive role models, with respect to educational achievement and the personal resilience needed to overcome hardships and opposition. Some teachers commit by staying with their school, in the knowledge that continuity could lead to stability and mutual trust. In both rural and urban contexts, commitment to the wider community through social or sporting involvement and contributions to local media, encourages the trust building that leads to respect from learners and their families. Being a fixture, who is not absent and who is not a short-term involuntary placement in the school and community, is seen to be valued, and especially in the more isolated rural school contexts. In schools serving Indigenous communities, consultation with elders lends sanction to, and reduces fears about, learning for some families.

Critical engagement with community

Fair Go teachers seek to communicate with parents and to involve them so they might understand that school is safe for their children and lifelong learning is valuable. Through class work practices, formal and informal interactions, going beyond the curricular activities of the school and bringing parents into the school, these exemplary teachers find ways to use the school system and classroom culture to be inclusive. As co-researchers, the teachers engage critically with their community. The difficulties of some families from low socio-economic contexts are evident to these teachers. For some teachers, it can be hard to hold on to a position when it seems to be challenged by parents. Through initiating and sustaining parental involvement, these teachers demonstrate non-judgemental attitudes and high expectations about learners' achievements. When gaps occur between parents' expectations and definitions of how learning success might be achieved, communication, respect and creation of safe learning environments lead to scrutiny for all about what is safe and what good teaching looks like. Because these teachers respond with empathy, positive reflection and improvement in attitudes are observed. These changes in parental understanding occur in very different contexts, from parents who are initially supportive, to some who display unrealistic expectations of academic results or its opposite: little confidence or interest in the processes of learning.

Conclusion

This chapter first introduced the different kinds of community contexts and student learning conditions embraced by the *Fair Go* teachers. It went on to present the nature of the challenges that the teachers work with in their local and wider educational community. At this point it was established that challenge was generally seen as a positive call to engage and conducive to productive pedagogical change. Finally, the chapter highlighted the common ways that the teachers responded to the challenges. The chapter provides a background to the more detailed narratives and analyses of the professional and pedagogical work to follow in the book. In summary, the successes attained by these exemplary teachers are ultimately not dependent on any individual context. Whatever the nature of contextual challenge, the *Fair Go* teachers' responses can be measured by the extent to which these teachers are able to change learners' attitudes. Many students in these case studies are able to articulate and recognize their improvement in learning outcomes and personal strengths. We want to suggest that appropriate and committed responses to low SES contexts are able to create places where learners increase academic participation and performance, and display higher levels of engagement with learning.

Note

1   Throughout the rest of this book the term 'multilingual' is used instead of EAL.

4 Learning and behaviour

Geoff Munns

'Learning trumps behaviour'. When the *Fair Go* teachers gathered for the cross-case analysis days this was a dominant pedagogical theme to emerge. Now while this is an important idea for the wider engagement project that underpins this book, there is a danger that, at first glance, it might hide some really important work that many of these teachers perform in challenging school and classroom contexts. It might also suggest the writers of this book naïvely believe that a strong focus on learning and the careful planning of high cognitive, high affective and high operative experiences will easily deliver a classroom full of model students. This is far from the case. Hence some caveats are first entered here about the research and learning and behaviour, before we briefly highlight some common classroom approaches employed among the *Fair Go* teachers that support those students who exhibit inappropriate behaviours.

Learning does trump behaviour: but . . . some caveats

The *Fair Go Program* has historically focused on the nature and processes of teachers' pedagogies as the key factors in student engagement. From the program's outset, the research teams (academics and co-researching classroom teachers) were clear that this was not a project about managing behaviour *per se*, even though we were researching in the kinds of community contexts where positive relationships between teachers, community and students are not effortlessly built. So at this level, the book, in its focus on teachers who successfully engage students, gazes through and beyond the 'tricks' of what is commonly viewed as 'behaviour management' to the wider and longer pictures of classroom relationships, as captured by the small 'e' and big 'E' theoretical framing outlined in Chapter 2. Considered this way, the book both is not, and is, about managing students' behaviour. Deeply embedded in the teachers' stories in Chapter 5, the composite image of the *Fair Go* teacher in Chapter 8, the pedagogical approaches with diverse students in Chapter 12, and the chapters highlighting different pathways to student engagement (Chapters 9, 10, 11, 13 and 14) are critical ways that productive teaching and learning relationships are developed. Implicitly then, there is much about behaviour at the heart of this book, albeit taken from the perspective of teachers' pedagogies and the notion of engaged and 'insider' learning communities. Notwithstanding the importance of this long-term view of classrooms, the research and analysis did uncover valuable insights into teaching in some very challenging contexts (for example, housing estates, inner urban multicultural suburbs and regional and remote schools serving predominantly Indigenous communities [see Chapter 3]). In these contexts the focus on learning is enmeshed with measured and consistent strategies designed to support learners as they develop more positive relationships with education, their school and their classroom. A summary of these strategies is now presented.

How learning trumps behaviour

The research and analysis brought forward a number of consistent themes at personal, whole class and individual support levels.

Personal

A focus on learning is facilitated when teachers show a professional commitment to, and knowledge about, the lives of students, their families and their community.

1   **Being a role model for learning** In the research classrooms this involves showing students the importance of learning and demonstrating the importance of co-learning relationships in the classroom. Students come to see that the teacher establishes learning as 'serious business' and 'the main game'.
2   **Establishing positive connections with the community** Data showed that connections become positive when relationships are built with community at a local level through participation in social and cultural activities. Communications with parents are mainly positive and there is ready and regular feedback when students do well and show improvements.
3   **Knowing kids' stories** There is a strong sense that the teachers are committed to the idea of 'knowing students well to teach them well'. This can mean knowing what they do and what interests them outside school, as well as getting a real feel for their home backgrounds. It also is about being able to read students and picking up early signs when students are unhappy and/or need special support. Teachers firmly believe that, in the end, students respond better when teachers show they care (and really do), and advise them and help them make better decisions for themselves both inside and outside the classroom.

Whole classroom

1 **Planning deeply** 'Plan hard and teach easy' is a mantra that sits easily with these teachers. Deep planning entails a strong focus on developing engaging experiences (high cognitive, high affective, high operative) that will involve all learners as 'insiders'. There is a consistency across the research classrooms in the relentless concentration on learning, including in the most challenging contexts, where historically compromise and lowered expectations are fallback positions.

2 **Focusing on learning goals with high expectations** High expectations of learner success have long been seen as a critical part of the work in low SES schools. The *Fair Go* teachers bolster high expectations with clear and negotiated learning goals, and provide thinking tools and strategies to achieve these goals. Tasks are set as reachable challenges. There is a strong sense of trust that in the end all learners can respond positively to high cognitive tasks.

3 **Being consistent and predictable** Consistency, in this case, means a regularity of responses that link to established learning practices. These 'repertoires of learning' provide predictable bases for student autonomy and risk-taking. Classroom routines are not necessarily about regularity of tasks (though they are in some cases), but instead about the learning focus.

4 **Sharing learning spaces** When learning is the 'main game', classrooms operate on the premise that all are important players. Teachers, individuals, groups – all are seen to be learning together with common goals to be achieved. Teaching often happens among the students as teachers move between foregrounding and backgrounding of their classroom presence.

5 **Being there** In these classes students can rely on their teachers to 'be there' for them: looking out for their needs at personal, social and learning levels. Students 'get' that their teachers are committed and interested in them and will not give up on them. As one of Sue's[1] students explains, 'She's like a stalker.' Being there often also means teachers are available and approachable outside of normal classroom hours.

6 **Having a 'long project'** A key theme emerging from the research is that *Fair Go* teachers view their classrooms as 'long projects'. Students are not to be easily 'solved' with short-term controlling measures. Implicit here is that teachers trust that the whole class measures described here will in the end bring all students 'on board.' Such a trust allows teachers to give attention to wider learning goals rather than getting caught up in the constant nagging of uncooperative students. This does not mean individual disruptive behaviour is ignored. Instead, it is handled in specific ways, and these are now discussed.

Individual

1   **Picking the 'battles'** It might seem unfortunate to employ this kind of terminology with respect these kinds of classrooms, but the idea of picking 'battles' supports the long project concept presented above. Minor transgressions are not so much ignored (see points 2 and 3 below), but don't become the main issue. More serious transgressions are openly treated as preventing learning and teaching.

2   **'Teaching through'** Many instances were observed in the case studies where teaching continues through inappropriate behaviour. In Eve's class, for instance, she quietly and dispassionately notes the behaviour and signals it will be dealt with later but would not interrupt the learning business at hand. This is a subtle and important distinction between merely ignoring disruptive behaviour in the messages about behaviour and learning conveyed to students.

3   **Deflecting and positively distracting** Closely aligned with the strategies of 'picking battles' and 'teaching through,' this refers to calmly and quietly reacting to minor situations by refocusing students. For example, in Nicole's class, when students are distracted and off task, she zeroes in to support them with task completion without mentioning behaviour. Elsewhere, Rebecca talks about 'continual inconspicuous assistance', positively distracting students from what they were doing back to the tasks at hand.

4   **Balancing emotion** Observations revealed the intelligent use and management of classroom emotion among many teachers in challenging contexts. Put simply, this involves employing high emotion in a positive sense (affirmation, praise, feedback, celebration) and low emotion in a negative sense (detached, quiet and calm censuring of inappropriate behaviours). Sue's classroom (see Chapter 5) is an excellent example of how classroom emotion works positively for both teacher and students.

5   **Working on a culture of belonging** While developing a culture of belonging has a whole class dimension, there is also a critical individual element in operation. Here individual students who are 'outside' the accepted patterns of learning and behaviour are embraced and encouraged to join the classroom community. Building confidence and ownership are particular strategies, supported by very specific and regular affirmations: 'You can now do this, which you couldn't before.' A good example of the culture of belonging is Dan's use of grouping. He joins the group of students with the least confidence and lowest academic standards as a co-learner, helping them with intellectual quality and frequently sharing their findings with the other more independent groups. In this way their ideas are validated and serve as a scaffold for other learners.

6   **Eliminating shaming** Across the board in these classrooms there is a philosophy that no student would be criticised negatively nor knowingly

have self-concepts lowered. Teachers work hard to eliminate feelings of shame associated with learning and behaviour. This is particularly significant in classrooms with large numbers of Indigenous students where shaming has strong cultural connotations.

Conclusion

The research has shown that under certain carefully constructed pedagogical conditions a focus on learning is able eventually to override difficult and disruptive behaviours, and this can happen in the most challenging of learning communities. As shown throughout this book, the work of exemplary teachers is complex and context dependent. The intention here is not to reduce the building of positive and productive classroom relationships to a set of strategies to be ticked off. Rather, it is to be read alongside the pedagogical stories that constitute the main fabric of the book, as a way of getting closer to understanding the ways in which this group of teachers has been able to use learning to trump behaviour.

Note

1   Teachers mentioned in this chapter are introduced in Chapter 5.

5 Introducing four of the teachers

Geoff Munns, Margery Hertzberg, Mary Mooney and Katina Zammit

Student engagement has rarely been the stuff of youth culture. Indeed, music and film consistently play out themes of disenchantment and disengagement, with messages ringing out about generation gaps and schools not working for students, especially those from poor and marginalized backgrounds. Think of The Who's *My Generation* or Pink Floyd's *The Wall*. And these themes echo throughout the research literature. Only occasionally do songs talk of great teachers, successful outcomes and bright futures. In one of these, the American post-punk band Timbuk3 sings about loving classes, things going great and getting better because of a teacher who opens up a future so bright they have to 'wear shades' (Timbuk3 1989). The research reported in this book picks up on the themes of engaging teachers, student achievement and possibilities for brighter educational futures. It acknowledges and understands the complex challenges faced by teachers and students in the poorest of schools, but is founded on the belief that there are many teachers who accept these challenges and are able to develop engaging classroom environments that offer better outcomes and brighter futures for their students.

This chapter introduces four of these teachers in detail before presenting snapshots of them all. Their pedagogical stories encapsulate many of the important themes of the research. They also highlight the commonalities and differences in pedagogical approaches of the wider group of teachers, and represent the diverse contexts and different stages of schooling in the research (see Chapter 3). Dan's senior primary class (11–12 years old) is in a large inner urban multicultural school. Sonia teaches a junior primary class (approximately 7–10 years old) in a relatively remote school in the Australian outback, where the majority of students are Indigenous. Sue is employed in a highly disadvantaged outer urban housing estate, where her teaching role is to help secondary school students (13–14 year olds) in transition from their primary school. Josephine is a creative arts teacher in an outer urban secondary school, and the research highlights her work with senior secondary school students (16–17 year olds). Considered together, the four classroom stories provide insights into the intellectual capacity and considered planning that characterizes the positive pedagogical work of all the *Fair*

Go teachers. Separately, the stories illustrate how these teachers creatively respond to the particular teaching and learning conditions of their contexts.

The *Teachers for a Fair Go* project's student engagement framework is used to present the pedagogies of the four teachers (see Chapter 2). In particular, the engaging messages around knowledge, ability, control, place and voice are utilized, showing how these teachers structure and negotiate the kinds of classrooms that work socially and academically for their students. The framework captures at the same time what is common and contextually unique in engaging messages produced in their classrooms.

Dan

Dan's students represent over 40 cultural-linguistic groups, the majority being Muslim and Arabic-speaking Australians. Almost 100 per cent of the students come from multilingual backgrounds. He was in his third year of teaching when his case study was conducted. Rejecting the 'detachment' of an earlier career in consultancy and policy, he had chosen to become a teacher as a way of making a difference and doing something important in the community. Both schools he has taught at brought him into contact with important and influential role models and mentors. Interestingly, two of these are also *Fair Go* teachers. His first school was in an extremely poor outer urban housing estate. Among the teachers there who accepted the very real challenges of working with many at risk and oppositional students was Sue, whose story is featured later in this chapter. Dan admired Sue's inspiring personal and professional qualities; she accepted responsibility for disadvantaged, at risk and challenging students, and was determined to make her classroom work for these students. At his current school, Dan found further inspiration in Georgia (see Chapters 10 and 12). What captured his attention were the ways their classrooms 'buzzed', and their determination to teach in ways they believed were best for their students. Engagement, reflection and change have become key factors in Dan's emerging pedagogies. Professional sharing and dialogue influenced him to 'personally develop his own practice, but also look outside the immediate practices'. Importantly, the school's leadership encouraged him to take risks and be innovative in his pedagogy.

Dan's class is typical of many inner urban schools in the developed world. Students are at different academic levels, with a significant number needing support to achieve syllabus outcomes. Some have experienced persistent difficulties in their school and classroom relationships. As discussed in Chapter 3, Dan views challenges as positive. He explains: 'These students really challenge me to be the best ... I need to think very deeply about what I do in the classroom to get the best out of them.' Planning and process are features of Dan's teaching.

> The challenge I face is to ensure every student will be an insider, totally engaged in what they do at school ... I always try to reflect on how I

might improve my planning and pedagogy for better engagement... Satisfaction is going home at the end of a day knowing the classroom was buzzing all day with self-motivated learning as a result of careful planning, informed pedagogy and deep critical reflection...

Interconnected engaging messages play out through his teaching.

Knowledge

Learning in Dan's classroom strongly connects with students' lives. Students are critical learners, continually being asked to think and solve authentic, hands-on challenges for themselves with the teacher as co-learner. 'My thought is "How can I bring that [syllabus] to them in a way that gets them on board, gets them thinking."' In the research year, students scientifically tested tennis balls, investigated the qualities of dishwashing detergent, produced multi-media photo stories of their local community and designed model cars for their kindergarten (5 year olds) 'buddy class'. Ownership and joint construction of learning are continually built and reinforced. 'How can your group decide? What performance tests will you devise?' Surprise is invariably the opening gambit of the learning experiences, and tasks develop with a sense of narrative and adventure. As a student enthuses, 'My teacher says in this class you can imagine.' The schedule is demanding, with high expectations that all learners will be involved with work that is cognitively challenging. The combinations of intellectual quality, active and authentic learning and consciously designed enjoyable experiences build engagement: hard fun. Importantly, students 'get it'. 'We do learning and it's fun at the same time.'

Ability

Dan includes all students in high intellectual quality learning. He aims to 'give enabling messages that create possibilities.' Students cannot opt out of learning. There are high expectations that all students are capable, and he facilitates this through student choice and carefully constructed cooperative learning strategies. Dan addresses different student needs and academic levels, and students understand different participation dynamics and accept how much collaboration they will receive with their teacher. As tasks are established, Dan becomes a team member with the students who are of the lowest academic standard and most at risk of resisting the work. Not unusual in itself, but as Dan scribes their ideas onto a large screen two things happen. The first is that the group's work is validated. The second is that the more self-directed groups use Dan's notes as their scaffold. 'This group has come up with some good ideas. Look at these words we could use.' In time, students appreciate that demanding high intellectual quality tasks are within their reach and respond accordingly. Critically, they appreciate that this classroom works more effectively for them. 'In other classes we just wrote stuff from the board and learnt nothing.' 'I have really improved . . . he gives us ideas.'

Control

Dan sees negative student behaviour as a symptom of failed planning processes and is clear that a stimulating and high affective learning environment minimises negative behaviour. 'As a teacher, my worst days are always those in which I choose to focus on managing the behaviour of my students above the quality of my planning and pedagogy.' Students comment that, 'When you step into the classroom it feels like we are on another planet . . . interesting . . . enjoyable.' Building student capabilities is essential. The classroom rationale is that no student is negatively criticised in a way that lowers self-concept. During the case study no student was in trouble, and student opposition did not compromise any activities. Dan does not 'back out' of lessons. The building of a shared pedagogical space is viewed as a long-term project that is his responsibility; students are not there to be blamed, changed or quickly 'solved'. 'My classroom is always a work in progress because every day is a challenge . . . I want every day to be trying to be my very best of teaching.' There is a real sense that perseverance is a key factor for both teacher and student. When issues arise (as they inevitably must), they are rephrased around learning, not compliance. This is done dispassionately, explicitly, calmly. 'It's just going to be easier for you and me if you move down there. You make the decision.'

Place

Learning experiences in Dan's classroom are inextricably linked with students' worlds (see *Knowledge*, above). Dan persistently shows, through planned activities and discourses, that he has a genuine validation and affection for the local community. This links with students' views: 'There are lots of people from different backgrounds. When you say "hello" you are saying "hello" to different parts of the world.' Acknowledging that some difficulties exist in the relationships people have with the wider culture, he argues that the community is redefining that culture. He works to build student resilience in the face of cultural barriers: 'Preparing students for a world they don't necessarily live in every day.' Not only does the learning connect thematically with students' lives, but also Dan strives to provide opportunities for students to share learning with their families. The testing of dishwashing detergent is a good example: learning that helps make more critical shopping choices. A key process is to develop conversations between students and parents that show that what happens in their classroom is worthwhile and can help them succeed in the future. 'Seeing kids starting to see that they can be learners and school can work for them.'

Voice

'Plan hard – teach easy.' While careful planning across the whole school day is a hallmark of Dan's teaching, student ownership and joint construction of learning are vital features. The classroom is not a place where he distils information, but rather learning is presented as a joint activity with teachers and students as partners. 'What did you find? You tell us.' Through this process, students are invited to be 'insiders' in the classroom, to personally value and participate in the day's activities. They are encouraged to be reflective, critical and test things out for themselves. There are spaces for all students to debate and come up with their own answers: 'Everyone's story won't be the same . . . not everybody thinks the same.' They make decisions as 'guardians of knowledge,' processes facilitated by open-ended and hands-on tasks. Consistent use of the second person ('. . . just do what you think is right'), and the enlisting of individual student engagement ('. . . I need your help to . . .') are coupled with a willingness to accept students' personal contributions. 'Thanks for that. What I liked about that was that he talked about processes . . .' In the end, classroom conversations are about learning. 'You might be the smartest person in the class right now.' And they believe it: 'He gives us a positive attitude.'

Sonia

> You can choose to make a difference in your life. I am here to help you learn and you need to tell me what I can do to help you learn or do better.

Sonia teaches in a school community where many parents did not experience success at school and distrust the education system. The literacy environment of the students is different from that of more affluent students. There is high mobility in the community and frequent turnover of staff. When Sonia first arrived, there was poor attendance and students often walked out of the classroom and did not return. They avoided work, especially literacy. If they attempted work they gave up easily, or would not attempt any work unless a teacher or aide was working with them. Within one term, Sonia increased attendance rates and decreased the rate of walking out. Students now attempt their work without an adult, are actively engaged and happy to display work. 'When I first started, the students were angry and only laughed at someone else's expense. Now we share jokes and fun times, and are able to laugh and know when to stop and get back to work.'

Sonia trained in Queensland, Australia, where she learnt about 'New Basics', 'Productive Pedagogies' and 'Rich Tasks' (Hayes *et al.* 2006). Her pedagogy involves strengthening and building relationships between her students and herself, creating an environment where learners are responsible for their own learning and providing systems that enable them to make choices and experience self-evaluation.

Sonia believes students should feel safe and have a sense of ownership: 'If people believe in you, it makes it easier to try new things.' Making good choices is prioritized, as these contribute to students' academic, social and emotional achievements. But there are clear boundaries. 'You chose to sit next to each other. If you aren't learning, paying attention, then you'll need to change who you're sitting with.' Students know Sonia is responsible for teaching them and it is their responsibility to learn. Each student is expected to respect that school is about learning. This includes the expectation of students respecting others' rights to talk by listening, and allowing others to learn.

Knowledge

Sonia builds on students' funds of knowledge, modifying her program to cater to students' likes and dislikes. She scaffolds students' learning, checks understanding of tasks, and ensures understanding is consolidated. Students receive explicit instruction on concepts, language and text features, complete hands-on activities and use technology to synthesise their learning. 'I talked with the kids about how they wanted to learn and gave the kids a sense of ownership and safety in the classroom environment and they thrived, loved it'. Sonia uses a range of strategies, differentiating tasks to ensure all students succeed. She uses a matrix for her integrated units, which she explains at the beginning, unpacking the tasks and commenting on the assessment tasks. Criteria for assessment tasks are explained and marked using a rubric, which is used on trial tasks. Students receive individualised feedback about what they did well and how to improve. Students elect to attend workshops to assist in their improvement. Sonia has the opportunity to work with different groups and address individual student needs. She uses questioning to assess students' understanding: 'I am confused, are you measuring in centimetres or pink elephants?'

Ability

Sonia won't settle for mediocrity. She has high expectations and co-constructs students' learning outcomes. The assessment rubric provides students with an understanding of what is required to reach a 'sound', 'high' and 'outstanding' level. They have a goal and the criteria to achieve it. All students are expected to reach 'sound' or higher. Sonia creates a learning journey on the interactive white board (IWB) for a new topic. A previous map provides a scaffold. Together they annotate the map using the assessment rubric with what needs to be learnt. Next to each annotation a tick, part of a tick or a cross is placed to identify what students know, what they know a little about and what they need to learn. Students concretely see how much they already know and the need to learn new concepts is reinforced. Sonia's language supports students to view themselves as capable. The message is, 'You can do this, it's easy'. Sonia believes students need to know they can succeed through persistence and building resilience, and ensures they understand mistakes are acceptable.

Control

Control of the curriculum is also shared. Students can choose to: work on tasks during class time, or during lunchtime; attend a workshop or not; play on the computer or work. But students must complete the compulsory tasks. While choice is provided there is no option that involves NOT being engaged in learning. Sonia emphasizes making 'good choices'. Choice goes beyond tasks. Sonia encourages self-regulation of disruptive behaviour. When a student behaves inappropriately (being OFF), she asks them to put their name on the OFF list. Later she talks to the student about their behaviour and its effect on the class and how they might change their behaviour (being ON) to 'ON thinking, feeling and acting'. The student decides how this will happen. 'Why's your name on the board? Go and tell me what you can do. I want you to go over and look and see what you can do.' Issues are rephrased around learning, not compliance or behaviour. Sonia believes students need to know you care. She focuses on 'respecting' her, themselves and others, 'You are not respecting my right to teach and the students to learn' and also being responsible for themselves and to the class, 'You need to respect yourself by learning'. Students also use this language.

Place

Sonia believes teachers need to have close connections with the community, to know what their expectations are and to keep in touch with elders to know what is happening in the community. She believes the community needs to see teachers beyond their professional role and have opportunities to interact socially. 'It is no good passing judgement on the community, they are who they are.' Dance groups provide awareness of, and inclusiveness for, the Indigenous culture and heritage. She tells the older students to be proud because they are the elders of the school. They should 'feel deadly'. 'We learn our lessons from nature. Aboriginal men do the dance. The emu dance teaches us to take care of and never neglect our families. We are not boys at the moment. We are warriors!' Sonia reinforces that school is a place for learners. She questions them about why they are coming to school and relates this to what they want in life.

Voice

Sonia's classroom is a place where students have a voice in their learning and how to organize their classroom. Students share their ideas using post-it notes stuck to the door: 'These are the good things; These are the not so good things; These are our questions; These are the things that would make it better.' She explains this: 'The rules, routines and consequences in my classroom have been jointly constructed, leading to ownership of the classroom and learning by the students.' Attention is on making the class a place for learning, asking students to explain new concepts to others. Rationales are provided for completing tasks and she encourages reflection and evaluation of students' work. Sonia has regular conferences with each student about learning, using a personal learning plan, the learning matrices and assessments. If a student is hindering the learning of others it is not their behaviour itself that is called into question, but the impact their behaviour has on the rest of the class. 'Do you think X is helping the class to learn or are they stopping it? Do you [the class] like Y [the behaviour] or appreciate it?'

Sue

Sue teaches in a secondary school in a housing estate. The school has 24 cultural and linguistic groups, including Indigenous students. There is a 25 per cent mobility rate among students. Sue is a Head Teacher responsible for students moving from primary to secondary school, a team leader for learning support and a mentor for beginning teachers.

While a teacher's aide at a nearby primary school, Sue completed primary education training. She taught in the support unit for students with intellectual disabilities and at the same time completed her fourth year of accreditation in Special Education. After gaining promotion to Assistant Principal, Sue moved into mainstream teaching.

Being an original member of the first phase of the *Fair Go Program* confirmed for Sue that 'It's okay to have a go at something educational that no-one else is doing.' Sue acknowledges support from various Principals, stating that, 'Adults need the same recognition and encouragement as kids to try something challenging that is going to benefit students and might change teaching practice.'

In 2008 Sue transferred from the local primary school and pioneered an innovative extension program for first year high school students. Sue integrates English, maths, social studies and visual arts. Students have other teachers for the remaining subjects. The extension program caters for learners identified as at risk, but with the potential to perform above their peers. Many students fall below national benchmarks for literacy and numeracy, and many (but not all) resist education and exhibit inappropriate behaviour. Sue firmly believes that

> Student misbehaviour can be turned around if schools accept the focus on teaching and learning... reject busy work, babysitting and compulsion as student control mechanisms... students can be engaged through rich tasks [because] rich tasks have intellectual quality but are open-ended so as to allow everybody to achieve their personal best... we can change behaviour through the curriculum.

Learning is a priority and other tasks are secondary to this core business. The bell rings, students enter and choose seats. With half the class seated, Sue begins the maths or English quiz (dependent on the forthcoming lesson) and within thirty seconds all are present and involved. After three minutes, the 'game' (a deliberate contextualized skills strategy) concludes. Sue introduces the body of the lesson. 'We're researching ancient Egypt and you'll need to use some of that spelling quiz vocabulary in your report.' Students regroup and begin their selected information report. It is only now that Sue scans the room and marks the attendance roll. As an observer, the inextricable links built between high cognitive, affective and operative are evident, as are the messages, to ensure success.

This school community is built on paddocks that in another era pioneered Australia's famous Australian Merino sheep industry. Where once a flock was herded by sheep dogs responding to the whistling messages of graziers, this present flock respond to very different messages as they interact together with their masterful teacher who disrupts the discourse – 'following like sheep' is the antithesis of this learning environment and all messages have intellectual rigour as their core, and this is now demonstrated.

Knowledge

'Tomorrow we will have our first piece of work to put around the room so it looks like we own the space,' says Sue on the first day of the school year. 'Change attitudes (to learning) through curriculum,' states Sue and this first rich task on the topic of 'seasons' will integrate English, maths, science and geography. Preparation includes a range of necessary resources that are both informative and culturally responsive. An information poster about the Aboriginal seasons of the Dharawal people is prominent as some students are Dharawal people. Emphasis is on students thinking creatively and imaginatively and Sue's intelligent and informed planning always incorporates scaffolds to ensure rigorous tasks that are within each student's zone of proximal development – an aspect all students quickly recognize and progressively value as the year advances. 'She won't let us give up and we're not allowed to say it's hard, we have to say it's challenging.' And '. . . work is challenging but it's easy to learn when we're having fun'. Sue moves between self-selected groups to monitor progress and provide constructive feedback to ensure intellectual quality. 'Remember . . . a little bit of good work is better than a lot of ordinary work.' And students believe that group work 'doubles the IQ, triples the IQ . . . we finish . . . we have friends in case you get lost in the question, instead of being alone, struggling.'

Ability

'Miss gives us a question and we have to calculate quickly, it warms our brains.'

'You've got to let them be clever,' says Sue and she ensures this in a multiplicity of ways that originate from a range of higher order cognitive tasks, usually negotiated with students to provide a choice of activities to achieve the mandatory outcomes. Feelings of ability are encouraged and promoted through self-reflective journals. For example, one student wrote,

> I enjoyed the reading assignment! It was very fun to do. We got to choose a book that interested us. I chose *Deadly Dare*... and it did keep my interest and I was able to give a good presentation... I was a little scared though everyone in my group made it easy for me.

Messages that it is okay to aspire to intellectual pursuits are further exemplified: 'I don't care if people think we're nerdy because I'll get a better job in life and be successful. I'll own my own building business.' His classmate added, 'and I'll own Microsoft.'

Control

Choice of tasks provides students with a sense of ownership of their learning but the emotional and physical environments also contribute. 'It's good to have choices,' explains Sue. 'You can sit by yourself if it gets too noisy. I will bring another table in for you to work alone when you want.' Student interview data verifies this powerful and consistent message. 'We choose to regulate our behaviour... she's not controlling us with seats... we're controlling ourselves.' Plentiful, appropriate and easily accessible resources also make tasks achievable with minimal fuss. 'Can I have a pair of scissors?' asks one student. 'Yes,' says Sue supplying a pair, 'but in future if you need something, just go and get it. You don't need to ask me.' 'Choose respect for yourself, your friends and your teacher' is the only class rule. Potential resistance is varied and quickly aborted. For example, Sue unobtrusively opens a book to the relevant page and places it on a student's desk en route to another group. This non-focused student looks up, looks at the book, smiles and studiously begins. Perhaps this is why a very resistant student stated, 'She's like a stalker... she's our right hand when we need help' and 'She doesn't rave on.'

Place

Physically and financially this is a tough place to live in and for many (but not all), it is also socially and emotionally dysfunctional. There is no appeal for Sue in the issues and disadvantages some of her students endure: 'their families are so complex and so complicated,' but she rejects overreaction and being judgemental.

> I want to expand their view of the world, not (expand) their view of [the housing estate]... I try to make the classroom as nice as I can, to make

school as pleasant as it can be. I'm hoping that there will be transfer to the rest of their lives . . . one needs to equip learners with skills for independent learning.

Overwhelmingly students respond that 'This classroom is like our second home . . . it's our room . . . it's free'. It is safe and accessible at all times including recess and lunch, an oasis wherein authentic learning occurs. Learners are nurtured to pursue self-directed learning and thus expand their world-view beyond the immediate challenges of intersecting disadvantage.

Voice

Students do not compete to have a voice nor to claim opportunities for substantive communication in both class discussion and group work. 'Here we stand up for our own opinions'. 'She gives us several choices of the same thing – we don't just do anything and we have to have a plan . . . she's the plan man!' And much of this is achieved by Sue's own planning of the content, ensuring that tasks involve creative and imaginative thinking, where risk taking is not just sanctioned – it is obligatory. For instance the prescribed mathematics text-book drill on Egyptian numbers is reconstructed so that students need to analyze and synthesise this information to construct a game that will teach Egyptian numbers to local Year 4 students. Sue challenges the group using a conventional dice because it does not display Egyptian numbers. Once students realise they will have to make one, Sue begins a considered conversation that deliberately uses the subject language (*cube* and *net*) to ensure students mathematically solve the problem and they succeed because, '[in groups], everyone shares and combines good ideas. We don't have captains, we're all captains.'

Josephine

> At the beginning of a new topic . . . you think . . . 'How am I going to be able to do this? It sounds really difficult.' When you actually finish that topic you feel relieved, you feel good about yourself because you've challenged yourself.

Josephine commenced her teaching career at a comprehensive secondary school working with secondary drama and English students. She had been teaching in this school for three years at the time of participating in the research. In addition to classroom teaching, Josephine undertook the student welfare roles of Year 7 Advisor and Co-coordinator of the school's positive behaviour team. The students who attend this school in Sydney's outer west live in a low socio-economic suburb of well-established residential housing. Indigenous students comprise 7 per cent of the total school population. Key people who supported and influenced Josephine's success during her first term as a teacher were her father (a Deputy Principal), the Principal and the English Head Teacher.

Josephine is an exemplary teacher because of the ways she challenges students' learning at the classroom level and through her ability to build school-wide engagement. She develops trust and respect across the school community by participating in, and organizing, a variety of student groups in debating, public speaking, donating blood and playing soccer. When Josephine presents information about these activities and students' achievements at school assemblies, she commands respect and students listen keenly. Mentoring individual students provides Josephine the opportunity to add value to the students' view of school life and their reason for attending. Her high self-efficacy as a teacher is apparent through the various ways she builds one-to-one relationships and community by embracing diverse groups of students.

Whole-school engagement is facilitated by Josephine through her student welfare responsibilities, where she strives 'to build positive expectations'. This motivated her membership of the positive behaviour team, which undertakes to develop a safe, consistent, school-wide and positive experience for the students to learn and socialise. Foundational to improved student wellbeing and learning is the negotiation of school-wide expectations, which are: being ready to learn, showing respect, being achievement focused and taking responsibility. As part of the behaviour system, Josephine adapted and explicitly communicated these expectations in the classroom by creating posters for the drama teaching spaces. In this process she included the students by taking their photographs engaged in positive behaviour responses and centred the photos on poster card. A glimpse at one of the posters shows a photo of students standing in a circle headlined by the caption, 'Meet in the centre of the classroom and wait for instructions', with the following text printed at the base, 'Achievement: Being ready to learn in drama', linking this start-of-lesson practice to the school-wide expectation. Here, Josephine demonstrates how she supports a systems and team approach to signal engaging messages to all students, including those at risk through low achievement aspirations and how, in spite of being in the early stage of her career, this drives her passion for, and success in, teaching.

Knowledge

'She shows you there are lots of different ways you could do that rather than being boxed in . . . She opens it and shows you way more stuff.' Students realise that knowledge need not be privileged; rather it can be open to them through embodied, active and inquiry-based learning. Josephine adopts an empathic pedagogy so that when the students step into role to play out everyday and prior experiences and imagined situations, they collaborate to create meaning; meaning that is relevant to the relationships of characters, such as the Year 11's masked characters of the *Commedia dell 'Arte* tradition, as well as to themselves. Through this facilitation of critical and performative skills, the students discover connections to what is significant. Josephine has developed a practice-to-theory approach of acquiring knowledge as a generative and creative process. It provides opportunities for the students to make reflective comments and ask questions, which lead them to explore other possibilities and create further understandings that are relevant to the curriculum and the students' personal contexts.

Ability

'We are all in this together,' is regularly conveyed by Josephine after introducing a drama lesson, such as the Year 9 ancient Greek theatre lesson. This saying encapsulates her pedagogy of affirming students as capable learners by inviting them to jointly construct the learning. This is physically achieved by establishing the class-commencing routine where the students and teacher stand in a circle. Circle dynamics is a feature of Josephine's 'all in this together' drama pedagogy, as it opens the space for everyone to communicate and relate across the group, be physically included and valued, and to collectively affirm the lesson goals as a community of learners. Connectedness is a feature of Josephine's circle practice and she facilitates this by referring to out-of-classroom interactions with the students, using her quick-witted humour and playing a circle game, bridging the introduction to the lesson's goals either physically, conceptually or symbolically. The students thrive in her classes because they, 'feel as though you can accomplish it no matter what,' and because Josephine focuses on the business of learning rather than behaviour. Setting 'achievable high goals' is a practice Josephine employs to acknowledge students' ability and to counteract the recurrent refrain by the students at this school, 'Why try when I'm going to fail?'

Control

'Let's work together to do the job,' is noted by Josephine as a key factor for success in the way that she shares control with her drama and English students. Josephine clarifies that, 'Maybe it doesn't foster any independent learning to begin with but I think it gives them the foundation . . . to get started.' 'Working together' is indicative of Josephine's democratic classroom and empathic pedagogy. Students attest that, 'She gets involved and has fun with us. It's like she's another student in the class.' Josephine employs a planned strategy to help initiate a unit of work or the exploration of a concept so that, 'It gives them the confidence to say, "I am capable of doing this now I've had a bit of a push", and I guess I like to see where it goes from there.' Josephine is flexible and open to not knowing the direction the students' learning might take and the different paths the journey leads them on. Josephine is responsive to providing differentiated support for students.

Place

The benefits of a physically appealing classroom as a factor in achieving positive connections to learning motivated Josephine to garner the support of the Principal to transform the drab-looking drama classrooms by redecorating them. After taking on the mantle of 'decorator' for a few weekends, the drama learning spaces contrasted starkly with the aesthetically unpleasing school environment, with its massive concrete buildings and pavement. She wanted to make the 'drama rooms pleasant environments to learn in (and) cheery and appealing to the students.' In this revamped classroom, photographs of the students doing drama work with captions adorn the walls to highlight learning processes. These also support student ownership of the drama rooms that also welcome parents and the community when they are invited into the school for drama assessment performances. Josephine is very keen for the students' families to make positive connections to schooling and to acknowledge the achievements of their sons and daughters. In doing so, she enhances the message that the school is a significant place in the community and articulates that, 'Connecting with the community to value public education and the learning needs of our students is terribly important [for] . . . success . . . within our school.'

Voice

'She's taught me how to believe in myself while I'm on stage and how to give your presence to the people who are watching you.' This is the voice of a drama student who feels they have performative presence with their peers and family, and control over the dramatic medium and its content. Gaining such cognitive, performative and social confidence is a great reward as the students are more willing to enter into classroom discussions and take advantage of the 'freedom to ask questions.' When presented with choices by Josephine, whether it is about group membership of the project, the study parameters, or the form of presentation, the students accept the teacher's offer, which assists in extending their work. Students are confident to also make offers to the whole class, putting forward suggestions for improvement to their peers or a change of direction. A shared learning space embracing student voice is the outcome of Josephine's facilitation of democratic relationships.

Conclusion

The pedagogical stories of these four teachers provide an introduction to the approaches of the wider group of *Fair Go* teachers. They highlight findings from the research that show not only the teachers' informed and creative ways of responding to their contexts, but also the commonalities of thinking and practice that exemplify what can make a difference for students in poverty. These differences and commonalities constitute the following chapters of the book. Before we turn to these chapters we present a short introduction to each of the teachers who were involved in the *Teachers for a Fair Go* research.

Early years (pre-school kindergarten[1] to 4th class[2])

Donna
Position: pre-school teacher.
Teaching context: small preschool in a large rural town – almost half of her students are Indigenous.

> '. . . I would like to instil a love of learning in these kids. If these kids are not engaged and don't love coming here I can't teach them anything.'

Georgia
Position: 3rd/4th class teacher.
Teaching context: large inner urban multicultural school with over 40 different language and cultural groups (mainly Muslim and Arabic speaking).

> 'Students love learning in my classroom. It may be the onions growing on the window sill, or because we blog or podcast, or the movies we make, or that we dramatise books, or because we pull things apart to see how they work.'

Harmonie
Position: 1st/2nd class teacher.
Teaching context: major rural centre serving a diverse student community.

> 'Kids need to know you believe in them: they know when you don't.'

Jo
Position: 4th class teacher.
Teaching context: outer urban suburb with a mixture of public and low cost private housing. Large numbers of multilingual learners and a significant Indigenous student population.

> 'It is good after teaching this long that I still care about what I do, and I am still passionate about teaching and I am still looking at ways to improve it.'

Jodie
Position: 3rd/4th/5th class teacher.
Teaching context: medium sized country town with over 75 per cent Indigenous students. School has a mixture of experienced and newer teachers.

'Make lessons meaningful, fun and engage and involve the students in the learning process . . . Develop positive relationships with all students at the school.'

Kim
Position: kindergarten teacher.
Teaching context: very multicultural school. The majority of students are Australians of South-east Asian backgrounds.

'It really disturbs me that people describe deficit views of students. I really appreciate the students' love of learning . . . children are the priority. They make you feel so good.'

Sonia
Position: 2nd/3rd/4th class teacher.
Teaching context: central school in a remote community.

'I really loved interacting with the kids . . . seeing their faces light up when they got something or learnt something . . . making a difference . . . make them feel safe, make them believe in themselves.'

Tammy
Position: 2nd class teacher (all boys class).
Teaching context: housing estate community with multilingual and Indigenous learners.

'I know I can help the community. I am like a role model for the young people in the community. I have really strong connections with this place.'

Vanessa
Position: 1st/2nd class teacher.
Teaching context: large outer urban multicultural school with Vietnamese, Spanish, Pacific Islands and Arabic background students.

'I think it's important, that love of learning. They have to see connections . . . Is it going to link in with anything else that we're doing or maybe their cultural background – is there something else I can draw into the lesson?'

Middle years[3] (5th class to 8th class)

Andrew
Position: teaching Principal, 4th/5th/6th class teacher.
Teaching context: very small primary school (80 students) in a large city.
Thirty per cent multilingual learners – largest groups from Somalia and the
Sudan (refugees).

> 'When working with [low SES] kids, your expectations have to be so
> high and you have to instil into your staff their expectations have to be
> high. It's not good enough just to hand out worksheets...you need to
> build rapport, find common ground with students...get out there and
> get involved in their lives.'

Chantal
Position: teaching Principal, 5th/6th class teacher (primary).
Teaching context: small urban multicultural primary school with 80 per cent
of students from multilingual backgrounds – Arabic the largest group.

> 'It's my job to offer students exciting and rewarding experiences. Show
> them you care. Support for educating the whole child and students will
> give you a lot – co-operation and progress.'

Dan
Position: 6th class teacher.
Teaching context: large inner urban multicultural primary school with over
40 different language and cultural groups (mainly Muslim and Arabic speaking).

> 'Seeing kids starting to see that they can be learners and school can work
> for them. My classroom is always a work in progress because every day
> is a challenge...I want every day to be trying to be my best day of
> teaching.'

Ehab
Postion: science[4] teacher.
Teaching context: small secondary boys' school in a very multicultural inner
urban community (over 30 distinct cultural groups – largest Arabic) with 96
per cent multilingual students.

> 'Challenge adds value to the role I am in now...I have a passion about
> igniting the flame of motivation and believing in my students...
> Education should be for everyone...not just students who can buy it.'

Kaili
Position: support teacher for students with English literacy needs (secondary).
Teaching context: large outer urban secondary school with over 50 cultural groups – 85 per cent of students from multilingual backgrounds.

> 'Some students try and derail the lesson but once you get them enthusiastic and involved . . . you manage the more difficult students and the rest fall into line . . . The day you stop learning is the day you stop teaching.'

Missy
Position: Indigenous language and culture teacher.
Teaching context: central school (kindergarten to 12th class) in a remote community.

> 'Never blame the kids . . . it's always about what we can do differently, catering to their needs, understanding why they do what they do.'

Nicole
Position: 3rd/4th/5th class teacher.
Teaching context: outer urban suburb with a mixture of public and low cost private housing. Sixty per cent multilingual background students and 10 per cent Indigenous students.

> 'Building a dream, keep a goal, something you want. Where do you want to be? What do you want to do? At the start of the year not one student could answer these questions. Now, so many kids have aspirations. Part of it is having these conversations about life.'

Rebecca
Position: English and support teacher for disengaged students.
Teaching context: small rural secondary school with 48 per cent Indigenous student population.

> 'Teachers need to modify the curriculum, never make students feel belittled about academic ability, never dumb down learning, never put a student down.'

Sarah
Position: 6th class teacher.
Teaching context: large outer urban suburb with a mixture of public (50 per cent) and private housing. Over 40 per cent multilingual students (18 per cent of Pacific Islander backgrounds).

'Have high expectations of yourself as a teacher constantly reflecting, refining. You can't expect students to have high expectations of themselves if you don't have them for yourself... Have fun. If you are excited, it will be infectious. You will be more likely to create those innovative, fun lessons and engaging opportunities.'

Sue
Position: 7th class extension teacher for students performing above their peers.
Teaching context: secondary school in outer urban housing estate community. Over 20 cultural groups – mainly Anglo-Australians and then Australians of Pacific Island and Indigenous backgrounds.

'Plan for success, so that kids succeed. This does not mean it will be easy. I do not let students say it is "too hard"... we say "it is challenging"... I will not lower myself to stand and rant – it punishes everybody.'

Later years (9th class to 12th class)

Bronwen
Position: English and social sciences teacher.
Teaching context: small secondary school in a rural community.

'Stepping back and getting out of the way' – this was an "Aha" moment for me. Kids know what they're doing and where they're going – they have their tasks and don't always need me to step in. Kids need to be able to do, express, talk.'

Danny
Position: English and woodwork teacher.
Teaching context: small central school (pre-school to secondary school) in a remote community where the students are 100 per cent Indigenous.

'Don't go in half-hearted to a lesson... don't go in unprepared... don't go in thinking that the kids can't achieve or can't do it... they are going to achieve some sort of success... even if it's minor, they have to achieve that.'

Diane
Position: English teacher.
Teaching context: medium sized urban girls' secondary school with 97 per cent students from multilingual backgrounds.

'I hope I'm giving students opportunities... so that they are students who are well prepared to meet new challenges, to be very confident, and competent in their interactions with others.'

Eve
Position: English teacher.
Teaching context: medium sized outer urban secondary school with
87 per cent multilingual students of whom 10 per cent have been in Australia
for five years or less.

> 'How I am going to make them more interested in their learning and
> engaged as opposed to more apathetic or hostile towards learning is a
> good challenge . . . I'll think, "What is the emotional connection the
> students make with this text before they read it?"'

Jennifer
Position: 10th/11th/12th class teacher, teaching 'Life Skills' syllabuses
(modified syllabuses across subjects with the aim of promoting healthy and
productive post-school lives for students with special education needs).
Teaching context: kindergarten to Year 12 school catering for students with
intellectual, physical and associated disabilities.

> 'My whole philosophy is dignity. All students participate in a
> Community Access Program . . . they all should have dignity, everyone is
> extended in the community as well as in the classroom.'

Josephine
Position: English and drama teacher.
Teaching context: medium sized outer urban community.

> 'Seeing a quiet student, who has low self-esteem and minimal confi-
> dence, grow into a strong performer who can perform in front of a live
> audience is the reward that I receive for my persistence and dedication
> to my students.'

Kate
Position: science teacher.
Teaching context: large urban multicultural girls' school with 43 different
language groups (largest Arabic), 98 per cent multilingual students and 15
per cent of students from refugee backgrounds, often with limited prior
schooling.

> 'A lot of our girls are completely disengaged in school. The challenge is
> finding ways to engage them, make them care about learning. One way
> is through technology. *YouTube* is my best friend. I relate it to the real
> world . . . find little snippets.'

Mark
Position: mathematics teacher.
Teaching context: small central school located close to a major regional city.

> 'I want to hear where they're at and how they're thinking...how they've come to that point and whether that view will change and how it will change...what questions they are actually asking...and where these questions are coming from.'

Nancy
Position: music teacher .
Teaching context: large outer urban multicultural school with over 96 per cent multilingual students – mainly Australians of Vietnamese and Chinese background.

> 'This bunch of kids...they're so thirsty for knowledge...and they have an incredible desire to learn...if you have a good product that you are delivering then you will not have any problem with management.'

Notes

1   In New South Wales' schools kindergarten (approximately 5 year olds) is the first year of primary (elementary) school. Primary schools are kindergarten to 6th class (approximately 12 year olds).
2   'Class', 'grade' and 'year' are often used interchangeably in NSW. We have used 'class' here as a universally recognized term.
3   Teachers in this group are either primary or secondary teachers. Secondary schools are Year 7 (approximately 13 year olds) to Year 12 (approximately 18 year olds).
4   In this chapter we use the terms for subject names that are used locally, but throughout the book we use more generic terms for school subject areas.

6 Teacher backgrounds

Anne Power, Les Vozzo and Leonie Pares

> A teaching identity is a more personal thing and indicates how one iden-
> tifies with being a teacher and how one feels as a teacher.
>
> (Mayer 1999: 6–7)

The teachers featured in this book are from different social and cultural backgrounds, and have had different pathways into teaching. Some are in their
early years of teaching, others have many years of experience. An important
aim of the *Teachers for a Fair Go* research (see Chapters 1 and 2) was to
explore each of their personal and professional journeys to find what had
brought them to their current pedagogical position. There were key questions to be answered.

- How have these teachers been 'formed' as educators?
- Who and what were their influences?
- What were the defining moments that affected their career choice and
  influenced their approaches to teaching?
- What has helped them develop a particular attitude to students' learning?

We approached these questions aware that teachers' unique classroom
approaches and professional identities are shaped in many ways. This chapter
is about using the teachers' stories in search of the seeds of success they have
shown in the formation of a teacher identity that enhances student engagement, improves student learning and hence develops them as exemplary
teachers. It explores three critical aspects of teacher identity identified in the
research. The first is community membership, the second is motivation to
teach and the third is the formative influences on teaching. These dimensions
have some resonance with Wenger's (1998) identification of 'dimensions of
identity', namely the way we experience ourselves, our community membership, our learning trajectory, our reconciling various forms of identity into
one identity and our relationship with the local and global. This chapter
commences with community membership, and the idea of teachers being and
becoming insiders in their communities.

The community membership: becoming an insider

Among the teachers in this study there are some who grew up and still live in the communities in which they teach. In this sense it could be argued they have a unique insider perspective into the culture of their community. The majority, however, teach in communities that are markedly different from where they live and where they have grown up. They have made their way into, and are making a difference in, inner-urban multicultural, outer-urban housing estate, regional and remote communities: accepting the challenges of teaching in the kinds of diverse social and cultural contexts discussed in Chapter 3. For these teachers, developing community membership is a different, and often a lengthier, more involved process.

The journeys of two of our teachers, Tammy and Harmonie, counterpoint each other. Tammy attended the same primary school where she teaches, and has lived her life in this poor outer urban housing estate community. Like many in this neighbourhood, she is Indigenous, and has been formed as a person and a teacher by her lived experiences and expectations of her community. As a student she had similar educational hurdles to surmount as the learners she works with, and so feels she has an understanding of their particular issues. On the other hand, Harmonie arrived as an 'outsider' in her regional community. Her strategy then was to build strong positive relationships with teachers, students and the community through her approaches to teaching and learning, and so has developed very positive relationships with her students and their families. The stories of these and other teachers in the project offer important insights into the formation of teacher identity and its impact on classroom pedagogies. Teachers with shared social and cultural backgrounds to their school communities might be regarded as having the 'insider advantage'. The classrooms of Tammy, Missy (Chapters 9 and 12) and Nicole (Chapter 9) illustrate what this cultural 'advantage' can look like through culturally sensitive teaching. How can others learn from the pedagogical stories they represent? Alternatively, what can be learnt through a consideration of the ways other teachers enter and become part of their school communities? Three examples follow that highlight some different ways teachers in the research worked on becoming insiders in their teaching communities.

The first is Vanessa, and it shows how she took up a contextually relevant way of developing a strong and enduring rapport with parents. At her outer urban multicultural school she involved bilingual parents in mathematics workshops aiming to show parents ways they could help their children. She explains,

> Just helping the parents saying, 'You do have a lot of knowledge that you can share with your children even if it's not in English.' All that mathematical knowledge that they do have they can share that they might not realize that they have – it's really valuable.

The inestimable value of these kinds of partnerships between teachers and parents is amplified elsewhere in this book (see, in particular, Chapter 13).

Danny is the second example. He is a secondary school teacher in a remote community, and has developed a deep understanding of issues affecting the majority Indigenous students he teaches. However, to apply the term cultural 'insider' to Danny would be misleading. Although he is Indigenous, he does not share the same background as his community and has had to work hard to gain acceptance from all members of his community. In his striving to break down stereotypes, he tuned into the individual needs and differences of each student. Believing that establishing a rapport with the students is essential, he became strongly involved in sport and contact with students outside the classroom. Danny also ensured he became involved in the social and sporting life of the local community. His teaching style has become typical of those in the research: he is calm, respectful, deeply sensitive to cultural influences on learning and constantly delivering engaging messages to students about ability. Danny's story supports research that shows the importance of developing positive and culturally congruent relationships with students from marginalized backgrounds and their families (see Byrne and Munns 2012; Tosolt 2009).

Donna has established an inviting literacy-rich pre-school that provides a sense of belonging for children and parents. This pre-school provided Donna's first opportunity to work with poor and Indigenous families and she knew it was highly significant to communicate and work with them. 'If I don't have the trust of their families they won't bring their children here.' Her journey as a teacher has deepened her insight and compassion that has further been enhanced by the support she received from community members. 'I learned how [Indigenous] people just needed to be supported. I learned about the community from working with community members, the teacher's aide, as well as the community support worker.' The messages she provides for students are about the importance of the place where they are and their voice in learning (see also Chapters 13 and 14). Donna became an insider in her community by learning about the community and by taking on appropriate teaching strategies for her learners. Her openness to teaching contextually has been her journey of 'becoming' and she has formed strong personal and pedagogical relationships that effect change for those students.

These three examples capture a widespread theme in the research. Similarly, other teachers in this study made explicit connections with the community with a focus on learning (see also Chapter 13). Their efforts confirm international research showing that partnerships between teachers and parents can support students' skill developments and optimize their achievements. Such collaboration with open, two-way communication and participatory decision-making makes an important contribution to improved student outcomes (see, for example, Alton-Lee 2003; Hargreaves 2000; Leithwood and Riehl 2003; OECD 2005; Webb *et al.* 2004). The *TFG* research has suggested that exemplary teachers of low SES students

eventually all become 'pedagogical insiders'. That is not to deny the important roles that teachers can perform in bringing 'outsider' perspectives to
their classroom as students are prepared for worlds outside their immediate
neighbourhoods. What we want to emphasize here is that 'outsiderness' and
'insiderness' are not fixed or static, rather they 'are ever-shifting and perme-
able social locations that are differentially experienced and expressed by
community members' (Naples 1996: 84). And so it is for these teachers as
they negotiate community boundaries. Collins (1991) argues that 'personal
and cultural biographies [are] significant sources of knowledge' for those
who would become insiders. This is perhaps a way that the teachers in this
study, who do not share the same cultural background as their students, can
be positioned. They have worked on building relationships, listened to and
talked with the community, and formed a conviction that curriculum and
pedagogy can be structured from the learners' standpoints in order to
enhance academic outcomes. The motivation to hold a socially just view of
teaching is an integral component of the learning trajectories of most of the
teachers in the research, and it is to this that the chapter now turns.

The motivation to teach

Not surprisingly, research has consistently shown that motivation to teach is
associated with a desire to work with children or adolescents and to impart
knowledge (Zammit *et al.* 2007). Interviews with the *Fair Go* teachers
revealed that they commonly brought particular attitudes to their profession.
Briefly, these attitudes included viewing challenge as positive (see Chapter 3)
and a belief that equitable outcomes can be achieved under the right pedagogical conditions. The professional journeys of these teachers provide varied
and interesting insights into their motivation to teach.

Some teachers chose teaching as a career after (and in some cases because
of) their own school experiences. For Sarah, her appointment under merit
selection to her housing estate school was her first and only teaching
appointment. Likewise, Josephine, Diane, Rebecca, Jodie, Chantal, Kim,
Kate and Nancy have only had teaching as a career. These teachers cite a
number of school, personal and professional experiences as instrumental in
their motivation to teach: enjoyment of particular school subjects, positive
teaching role models, commitment to helping the community.

Others in the research had a range of personal and work experiences, with
many interesting twists and turns, before settling on teaching as a profession.
Both Sue and Missy worked as teachers' aides in their current school
communities, periods that turned out to be a bridge for their career path into
teaching. In several instances there have been experiences or encounters that
have been catalysts for change. Danny took a degree in physical education
and while he was doing it he realized that through teaching he could help
young people. Mark's previous training was in accountancy, but an account-
ant mentor taught him that money did not necessarily give satisfaction in life.

This encouraged Mark to think about new directions, and he became a mathematics teacher. Ehab worked in business management, youth work, adult migrant education and a charitable organization before he decided he wanted to teach in schools. Georgia completed an information technology degree and was a software engineer with IBM. This background has helped her become a high-end user of technology in her teaching (see Chapter 11). Andrew chose primary school teaching after commencing an engineering degree that he realized was not the qualification for him. He worked in various positions: labouring, car sales and professional rugby playing. Andrew envisaged teaching as a profession that allowed him to 'be busy' and would challenge him. Before Eve completed her teaching degree, her concern for social justice prompted her to work in the disability sector for three years in vocational training for adults with a moderate intellectual disability. For these and other teachers in the research, these formative experiences influenced them in their current attitudes towards student learning. As interesting as these pathways may be, the stories are not intended to privilege 'having the other career' as a prerequisite for becoming the exemplary teacher. Indeed, the research has shown that there is no particular pathway into the teaching profession that seems to predict future teaching success. Teachers straight from university, those with many years of teaching experience, career changers – what appears to count is what ideas and values they have gathered along the way. That is, whatever the journey towards teaching, these teachers have collectively reached a point in their careers where they see the importance of providing messages to their students about the enjoyment of knowledge and their right to a voice in their learning.

Beyond initial teacher training, many of the *Fair Go* teachers have extended their qualifications through professional development and further study. It would be reasonable to conclude from the research that across the board these teachers are strongly engaged in professional learning. Jennifer is an interesting case. While working five days a week in a school for children with intellectual and physical disabilities she completed a postgraduate degree in special education at night. Following a similar path, after working casually supporting special needs students, Kaili realized that special education was what she wanted to do, so she returned to study in that area and was posted to her current high school as a teacher for students needing learning assistance. For two others in the group, further study into their teaching at postgraduate level extended their professional knowledge. Nicole completed an honours degree after her initial qualification and graduated with first class honours and the university medal. Eve is currently enrolled in the USA in doctoral studies studying student voice and low SES students. These examples give strong weight to the argument that the pursuit of quality teaching is a long journey. Perhaps also it challenges the notion that great teachers are 'born' rather than 'made'. The next section of the chapter considers important influences in their 'making' as exemplary teachers.

Influences

The influences on their pedagogies described by the teachers in this book can be grouped into four categories: Principals and executive teachers; colleagues; family; and previous teaching experiences. Although these influences are not the same for all teachers, a number of recurring themes were revealed in the research.

Principals and executive teachers

Many of the *Fair Go* teachers named current and previous Principals and Deputy Principals who have influenced their work in schools. This backs up research literature that has found that teacher agency (the ability to act to improve a learning situation) shapes, and is shaped by, the structural and cultural features of society and school cultures (see, for example, Lasky 2005). Our findings have shown that Principals, as leaders within school cultures, have in the majority of cases encouraged the abilities of the research teachers, and modelled for them ways in which to challenge and engage their students. In interviews different teachers made comments such as:

- his sayings tie in with my philosophy of education;
- he is a leader;
- you aspire to be like her;
- she instils belief in one's ability, with high expectations of us as teachers and this permeates to the students.

These comments capture common research findings about the relationships between exemplary teaching and effective leadership. The importance of positive role models that provide support for teachers to be innovative in their teaching emerged as a significant factor in the development of the *Fair Go* teachers' pedagogies. The following three examples typify this level of support and belief for teachers across the research, particularly those in the earlier stages of their career. Importantly, they show how this helped in the development of teaching practices that engaged students from low SES backgrounds. The first is Sonia, whose pedagogy has been influenced by research about improving thinking skills. This research provided her with an opportunity to learn new ways to strengthen and build relationships between the learner and teacher, create an educational environment where learners are responsible for their own learning and build systems that enable learners to make choices and give them experience in self evaluation. Sonia believes that she was very fortunate to have a Principal and Assistant Principal who both encouraged and supported her with the changes she was implementing in the classroom. The second example is Dan. At his current school, leadership and an encouraging culture have contributed to his success. His Principal and the school executive have been important in facilitating Dan's capacity to take risks and innovate within a context of strong support, professional dialogue and high expectations. He feels his Principal believes in his approaches to teaching and so urges him to lead and participate in whole school professional learning. Dan believes that in this early stage of his career, this has strongly contributed to the innovations he has brought to his teaching practices. Finally, Nicole valued the mentoring relationship of an Assistant Principal, who continually challenged her to 'acknowledge work done, rigorously scrutinize, reflect, process and come up with your own answers.'

By comparison, two of the more experienced *Fair Go* teachers, Andrew and Chantal, have had strong models and mentors for their respective positions as teaching Principals. Inspired by teaching colleagues like the current Principal of a nearby high school, Andrew was taught 'about teaching literacy and leadership.' He also explains how another Principal 'taught me about how you communicate with the community, raise a school profile, be visible, get in front of issues, do home visits and communicate directly with parents.' In a similar way Chantal was inspired by the Principal in her first school, and was challenged to develop her leadership skills, encouraged to gain the Deputy Principal role at a suburban primary school (where she was teacher mentor for a large group of beginning teachers) and move on to the teaching Principal position she now holds at her primary school. Through this influential role model, Chantal developed and accepted responsibility for disadvantaged, at risk and challenging students, and this has helped build and embed her philosophy and strengthen her commitment.

Other colleagues

As well as Principals and executives, the *Fair Go* teachers mentioned a range of other colleagues who supported them, influenced their teaching practices and broadened their communities of practice. In this sense leadership has a much wider definition, and includes teacher-leaders, defined as 'teachers who are leaders within and beyond the classroom [who] identify with and contribute to a community of teacher learners and leaders and influence others toward improved educational practice' (Katzenmeyer and Moller 2001: 3). The teachers talked about how colleagues helped them to stay positive, understand the teaching context, remain committed to the community and develop key pedagogical qualities of patience, perseverance and knowledge of content.

Family

Memories of childhood and family support were cited as strong influences for some of the teachers in the study. This was especially the case for the Indigenous teachers who were driven by a passionate need to advantage their community and their people. For example, Missy commented on the support and inspiration of family members who were fighters for Indigenous rights.

Nicole mentioned influences that included her father (the Principal of an urban high school who talked to her about learning) and the support from her mother and family. In particular, Nicole believed that her Indigenous 'Nan', who worked in Indigenous pre-schools, inspired her approaches to teaching: '...the stories, songs and warmth between her and the kids.'

Among other teachers, the story of Georgia stands out for the way she was influenced by her parents' views to develop a style of teaching consistent with the approaches of others in the research. She recalls her mother saying, 'Don't ever say you can't. Have a go at everything and just do your best.' Her father was very patient and allowed her to always try things in different ways, and this gave Georgia opportunities to make mistakes and learn from them. This ethos carries into Georgia's approach to working in the classroom with her students. It helped her understand that whilst learning might be challenging, one needs to keep 'having a go': 'I pounce on the students, not when they make a mistake, but when they utter the words, "This is too hard", or "I can't do this"'. Georgia comments further, 'I am engaged in reading, thinking and reflecting every day'. She also acknowledges the influence of 'numerous memorable teachers who always had high expectations and always believed in students...supporting us to go that one step further and believing we could'.

Previous teaching experiences

Previous teaching experiences were also cited by a large number of the *Fair Go* teachers as significant in the development of their teaching philosophies. A fifth of the teachers previously worked with disengaged adolescents and students at risk before their current school. Those early experiences were triggers for future approaches to teaching and learning. They were formative of intentions to offer opportunities to low SES students. They learned from students' contexts and found ways to encourage them to learn. These teachers carried and adapted a collection of engaging strategies to their new locations. Mark, Diane and Kim are interesting cases in point, showing how previous teaching influenced their attitudes and approaches to student learning.

Mark's case is an illustration of how a focus on social development can allow teachers to subtly influence academic development. He formerly ran wilderness outdoor education courses for students at risk from disengaging from education, and this experience helped him understand the relationship between social and academic outcomes, which he subsequently adapted for his classroom. As he explains:

> What I do is get them socialized, telling them, 'You are an important member of a group and you are responsible for each other.' Kids respond to that brilliantly. I do maths with them on the spot, where correctness matters, e.g. rope lengths, map-making, compasses. They take significant abstract concepts on board because they are now imperative. The facades

that these kids put up are often facades to get by each day, to fend for themselves, that can lead to a delinquent peer mentality. When these facades are taken away...then they do become responsible, become someone different. Poor behaviour is almost unknown by the end of the camp.

At an early stage of her career, Diane was involved in a project for girls' education strategies. She was also chairperson for a social justice initiative where she gained insight into the need to empower students from low SES backgrounds through literacy and numeracy and through providing opportunities for them to have a voice. These insights subsequently developed into her pedagogical approaches to teaching English in her secondary school.

Finally, Kim is one of the many *Fair Go* teachers who have taught in schools in socially disadvantaged communities with a majority of learners from diverse cultural and linguistic backgrounds. These experiences have helped her nurture professional learning and cultural understanding with a resultant improvement in student engagement:

With time, I realized changes occurred in my challenging [disruptive] students. More students were on task and class atmosphere improved and was calmer. I recognized the importance of high expectations, building students up, helping them to be proud and I grew in understanding of [their] culture.

In summary, these final three teacher's stories as well as those before them have highlighted the different kinds of influences that brought this whole group of teachers to their current pedagogical positions. While these influences have been varied, they help to bring forward a picture of the general approaches to teaching that are typical of the *Fair Go* teachers.

Conclusion

An investigation of the teachers' backgrounds has provided the research with insights into how they have been formed as educators, their main influences and some defining moments impacting on their choice to become a teacher. The research has explored how the teachers' pedagogies have been shaped in ways that are reflected in the work they do in their classrooms. This chapter indicates that there are personal qualities and professional dispositions developed through entering teaching communities, professional and mentoring relationships, professional learning, family backgrounds and previous teaching experiences that have been instrumental in the formation of these teachers as exemplary teachers of students in poverty. Throughout this book, the presentation and discussion of teaching practices demonstrate that there are many different approaches and these are invariably context dependent. Nonetheless, the book also shows that the teachers are strongly united in core beliefs about what really counts in classrooms for students in low SES settings. Although these teachers do not all share identical practices, there are primary pedagogical goals that bring them together. To generalize across the group, these pedagogies demand high intellectual quality with students substantially involved in their learning experiences, especially so when these connect to their own lives. Their classrooms have a palpable sense of student engagement, their students have a voice and feel valued and respected as members of a learning community. The research reinforces the importance that relationships have in the teaching-learning environment (see also Zammit *et al.* 2007).

This chapter opened with a quote that evoked the significance of teacher identity in the teaching relationship. Evidence has demonstrated that one of the invaluable characteristics that has emerged from this study is the teachers' attitude and ability to understand their students and then to consider what they might want and need, in order to engage them in their learning.

7 Professional qualities of the teachers

Les Vozzo, Anne Power and Leonie Pares

In Chapter 1, attention was briefly drawn to Bransford *et al.*'s (2007) comparison of teaching to conducting an orchestra. Here is a more extended quote from that comparison:

> Hidden from the audience – especially from the musical novice – are the conductor's abilities to read and interpret all of the parts at once, to play several instruments and understand the capacities of many more, to organize and coordinate the disparate parts, to motivate and communicate with all of the orchestra members. In the same way that conducting looks like hand waving to the uninitiated, teaching looks simple from the perspective of students who see a person talking and listening, handing out papers, and giving assignments. Invisible in both of these performances are the many kinds of knowledge, unseen plans, and backstage moves – the skunkworks, if you will, that allow a teacher to purposefully move a group of students from one set of understandings and skills to quite another over the space of many months.
>
> (Bransford *et al.* 2007: 1)

The teachers we profile in this book achieve this 'purposeful movement' based on a set of pedagogies which the book will discuss in some detail, especially in Chapters 8–12. It is important to note that the impact of these teachers is connected to this pedagogy, for example to the engaging messages (Chapter 8) which they relay in specific contexts to specific students. The *Fair Go* teachers 'move' their groups of students using informed planning and classroom-based strategic thinking. As a group of people, as Chapters 5 and 6 show, they are different from each other and they have been formed from a range of different experiences. Nevertheless, collectively, they possess certain professional qualities we believe it is important to discuss before moving on to consider their pedagogies – and that discussion is the aim of this chapter.

What qualities do we know are important for exemplary teachers of low SES students?

Haberman (1995) argues that his 'star' teachers of children in poverty have particular 'functions'. In detailing these, he, in effect, deals with particular personal and professional qualities, as well as pedagogical decisions among those he considers 'stars'. Some of the key personal and professional qualities include:

- persistence – feeling a constant responsibility to make the classroom interesting; catering for individual needs and interests; gaining the interests of 'problem children';
- being able to put ideas into practice – seeing purposes and implications and key concepts about teaching but also being able to put these into action; being reflective and able to move from thought to action back to thought again; having a sense of the generalisations that their specific behaviours add up to;
- being able to admit to errors;
- having emotional and physical stamina;
- having organizational ability – managing space, time, the grouping of children, the use of materials and equipment.

(Haberman 1995: 21–92)

Whilst the *Fair Go* teachers' stories are unique, they too contain some commonality around what we refer to here as 'professional qualities'. Their qualities, reflected in their teaching, are shaped by factors such as life experiences, training, individual characters/personalities and the particular contexts in which they find themselves at any given time. Data emerging from our research shows how their specific qualities and dispositions manifest in what they do and are also evident in their thinking and beliefs. This chapter draws on that data to discuss the kinds of professional qualities that these teachers bring to their work with students from low SES backgrounds. These qualities are now discussed below.

Creating an environment where risks are worth taking

The concept of risk-taking is a double-edged sword. On the one hand, 'risk', particularly for students not used to success in school, carries with it the possibility of being rejected. Risk of failure, of embarrassment, of criticism, is what can drive the attitudes to learning of many such students. Risk, therefore, is to be avoided and the creation of a risk-free environment something at which the teacher should aim. On the other hand, risk-taking, moving into new territory, trying out new skills and ideas, ought to be the defining characteristic of learning. From this view, the creation of a risk-taking environment ought to be something at which the teacher should aim. The solution to this paradox, of course, is an environment in which students perceive risks as worth taking. When these teachers spoke about 'caring' for their students, they were not thinking only of students' physical wellbeing but also of their emotional navigation of the difficult waters of school.

When Diane's English students participated in the design of a travel expo as part of an English unit, *Getaway: The Language of Travel*, Diane made contact with representatives of the travel industry and the students knew that their project – designing a multimedia promotion of a travel destination with a group-designed brochure as a central product – was to be viewed and judged by the industry. They knew that their learning journals, brochures and feedback data from teachers, peers and travel agents were also to be presented publicly at professional association conferences. They saw the initiative as bringing distinction to themselves, their class and their school. Further, they saw their school as a place where they were trusted to take control of their learning – planning, thinking, solving problems, collaborating, using ICT effectively – and a place where such initiative was celebrated and shared.

At one level this is a story of authentic learning, where a teacher has actively made connections between curriculum and the world outside school as a consistent focus for quality learning and teaching. At another level, it is a story of a teacher's encouragement of students and her use of engaging messages to develop student self-confidence and a sense that they can achieve at high levels.

Professional determination

Teaching in the contexts which we are describing in this book throws up many challenges. The ability to acknowledge obstacles, meet them and deal with them – in fact to make a positive response to them and see challenge as a 'call to engage' – is a mark of these teachers. We would like to call this 'professional determination'.[1] As Haberman himself says, ' . . . they believe problems are part of their job . . . They assume problems are the reason for needing skilled practitioners' (1995: 3–4). For us, one key quality that marked this characteristic was a resilience resulting from the teachers' capacities to be open to new ideas, flexible and positive. When the classroom took off in directions that were perhaps unanticipated, these were often seen as new possibilities not to be shut down. Of course, some things needed to be shut down, but the mark of these teachers was the strategic on-the-spot decision about the value of a new direction in terms of the learning of the whole class or of individuals. These teachers are both optimistic and realistic and consistently demonstrate that they care about the 'main game', that is, the quality of their students' learning. Jen's desire for her students with special needs to become as independent as possible supported by her determination to make a difference meant that she saw, as a personal motto, the need to 'be persistent, be consistent and have high expectations'. Being persistent, consistent and being prepared to come back each day with high expectations are markers of resilience, but also of a determination that students will be given every opportunity to succeed. Part of this determination among these teachers is also strong advocacy for their students and being strategic exploiters of opportunities on their students' behalf.

Reflectiveness

Resilience is also marked by growth in the abilities of individuals (and communities) to deal with changing and challenging circumstances and dynamic conditions. The notion of the 'reflective practitioner' (Schon 1983) has become a bit of a cliché in discussing the work of accomplished teachers, however, it is true that these teachers tend to both engage in ongoing conversations with their students about learning itself and also continually question and reflect on their own practices. This was especially marked in the way they grasped the opportunity provided by the six-day cross-case analysis that followed the individual case studies.

The ability to 'think outside the box' is particularly prevalent among these teachers, benefiting students in numerous ways, but ultimately in terms of their engagement with schooling. Students from Georgia's Year 4 project-oriented classroom said, 'I don't want to go out into the playground – I like being in the classroom' and 'When I go into the room it is a new day, a fresh day'. Part of the reflectiveness that these teachers bring to the job is their inclination to make their classrooms feel fresh. Every day is treated as a new day. Any problems, for example, from the previous day are, yes, dealt with deliberately and strategically, but not allowed to dominate as the main concern of a new day. 'Breathing space' is created for new beginnings to occur – incubation for new ideas and opportunities for students to make new knowledge their own.

Respect

Some of the teachers, as we have seen in Chapter 6, share particular back-grounds, such as Indigeneity, with their students. Tammy has lived her life in the south-western Sydney community where she teaches. She herself is Indigenous and has been formed by the experiences and expectations of that community and feels like 'a role model for (its) young people'. Missy, too, is an Indigenous woman who uses the language and the cultural concepts of natural places that hold significance for her students.

However, not all teachers are, or can be, cultural insiders – ethnically or racially, or even insiders in terms of class. What these teachers cultivate and convey to their students, however, is respect – for them as individuals and for their communities. They listen respectfully and convey attitudes of 'I'm here for you' and 'we're all in this together'. They find time for individuals and their students see that clearly. Diane capitalizes on cultural diversity as a vehicle for enrichment. Eve also draws on her students' cultural diversity and constantly activates prior knowledge. In the course of achieving their outcomes, what all these teachers tend to do through questioning, effective listening and responding is to be in constant dialogue with students. Learning effectively becomes an ongoing conversation. Josephine's students talk of her trying 'to see things from your point of view... Even if she's just writing on the board, she's talking to us about it as well... not like you're just writing notes from the board, like you're having a conversation with her as you're doing it'.

Jen's respect for her students is reflected in the way she consistently conveys high expectations whilst ensuring each student's sense of individuality and dignity is maintained. When taking her students into the community, she provides many rich, tactile experiences, with her students experiencing what it's like to be at a restaurant with a group, having to wait turns, interacting with others, picking up on social cues and being able to order from the menu. She sees her job as setting them up with social skills necessary for a relatively independent life in the world. Jen places great importance on being in constant communication with the families:

> My current teaching is very much driven by individual needs, goals and outcomes that families want them to achieve... My whole philosophy is based on dignity, and that everyone is extended in the community as well as in the classroom

Donna also is very proactive in establishing rapport with the community in which she works as well as in the classroom itself. Her philosophy is that teaching is about respect and empowerment.

Effective communication and building strong bridges with community and family is important for the *Fair Go* teachers. Rebecca says of arriving in her rural town, that 'The first thing I needed to do in this town was take an interest'. In involving herself in many community activities, she says, 'I fell in love with the people, the place, the atmosphere'. This view is echoed by Sonia who says, 'I always feel I am coming home when I get back out here. That is a nice way to be. I don't feel I am stuck out here for three years to get points for a transfer back to the coast'.[2] Sonia believes that 'The community needs to know you care' and become convinced that 'you want to make a difference'.

These teachers do have a sense of their mission for their students and a determination that their students' life circumstances should not be an insuperable barrier to their success. One has to be careful when using a word like 'mission' not to give an impression of a kind of middle class version of *noblesse oblige* towards their students. Certainly each teacher has a sense of social justice about their current role, but this is rooted in the very positive attitudes held by them about their students. As is evident throughout the book, there is no deficit view of what their students can achieve.

And not to forget...

There is also a 'grab bag' of other important qualities that characterise these teachers: compassion, warmth, friendliness, humour, passion, curiosity and courage. Josephine, Danny and Kate express these qualities through their willingness to embrace students' different learning styles. Eve and Diane, in encouraging emotional connections to the English texts they teach, demonstrate a similar willingness, as well as their own passion for those texts. Vanessa and Georgia bring a quality of excitement to learning that results in highly energized classes. A striking characteristic of Eve's teaching is energy fired by enthusiasm. Kate's classroom is also characterized by enthusiasm and passion for science itself. This passion also reflects a strong commitment to their own learning which is characteristic of this group of teachers.

Vanessa's classroom, a composite Year 1 and 2 class in western Sydney, also buzzes with the children expressing their exuberance for learning. She engenders excitement in teaching and shares her enthusiasm with the children: '...if they bring information back I get excited. "Oh, you found out" and I try to make it a big thing that they found out that information. "Isn't it exciting we can share it and how did you find it?"'

Finally, as Jen says, and perhaps above all else, 'be prepared to work hard'. Meaningful learning is achieved through thorough preparation, resourcing and teaching processes that elicit student problem solving – none of which comes ready-made.

Two teachers' journeys

Andrew and Sarah – both middle years teachers in the *Fair Go* project – typify many of these qualities.

Andrew chose primary school teaching after a number of jobs because he saw it as a profession that would challenge him. He made a commitment quite soon into his career to teaching in rural areas. On appointment to a very remote school, though still relatively inexperienced, he grasped an offer of executive leadership, developing his capacities 'as a leader and manager', one who would 'lead by example and by being visible'.

In his next appointment to a school in a larger rural town, Andrew found he was working with a disadvantaged community and students and developed a stronger commitment to social equity. His next appointment was to a Priority Action School (PAS) – a particularly disadvantaged subset of schools within the NSW Priority Schools Program. These schools, in fact, are targeted as centres of innovation for improved teaching and learning practices through specialized programs. Here he had a 'considerable amount of time to consolidate skills and gain a significant amount of professional learning'. Significantly, he argues 'there is a need for accountability in the PAS Programs. If you get all this professional development you should not be just handing out worksheets'. He tells of one of his role model Principals teaching 'me about how you communicate with the community, raise a school profile, be visible, get in front of issues, do home visits and communicate directly with parents'. As a teaching Principal, Andrew's expectations of himself and his staff are that 'we don't waste time (but) teach kids what they need to know'. His own professional development directions are personal, purposeful, ongoing and related to his colleagues and the wider professional context. The ideals and objectives he applies to himself and colleagues are captured in the following quotations:

> when working with PSP kids, your expectations have to be so high and you have to instil into your staff that their expectations have to be high. It's not good enough just to hand out worksheets, shut up sheets

> you need to build rapport, find common ground with students... be able to chat, to get out there and get involved in their lives

> the longer you are in PSP schools, the easier it becomes. You gain a level of trust with the community and the kids

Sarah has a passion for maths and enjoys programming. Her work ethic is 'when I do something, I like to do it really well'. Sarah highlights a capacity to be not only knowledgeable about good practice but also open to new programs and ideas. Sarah values the attitudes of her current Principal, which stress high expectations of the teachers, that 'permeate... to the students'. Sarah's own professional directions are to: keep learning, reviewing, refining; seek more leadership opportunities; mentor early career teachers; find more ways to engage students, and be open to new things. She 'always wanted to be a teacher, have a career where I feel like I can influence people, make a difference, be accountable (by the) amount of impact on people's lives'.

In these stories, we see particular manifestations of the qualities outlined above: rising to a challenge; a commitment to social justice; a sense of giving back to the profession itself; high expectations of oneself, one's colleagues and one's students; a commitment to high quality learning; a valuing of the community of the school; a passion for the subject being taught; a commitment to ongoing professional learning and a desire to make a difference. What these mean in terms of classroom action is the subject of the following chapters.

Notes

1   We owe this phrase to Professor Susan Groundwater-Smith (University of Sydney), who was a key critical friend to the *Teachers for a Fair Go* project.
2   In NSW, public schools are still largely staffed by a central office. Sonia here is referring to a system of staffing rural and remote schools by having teachers accumulate 'transfer points' by teaching in such areas – points which then give them priority for a transfer to more 'desirable' areas, such as the coastal regions.

8 What exemplary teachers do

Wayne Sawyer, Jon Callow, Geoff Munns and Katina Zammit

Introduction

By now, readers will be well aware of the importance of the MeE Framework to the work of the *Teachers for a Fair Go* project. As a brief reminder from Chapter 2, the key elements are:

- classroom learning experiences conceptualised as high cognitive/high affective/high operative;
- the notion of the 'insider classroom' expressed through the areas of: student self-assessment; student community of reflection; teacher inclusive conversations and teacher feedback;
- engaging messages in terms of: knowledge, ability, control, place and voice;
- individual support strategies.

Now, clearly these are aspirational (in the sense of describing ideal situations) but they are so in different ways. Classrooms will always have some measure of cognitive/affective/operative experiences. We were looking for these to be 'high' in terms of student engagement. Similarly, all classrooms send messages about knowledge, ability, control, place and voice. The key question is whether these are engaging or disengaging messages and we were looking for the former. And though all classrooms necessarily involve teacher feedback in some form, not all classrooms necessarily involve student self-assessment, student communities of reflection, teacher inclusive conversations, or even individual support strategies. These could be considered aspirational in existing at all. However, in our terms, engagement is actually defined by the presence of all of these elements. 'Busywork' (working, but with a low level of intellectual stimulation) is not engagement in our terms. These elements were what we were looking for in the work of the teachers on the project.

At this point an objection might be raised about potential circularity in the methodology. Were we simply defining engagement in certain ways, choosing teachers on that basis and then finding them doing the very things on the basis of which they were chosen? As Chapter 2 pointed out, nominators of the teachers were expected to define in their own terms what successful student engagement by their nominee teachers looked like. Similarly, when asking the teachers themselves to provide evidence of successful engagement, this was not structured in the terms of the MeE Framework. Part of our aim in the project was to test the robustness of the framework itself. Could the work of a set of teachers who were regarded by their peers as highly successful at engaging students be explained in the terms provided by the MeE Framework? In other words, could the model itself move beyond a theoretical model for engagement and demonstrate robustness as a way of explaining engagement?

We now feel that that this is so. Firstly, as discussed in Chapter 2, quantitative research (Munns and Martin, under review) using confirmatory factor analysis and structural equation modelling across a data set of more than 3000 Australian secondary school students has supported the validity of the hypothesised model. It is also worth remembering that the framework itself was originally derived from both an extensive review of literature, and then inductively from earlier research in the total *Fair Go Program* with both the literature review and the action research as simultaneous, iterative processes. Importantly, the teachers themselves – especially in the six day cross-case analysis workshop – felt that it provided a framework that explained what they were doing in their classrooms. Eve, for example, speaks of the framework working for her as a reflective tool 'on my pedagogy' and 'on my interaction with students'. This view has also been confirmed by teachers in other action research projects in NSW Department of Education schools across all school years (see Cole *et al.* 2010). Most importantly, however, the *Teachers for a Fair Go* project itself provides a wealth of data which seems to confirm the framework's explanatory power – as we attempt to show in this book, especially in Chapters 8–13.

The process of analysis

Each case study report included sections on 'learning experiences' ('e'ngagement), the 'insider classroom' ('e'ngagement), 'individual support strategies ('M' motivation) and 'engaging messages' (the processes of engagement). To discuss each of these areas, we returned to each case study report and looked for commonalities within each of the sections and also within the stages ('early' 'middle, 'later') and then looked for commonalities across the stages ('early' 'middle, 'later'). In addition, we carried out a similar analysis on the six-day cross-case workshop in which all of the teachers were involved.

The learning experiences

The learning experiences directly correspond to the *Fair Go* definition of student engagement. Chapter 2 explained how substantive engagement is understood as the multifaceted coming together of high cognitive, high affective and high operative learning experiences. These experiences are fundamental to teachers' planning and constitute the central circle of the 'e'ngagement frame. The following list of six key commonalities[1] were found in all the *Fair Go* teachers:

High cognitive

• classroom experiences are intellectually challenging;
• teaching and learning are the focus of sustained and ongoing classroom conversations.

High affective

• classroom practices build a community;
• classroom environments are such that students feel able to take risks.

High operative

• learning is prioritised, which in turn targets and minimises student resistance;
• there exists a thoughtful repertoire of practices.

Below we discuss each of these areas in further detail.

High cognitive: classroom experiences are intellectually challenging

The *Fair Go* classrooms value higher order thinking, problem solving, problematizing knowledge and analysis. Research and experimentation are common activities and students are encouraged to question their conclusions ('How did you work that out?' 'Did anyone have a different conclusion?' 'Would anyone do it differently?' 'Are there other ways of looking at this?'). Part of this is a 'culture of enquiry', both in terms of set tasks ('enquiry learning') but also in terms of questions asked ('What do we know about...?' 'What can we tell about...?' 'What would happen if...?'). This culture of enquiry is also one of the ways we believe 'high operative' is achieved and demonstrates the fact that teachers build links between the 'high cognitive', 'high affective' and 'high operative' areas. Although we have separated these three areas for the purposes of identification, analysis and discussion, they are largely not separated in teacher practice. Judicious questioning is a key strategy around this culture of enquiry. On occasions we would refer to teachers' habits of 'relentless questioning'. Teachers respond to student questions with questions. Students are asked to create questions for others to answer/investigate. This culture of enquiry is a shared culture – with students working together and teachers 'down there with them' and seen to be also seeking answers to problems. Student–student discussion is also a dominant feature of lessons, usually in pairs or groups.

This is not to say that explicit instruction does not occur. Modelling is one strategy, used widely by both teachers and peers. Vocabulary is also a consciously considered aspect of lessons, whether it is developing vocabulary, exploring word meanings, using a metalanguage or focusing on key terminology (including the spelling of such terms). Sarah, for example, engages in a number of etymological activities as part of vocabulary development. 'Explicitness' in this context also refers to clear articulation of content, goals, key concepts and criteria for achievement. All of these are foregrounded by teachers. 'Transparency', 'visibility' and 'lucidity' are important synonyms for this foregrounding work. Such foregrounding and lucid task analysis creates the sense of security which assists students towards independence.

Teachers draw on, and make links to, student lived experience and funds of knowledge, often through questioning. They are also careful to make explicit links between existing student knowledge and experience and new knowledge. Teachers also make strategic and judicious use of resources, including ICT, which tend to be integrated into rich tasks and which are not used as an add-on or stand-alone. Student engagement is on occasions initiated and sustained through 'hands on' experiences with ICT.

High cognitive: teaching and learning are the focus of sustained and ongoing classroom conversations

A highly notable feature is the degree of explicit focus in classrooms on the topic of teaching and learning itself, quite apart from the curriculum content at any one moment. Discussing aspects of learning, and, indeed, of pedagogy, is part of the day-to-day experience of students in these classrooms. Even very young students are discussing Bloom's taxonomy or sitting in sharing circles explaining why certain things are done in certain ways or discussing what they can do to 'switch on'. Some teachers begin the year with a unit on 'learning to learn' which can focus on areas such as 'how everyone learns differently' or may negotiate aspects of quality learning for each student. Sonia constructs 'matrices for learning' for her class that effectively develop a learning management plan for each student.

These conversations mean, in turn, a valuing of the process of learning, as well as the content knowledge itself. Teachers explicitly focus on questions such as, 'How did you get there?' 'What was your process?' This also means that reflection is ongoing in these classrooms: reflection about what students 'now know/can do/have discovered'; what strategies are used to get there; what students find challenging; what students needed more practice in, or help with. This degree of metacognition is regular and planned.

High affective: classroom practices build a community

The key high affective issues are student commitment and 'buy in'. The first key principle is ownership. In the early years, this is manifested in: a physical environment which is inclusive of students and reflects their work; easy access to resources; flexible planning; students being trusted to use technology, and developing a sense of student responsibility through strategies such as using them as teaching assistants and through expecting accountability. The use of inclusive 'we' language is also notable in the early years: 'we make the decisions', 'we can work with others or by ourselves', 'we are learners together'. In the middle years, this language is more 'you' focused and tends to encourage students to see the classroom work and related decisions about it as 'theirs'. In the later years, areas such as having students design assessment rubrics for the class also demonstrate the principle of ownership. An important part of this principle is negotiation of the classroom curriculum at all levels, including pre-school. This is sometimes to reflect students' interests and tends to give a keen sense of agency. It also conveys a strong message about student capabilities. Teachers do not see this as relinquishing their power, but as sharing decision-making. In turn, then, choice within boundaries is a strong principle, whether reflected in choosing tasks, topics, texts, or presentation modes, or students choosing with whom they work. The accountability expected of students brings with their sense of agency a sense of responsibility and self-regulation. Teachers also promote a sense of inclusivity through attending to a range of learning styles, abilities and problem-solving approaches. 'We're all in this together' is the culture of these classrooms.

High affective: classroom environments are such that students feel able to take risks

These classrooms are not risk-free environments. Rather, risk is encouraged, but students are made to feel assured about risk-taking through the scaffolding (in the Vygotskian sense) and modelling in which teachers engage (see 'High operative' discussion below). Fun also has a role in creating this security. The phrase we used to describe this was Papert's (1996, 2002) 'hard fun'. Students enjoy what they do and gain satisfaction from it, but that satisfaction is a sense of achievement related to the cognitive challenge and also related to the ways in which teachers arouse their curiosity. Because effort and contribution are valued, challenge is accepted.

Also valued is students' prior knowledge. This also links back to 'High cognition', often reflecting the cultural diversity which students bring with them to the classroom. Linked to this in turn is the respect shown to students, giving them full attention when listening, acknowledging individual students and their contributions and questions, providing constant feedback and affirmation, often through expanding student contributions, and offering individual assistance. Mutual respect between students is also insisted upon. All of this creates what are largely calm, relaxed, friendly but focused classrooms. The teachers' own humour also plays a role in creating this environment.

High operative: learning is prioritized, which in turn targets and minimises student resistance

It is easy to state that in these classrooms 'learning trumps behaviour' as the prime concern, but how do these teachers achieve a state in which students are centrally focused on learning in what are often very challenging environments, where other teachers might spend the bulk of their time dealing with behaviour issues? When poor behaviour occurs in the early years, teachers tend to acknowledge the behaviour but not give attention to it, or, alternatively, put to the whole class the question, 'Do you like that our learning is being interrupted?' In the later years, this is partly a matter of setting up expectations from the early days with a class that 'we are all here with a contribution to make' and that 'I will provide the conditions that give you no excuse not to learn' so that non-compliance eventually disappears as an option. Eve was observed with a class in which resistance could easily have become a problem. She dealt with this by a strategic mix of: clear routines; keeping the momentum of the lesson always going with no dead moments, and unobtrusively making students aware that she had observed inappropriate behaviour but had chosen not to let it distract the lesson. Out of this mix, students receive a clear message that 'we are here to do business and the business of the lesson is not to have confrontations over your behaviour'. She continually moves past distractions to get on with this 'core business'. Sue has a conscious philosophy of contrasting high and low emotion. Poor behaviour is acknowledged and dealt with, but with 'low' emotion. Learning achievement is acknowledged with 'high' emotion. Other teachers set out to focus on students managing their own behaviour, by, for example, having them set their own consequences and collaborating in setting up the routine workings of the class. Establishing respectful relationships early is seen as important, as are boundaries and structures, before the class can move into risk-taking challenge. Building 'relationship capital' in the playground and in extra-curricular activities that would have payoff in the classroom is also seen as important.

Teachers emphasize the importance of changing student belief structures – and that means making the time for individual conversations that give students a sense that they can learn and achieve. Building students' sense that they are valued begins with these conversations. Feedback from the earliest days conveying a message that 'I am interested in you' is also seen as important, as is focusing the early language on learning itself. When Sue inherited a new class with students who had challenging behaviours, rather than trying to exert increased overt control over them, she initiated a project in which the students became researchers of learning in the school. They were trained in letter writing and interviewing and writing reports of lesson observations. These students observed lessons in a number of classes in the school, interviewed teachers and students about learning and wrote research reports that showed them that they could achieve well, many of them experiencing success for the first time. A number of teachers talked of the importance of contacting parents early with positive things to report about their child, which in itself could shift the dynamic of the relationship with some students.

High operative: there exists a thoughtful repertoire of practices

Students 'bought into' the message of 'learning trumps behaviour' because of the repertoire of practices that teachers used, including 'scaffolding'. This term has quite a precise meaning in Vygotskian theory. Vygotsky postulated the idea of the zone of proximal development (see Vygotsky 1978), a cognitive region that lies just beyond what the child can do alone. Anything the student can learn with the assistance and support of a teacher (or more capable peer) lies within the ZPD. Strategies for mastering the tasks within this region are metaphoric 'scaffolds'. Building begins on the foundation of what is already known and can be done. The teacher provides the scaffold to support the building task, which moves towards the previously unknown. The scaffold is the instructional support, which, like a literal scaffold, will eventually be withdrawn as the student masters tasks (see Hedegard 2005, Cheyne and Tarulli 2005: 135). Part of scaffolding is the judgement about when a student is ready for independence. This overall sense of 'scaffolding' – which has links back to the high cognitive area – is central to these teachers' practices. In a special education setting, for example, Jennifer scaffolds students' activities through clear instruction and demonstration, but also by clearly rehearsing why students would need this particular skill in other contexts. Across other teachers, scaffolding might take the forms of demonstrating, modelling, questioning, clarifying, summarising and explaining with groups and individuals. It also involves re-framing tasks through clarification, ordering, reorganizing and elaborating. A further major strategy across all years is making use of group collaboration. Sharing is part of this – in early years, students are part of sharing circles, which creates the expectation that all class members can view each others' work (though this is not necessarily made compulsory). Sharing ideas more generally is common. Discussion is widely used to demonstrate ideas, but also to provide an opportunity for ideas to be formulated through talk. As part of classroom talk, role-play is also widely used. The use of ICT also assists student 'buy in', particularly as ICT gives some students an opportunity to demonstrate an area of competence when they may have lacked confidence in other areas. Task variety is also a strong principle, sometimes occurring through rotating activities. However, the strongest overall principle that teachers employed across all years is that students are active participants in learning – and this was commonly manifested through 'hands-on' activities.

The insider classroom

'The insider classroom' is the second key component of the *FGP* student engagement framework. This was reinforced strongly in data from the research. To recapitulate from Chapter 2, insider classroom processes help learners become part of the learning community, and become recognized as valuable members of the community who play meaningful roles for the benefit of all learners. The following set of commonalities was analyzed across the early, middle and later years:

Student community of reflection

- learning as shared responsibility;
- support and time for reflection about learning;
- whole class responsibility for self-regulation of behaviour.

Teacher inclusive conversations

- conversational tenor – balances foregrounding (clarity) and backgrounding (support);
- task design invites conversations across the learning community;
- focus on learning over behaviour is supported by task design.

Student self-assessment

- whole class focus on reflection through an environment of questioning;
- conscious building of cooperative learning processes involving peer support for each other's work;
- encouragement of, and support for, personal task assessment processes.

Teacher feedback

- positive focus on learning with high expectations;
- learning focused, refocused and extended;
- emphasis on reflection and self-regulation.

Each of these is now discussed in detail.

Student community of reflection

A key feature of the *Fair Go* teachers' work is the considered crafting of a learning community. Learning is a shared responsibility and there is a very real sense that all students are involved in thinking and doing. This happens from the earliest of ages, as in Donna's preschool, where learners are encouraged to listen to each other and share ideas, taking important steps towards cooperative reflection on experiences with shared responsibility and owner-ship. Elsewhere, teachers promote lateral thinking, decision-making and the communication of knowledge widely across all learners. Groups are asked to challenge each other in ways that give all students access to learning experi-ences. Eve explicitly asks later years' students to value opinions and embrace different perspectives. Importantly, teachers' planning builds in support and time for reflection about learning, operating at individual, group and whole class levels. In some classes (such as Dan's and Chantal's), teacher support and feedback serves the dual purpose of assisting needy students and provid-ing a scaffold for the more self-directed students. In the later years, reflection often takes on a stronger formal assessment focus, with students sharing responses to examination questions. Nancy's class is a case in point, where students use official marking guidelines to award each other grades and build collective exam competence. Building a reflective learning community provides particular challenges in some of the research contexts. In these and other classes, *Fair Go* teachers consciously work on shaping a whole class responsibility for self-regulation of behaviour. It is clear in Sue's classroom that the class is expected to operate as a unified group. Sonia's Indigenous students are given opportunities to reflect on disruptive behaviour and why they are 'off'. Addressing student bullying, Nicole offers explicit guidance while still allowing student ownership of their actions: 'We are learning together about this so we can help. We need to understand and support. It's not time for bullying. You need to explain. That's your job now'.

Teacher inclusive conversations

The idea that classroom discourse is predominantly conversational is central to the student engagement framework, and was borne out in the data. Across all stages, teachers adopt a conversational tenor, invariably positioning them as co-learners rather than prime deliverers of content. That is not to say that they abdicate responsibility for planning focused on achievement of learning outcomes. Rather, it is about the rhythm of classrooms where learning is the main game and students are key players. A balance is struck between fore-grounding, when tasks are clarified and criteria and purpose are established, and backgrounding, when teachers adopt supportive roles with groups and individuals. This balance allows time for teachers like Georgia to 'unpack' chal-lenging tasks, or for Vanessa to move between private and whole class conversations about learning. Jennifer continually converses with her students, creating a sense of belonging as she establishes rapport and connectedness. Task design that invites conversations is a critical component of the teachers' pedagogies. Consider Dan's classroom where tasks and talk relentlessly urge students to talk about their learning. 'What did you find? You tell us. What do we know? Can we trust that?' And Andrew's reflective conversations: 'The word doesn't look right. We use our visual knowledge, don't we?' The nature and quality of task design helps the teachers focus on learning over behaviour.

As discussed above, this is not always straightforward, but is a feature of all classrooms. The central business is learning, dominating the discourse, whether in Ehab's science room where challenges from individual students are met with comments about the task at hand, or Josephine's well-organized lessons that are delivered in an engaging and dynamic way. That a focus on learning wins out over behaviour in the kinds of contexts where firm control is often seen to be the only effective strategy, is evidence that these teachers can push through to more productive environments.

Student self-assessment

Common across the classrooms are frequent opportunities for qualitative self-assessment, allowing students to think and express ideas about the processes of their learning. This is an important student engagement practice promoting a movement away from the teacher as the sole judge and towards students taking more responsibility for the evaluation of their learning. Self-assessment (a strong metacognitive quality) operates among the *Fair Go* teachers at whole class, group and individual levels. At a whole class level, the kinds of learning conversations described above promote a focus on reflection through an environment of questioning. In the early years' classes like Kim's, students are briskly challenged to express ideas and their responses form a substantive conversation among themselves: 'Tell me what you think'. In the middle years, students are encouraged to consider multiple perspectives and recognize that choices exist in the way they construct and access knowledge. Among later years' students, self-assessment has a clearer formal assessment orientation. For example, Diane teaches reflection through student evaluation of sample essays using published examination criteria. Mark asks students as they consider different perspectives to answers, 'What do you think? How would you test that?' At a group level there is a conscious building of cooperative learning processes involving peer support for each other's work. A variety of strategies are employed (for example, learning logs [Jodie, Josephine], digital tasks involving self-correction [Kim], assessment grids [Sonia], check lists [Vanessa]). Chantal's students self-monitor results through bar graphs so progress is transparent and this in turn motivates effort: 'Be honest with yourself, no need to cheat'. At individual levels, teachers offer encouragement of, and support for, personal task assessment processes. At all three levels, self-assessment brings students closer to student engagement through a focus on learning and a sense that 'we're all in this together'. As one of Sarah's students puts it, 'I learn about different ways to learn and discuss . . . make more friends, see how different people react to things'.

Teacher feedback

Teacher feedback plays a key role in reinforcing the pervasive emphasis on learning observed in the teachers' pedagogies. Again the tenor is invariably conversational, and there is a positive focus on learning with high expectations. This happens at individual, group and whole class levels. Working hand-in-hand with teacher inclusive conversations, feedback aims to build confidence in children as learners, across all the research classrooms and all ages of schooling. As an example, Harmonie regularly uses a learning circle in her early years class where explicit positive feedback delivers consistent messages about the importance of learning. This also happens in Jodie's teaching, where students are invited to reflect as an integral component of the feedback loop: 'How did you feel? What did you learn? What do you know?' With much older learners, Danny's classroom moves along with a constant and easy flow of praise and instruction.

Feedback in these classes spotlights high expectations. Students are continually reminded that their teachers believe they can succeed at higher levels through conversations that focus, refocus and extend learning. In Tammy's young class explicit tasks are developed to encourage sharing of ideas and provide opportunities for her to shape the technical language as students respond. In the middle years, effort and persistence develop as a particular feedback focus. In quite different contexts, Kaili, Sarah and Missy employ teacher and peer modelling alongside feedback to build student belief and foster success. Rebecca assists lower academic standard students with explicit and guided strategies while prompting and affirming student choices for the others. Whereas feedback to later years' students is more strongly targeted towards formal assessment, the emphasis on reflection and self-regulation persists as a constant research theme among all teachers. Diane and Bronwen provide detailed, comprehensive and individualised oral and written feedback with positive strategies for improvement. Similarly, Kate differentiates for individual students and maintains the direction on building student negotiation of learning. In all these classes, students are invited and expected to be fully involved as insiders in the processes of their learning.

Motivation: individual support

The motivation element of the model is where the distinct role of the individual is considered. While we would argue that all facets of the framework are critical, it is often this facet in which teachers, and particularly new teachers, are interested. Questions such as, 'So what do you do about behaviour management?' or, 'How do I work with individuals who aren't engaged in learning?' are often paramount in the minds of early career teachers.

The most common themes from the data are presented in the sections below.

Support for individuals to develop a belief and confidence in their own ability to succeed at school, overcome challenges and perform at their best

- high expectations, supporting achievement, setting them up to succeed;
- clearly explained learning experiences with a focus on cooperative learning and reflection;
- simultaneous scaffolding of learning tasks and self-concept;
- variety of learning styles.

Individual encouragement and skill development

- clarity of task and purpose with balanced teacher assistance as a scaffold;
- negotiated learning using varied approaches to cater for student interest, ability and prior knowledge;
- encouragement for students to see that things are achievable;
- use of a variety of resources to motivate learners,

Indications that school is useful, important and relevant

- individual feedback about the value of school and learning;
- building connections with real life and community.

Individual help to overcome anxiety, take risks and have more control over learning

- provision of clear guides and scaffolds to support learners;
- consistent guiding by the teacher, making it appear 'easy to complete' with less risk but challenging fear of failure;
- praise for success – making success happen and building on it.

Promotion of effort and persistence

- persistence and reinforcement of learning, including inclusive strategies, encouragement of positive student input, and not letting 'behaviour' get in the way of learning;
- variety of tasks, learning styles and resources;
- high positive feedback.

Fostering of self-regulation

- concentration on learning rather than behaviours;
- respectful teacher practices based on knowledge of each student to help minimise maladaptive behaviour;
- individualised strategies to assist students to focus on the task, including visual/verbal/gestural prompts.

Support for individuals to develop a belief and confidence in their own ability to succeed at school, overcome challenges and perform at their best

From the early years to the later years, *Fair Go* teachers develop students' confidence and belief in their ability to succeed. Having high expectations, supporting student achievement and setting their students up to perform at their best are common across the stages. Teachers explicitly encourage students with positive comments and feedback ('You might be the smartest person in the class right now') as well as carefully setting up learning experiences for students to succeed. Foregrounding information and modelling of tasks is a key feature across the case studies, where skills are carefully explained and demonstrated. Again scaffolding helps the high cognitive, affective and operative engagement work in concert with motivation. This scaffolding is not only around academic work but also individual building of confidence. In Tammy's Year 2 boys-only class, not only are activities carefully modelled, and students scaffolded to be able to read a text, interpret images or develop a mathematical concept, but she also scaffolds their confidence. Having explained the task, she asks them 'Do you feel ready? Do you know what to do?' This is teamed with positive reinforcement at the beginning of a task where Tammy tells the students, 'You are superstars. Give yourselves a pat on the back, both sides!'

Other common features which support individuals' belief and confidence in their ability include using a variety of teaching styles and activities, the use of grouping and cooperative learning activities and reflection by students about their learning. One feature highlighted by early years' teachers in particular is the idea that learning, like play, should be fun and positive. Permeating learning is a high expectation for students to do well at their level, but also to do well in an absolute sense. As Sonia says to her class, '...you can't be less than basic but you can be higher than high.'

Individual encouragement and skill development

Teachers encourage individual skills with clear and purposeful lessons, using varied resources as well as negotiating learning based on the needs of each student. In very similar ways to developing confidence and ability in oneself, strategies and approaches that encourage individuals and their skills include scaffolding and foregrounding information.

As with the effective use of scaffolding noted above, there is a balance of teacher assistance and direction that is withdrawn as students move towards independent control of their learning. Missy, working with a middle years class, models the same stems of questions and answers in a social science lesson, building students' confidence, showing them the whole sentence structure so they could vary the overall pattern by supplying their own choice of words. For example, she says, 'She lives at – the river/hills/billabong... My totem is – fish/goanna/eagle'. There is also a sense of negotiation in classrooms, depending on student need. Kate, after explaining and setting a task for her Year 10 science students involving viewing a video says, 'If you get overwhelmed, just ask me to stop the video and we'll work on the answers in the booklet together.'

In order to support skill development, careful planning is crucial. As with many good teachers, what they do in the classroom appears to happen 'naturally', but as Dan in the middle years notes, you need to 'Plan hard and teach easy'. Nancy, teaching music to upper secondary, commented that some students are often hard on themselves and lose confidence rapidly when others around them understand more quickly than they do. She observed that this was where a type of 'shutdown' often occurred, similar to a performance avoidance orientation (Anderman *et al.* 2011). In order to counter this, and encourage them to see learning as achievable, she spends time before lessons making sure students are assigned parts that they can manage and which suit their ability level, whilst ensuring they learn and progress. She remarks, 'I make it look like I randomly choose groups but it is all pre-planned.'

Indications that school is useful, important and relevant

Building a sense of the usefulness and value of school is promoted at the individual and the classroom level. Some feedback is more general on the value of schooling while other feedback is related to a specific activity, such as when Jo asks, 'Why do you think I want you to be able to learn to read?'. Georgia consciously seeks to change her students' 'story' in terms of giving them a positive experience of schooling. The way teachers encourage students to understand the relevance of school involves creating tasks and developing skills that link to real life situations, experiences and to the community. While not every lesson or skill can be linked to 'real life', teachers often work to make connections where possible. For example, Chantal incorporates the measuring of area as part of the design of an actual school courtyard, relating landscaping processes to TV renovation shows. Dan's class tests sports products and discusses how the information could be made clearer for an audience unused to reading graphs. Andrew's class writes brochures about a local topic for another school, where audience has to be considered. Sometimes longer-term motivation is discussed, such as when a young child in Sonia's class wanted to finish school so he could get a job and buy his own car. For that child, at that place and time, this is an appropriate reason for the teacher to affirm and encourage that wish, as a motivating factor in his life.

Individual help to overcome anxiety, take risks and have more control over learning

Disengagement and self-handicapping can flow from anxiety, lack of control and failure avoidance. Conversely, developing a sense of self-efficacy and mastery may flow into behaviours such as persistence, planning and study management. Overcoming anxiety in order to take risks and have control over learning requires experiencing success regularly in a safe, supportive environment. From the data, clear guides, both in the pedagogy and in resources that support the students' learning, are a common feature of these classrooms. This includes discussion and clarification of tasks, which give a sense of control to students. Teachers persevere with tasks that are intellectually challenging but set up in such a way that success is achievable for each student. Danny carefully sequences tasks so that students build on the success of the previous task. Teamed with clear teaching and sharing some control was praise, which is a key feature in all classrooms. Whether it is Mark in secondary maths simply stating, 'I'm really pleased with your efforts' to Nancy saying to a boy in music class, 'You have a lovely voice', public recognition is important. It needs to be noted that feedback is in the context of high cognitive learning experiences, where praise provides accurate, informative feedback to learners (see previous discussion on feedback in 'The insider classroom', page 99).

Promotion of effort and persistence

The promotion of effort and persistence is realised through substantial encouragement, where teachers model persistence in their classrooms and (as discussed above) do not allow 'behaviour' problems to take away from the focus on learning. Teachers encourage effort, even when initial responses aren't yet correct ('You got that one right', or 'You maybe didn't get it right today – but you can get it right tomorrow'). Some of the early years classrooms combine verbal affirmation with extrinsic rewards, giving students many chances to shine and experience success. While off-task behaviour is often dealt with dispassionately (see also Chapter 4), effort is strongly praised and rewarded ('You can, you can, you can, you can and I might even be able to help you'). As with any learning experience, the quality and relevance of the tasks in which learners are invited to participate influences the effort and persistence that they might choose to show. Rich, interesting and varied tasks from singing to woodwork, community activities to digital movie-making, promote student effort and persistence. Lessons are also designed to cater for different interests and learning styles in the class.

Fostering of self-regulation

The focus on learning rather than behaviour which we have drawn attention to on a number of occasions in this chapter is also important in fostering student self-regulation. While various management strategies may be used in the classroom, teachers who focus on learning deal quickly with off-task behaviours and return to their main focus on learning. Teachers also commented on the need to know each child, to care and listen, and pick up on any signs that indicate something may be upsetting a student. Individualised visual, verbal or gestural prompts are also used, in order to assist students to focus on the tasks at hand. When lack of self-regulation occurs, practical strategies are also used, such as providing alternative work or seating when appropriate for students who are unsettled, allowing students to save face after an outburst by letting them re-enter the classroom and calm down before speaking with them.

Engaging messages

The message systems are a key block in the architecture of the MeE Framework. What became apparent in the analysis of the data was the inter-weaving of the messages through pedagogy, curriculum and assessment. What also needs to be acknowledged is that the messages were not all identified in a single learning experience or lesson. It was an accumulation across time that conveyed engaging messages around all of the discourses of power. That is, there was a consistency of messages carried in the *Fair Go* teachers' overriding classroom philosophy. Maintaining the focus on learning helped sustain positive engaging messages even in the face of disruptive responses in some of the classrooms. The commonalities drawn from the case studies were:

Share the experience (knowledge)

- use of scaffolds;
- use of guiding questions;
- endorsement of, and drawing upon, students' knowledge;
- use of technology for learning and to present new knowledge.

You are capable (ability)

- high expectations for all students;
- provision of reinforcement for individual students about their ability;
- praise frequently heard.

Focus on learning not compliance (control)

- explicitness about tasks so students knew what and how to achieve success;
- provision of clarification of tasks when required;
- expectations that students would behave.

Foster a sense of belonging (place)

- respect for students and their community;
- encouragement of links to the wider community beyond the school;

- classrooms as places for learning: students had the capacity to learn through authentic tasks;
- students feel valued, relaxed and productive.

We have a say (voice)

- use of collaboration;
- sharing of information, time, attention and space;
- reflections, discussions and sharing of responses to learning.

Share the experience (knowledge)

Engaging messages about knowledge are provided when teachers employ scaffolds, guiding questions and endorsement of students' knowledge. They are also conveyed when students draw upon and develop their own prior knowledge, relate their learning to different audiences and purposes and reflect on their learning. Teachers and students use technology for learning and to present new knowledge. For example, Sonia scaffolds her students' learning when she draws a learning journey from the learning matrix of what was to be learnt, demonstrating to students what they already knew and what they needed to learn. Andrew positions his Year 4/5/6 students as joint constructors of knowledge: predictors, interpreters, evaluators and reflectors within tasks that involve higher order thinking and metacognitive reflection. In the later years, Kate connects learning in science with real life situations, skilfully integrating the use of digital and virtual learning contexts to stimulate student interest, confidence and consolidation of learning.

You are capable (ability)

Engaging messages about ability are present because the teachers hold high expectations for all students in their classes. They also provide reinforcement for individual students about their ability. Praise is frequently heard. There is a close connection between messages about ability with messages about knowledge and voice. In Georgia's class, students are encouraged to take risks. Individuals working within a group on a particular habitat are asked to think about what they could contribute to the group's learning about, and presentation on, their habitat. All students are expected to contribute and Georgia encourages students to attempt different tasks, such as creating a Scratch animation, instead of Powerpoint slides as part of their group's presentation. Sue's Year 7 students are all encouraged to be part of discussions. They are comfortable giving limited responses, which could be built upon by other members of the group or in discussion with the class. Different scaffolds are used to assist the diverse student population to succeed at activities. Eve uses scaffolds with her English and multilingual classes, always extending students to go beyond the security of the scaffolds towards more sophisticated language and synthesis.

Focus on learning not compliance (control)

Once again, in the 'engaging messages' frame, the focus on learning over behaviour is paramount. Behaviour issues are rephrased around learning, not compliance. The teachers remain calm and exercise patience. They provide clarification when required and are explicit about tasks so students know how to achieve success. In Sonia's classroom, her students could choose which workshop in mathematics to go to which met their learning goals in the area. A student could change workshops if they felt it was necessary but they had to be actively engaged in learning and not stopping others from learning. It was the students' choice whether to work during class or during lunchtime. Rebecca's rationale is that no student should be criticised negatively, nor have their self-concept lowered. She provides her students with opportunities to take responsibility for their learning and to self-regulate their behaviour. Nancy has a similar view. She defuses situations by redirecting students to the business of learning.

Foster a sense of belonging (place)

Engaging messages about place are provided through the teachers' respect of the students and their community, encouraging links to be made to the wider community beyond the school. Classrooms are places for learning, where students have the opportunity to learn through authentic learning tasks. In the classrooms, students have the sense of belonging, being comfortable, and feeling valued, relaxed and productive. Teachers in the early years create an environment where students feel comfortable moving around the classroom. Kim's kindergarten students move around the room independently and in an orderly manner, knowing where objects go and where to get materials they need. Nicole includes learning experiences often related to her students' known contexts, and connecting with their culture and the environment.

We have a say (voice)

Engaging messages about voice are conveyed through the use of collaboration and the sharing of information, time, attention and space. Practices in the classroom employ reflections, discussions and sharing of responses to learning. In Harmonie's class the students work in groups so they can share information to assist if another student is unsure of what is required for the task. Students use a reflective journal, with one student reflecting on why it is important to know how to learn: 'So we can help people out that don't know.' In Sarah's class engaging messages about voice are generated through a choice of learning options, within the structure of her learning design. It is also facilitated by frequent authentic activities and her attention to student responses. Josephine also provides choices in selection of activities for her English and drama students. She uses relevant questioning (which her students also employ) to get students to articulate their decision making and their choices: 'Why have you chosen this individual project?' and 'What are you trying to achieve?'

Conclusion

The headings and sub-headings we have used in this chapter provide a framework for explaining the work of these teachers that fills out the overarching MeE Framework. One other key message, however, is that the elements of the MeE Framework do not exist in separate boxes as discrete items to be ticked off in order to achieve successful teaching in low SES contexts. Rather, the elements interact and overlap, with items from the motivation/individual support area, for example re-occurring in the learning experiences area and among the engaging messages. That is why there has been so much emphasis on the idea that learning in these classrooms is both a central focus and an explicit focus and does not become lost in battles over inappropriate behaviour. It was a recurring theme in all areas of the framework. There is some discussion of how this is achieved in the learning experiences area (page 91) and in Chapter 4 (page 47). A brief list of other key areas of overlap could include:

- building students' sense that they are valued;
- students as active participants in learning;
- support and time being given to reflection about learning.

In the rest of the book we now focus on specific areas of curriculum and associated pedagogy in order to flesh out further the important principles given here.

Note

1   This is a refinement of an earlier analysis contained in Munns *et al.* (2011)

9 Literacies in challenging contexts

Katina Zammit and Jon Callow

> Literacy is about empowerment. It increases awareness and influences the behaviour of individuals, families and communities. It improves communication skills, gives access to knowledge and builds the self-confidence and self-esteem needed to make decisions.
>
> (Koïchiro Matsuura, Director-General of UNESCO on the occasion of International Literacy Day 2008)

In their modelled reading lessons, Nicole and her class of nine-year-olds have been learning about Indigenous Australia, reading a book by 'Uncle' Bob Randall called *Nyuntu Ninti* as well as viewing an online video featuring Uncle Bob. Nicole understands that Uncle Bob's intended message is to promote Aboriginal culture and reconciliation. While she strongly supports this message, she also wants her students to develop the literacy skills to understand how Uncle Bob puts forward his perspective, his world view. By incorporating higher order thinking questions about text purpose into her literacy lessons, Nicole says that

> Students amaze me with their ability to see Uncle Bob's perspective. To understand that his message, that is hidden within his words, is to promote an understanding of Aboriginal culture in an effort to have true reconciliation. Students are able to articulate that they are being positioned by Uncle Bob to feel this way. It is once they understand that this knowledge is constructed, that they have true power. Critical literacy encompasses this thinking. Students then continue this now shared knowledge and create their own narratives around reconciliation and what this means in our context.

Nicole's understanding of literacy is broader than a set of simple, functional skills. She understands that literacy is also shaped by political, ideological and economic influences (Luke and Elkins 2002), educational practices and settings (Luke *et al.* 2000) – and also, as shown in her lessons, by technological change and innovation (Lankshear and Knobel 2007). Literacy can also provide access to educational attainment and various careers (Reder

2000; May 2007), to the language of power and production (May 2007), and to social, economic and cultural capital (Patel Stevens 2011; Luke 2003; Luke and Luke 2001). Access to print literacy 'influenc(es) (not determin[es]) one's capacity to engage with social fields – traditional and emergent, corporate and institutional, cultural and economic' (Luke and Luke 2001: 95).

Being literate, however, is also more complex than simply being able to read and write the printed word (UNESCO 2009; Gee 1990). Literacy for a twenty-first century context is understood as a complex phenomenon, set in broader social contexts (Gee 2001), multiple rather than singular (New London Group 2000) and incorporating a variety of media (spoken, print, screen) and modalities (Kress 2003). It is about being able to engage with, and create, a range of texts, employing combinations of semiotic resources (linguistic, visual, gestural, audio, spatial) in different contexts (New London Group 2000; Zammit 2010).

This chapter examines the types of literacy practices that were evident across the case study data, from the early years to the later years. Given that all classrooms are situated in particular contexts and communities, with their own needs and challenges, the chapter begins with a review of the theory and associated pedagogy which might generally characterize effective and appropriate literacy practices. Using this as a benchmark, the literacy practices from each of the three stages of schooling which we investigated are here analyzed and discussed in relation to both effective literacy practice and the student engagement framework.

Literacy

In the broader international context, literacy theory and related practices draw on a variety of traditions and research fields. Notwithstanding the challenges of attempting to define literacy succinctly, Freebody argues that there is a sense that societies are now more dependent on literacy and that we therefore need 'more complex and sophisticated literacy capabilities' (Freebody 2007: 6). This is reflected in the recognition of the need for multiple literacy skills (New London Group 2000; Zammit 2010), the evolution of new literacies associated with technology (Lankshear and Knobel 2007), as well as the social, political and economic aspects of literacy, represented by a diversity of policy and curriculum statements internationally (see Freebody 2007: 8 for a selection of such policies). Given the complex and global nature of contemporary society, literacy needs to be understood in these wider cultural contexts, where technology, diversity, multilingualism and changing labour markets are key elements in students' current and future lives. This changing global context also impacts on what types of texts are studied in schools and what counts as 'reading' and 'writing', as well as how these are best taught. While Freebody acknowledges the ongoing nature of debate around pedagogy, he argues for a 'range of pedagogical approaches, some involving more authoritative and direct teacher intervention, some involving more encouragement, support, and indirect guidance on the part of teachers' (NCB 2008: 7). In order to hold these approaches together, with their sometimes varied theoretical underpinnings, a broader literacy paradigm has become dominant in many literacy and curriculum documents in the Western world (IRA 2012; UKLA 2012; NCB 2008).

Luke and Freebody's four resources model of reading (Freebody and Luke 1990) has strongly informed theoretical frameworks for conceptualizing reading in both Australian educational settings and internationally. More recently Freebody has rearticulated this model in terms of literacy in general, which he defines as the:

> orchestration in action of resources relating to the peculiarities of the demands at hand for:
>
> • cracking the relationship between spoken and materialized language;
> • using and extending cultural knowledge to make texts meaningful;
> • drawing on, using and making a repertoire of texts that effectively advance the individual or collective purposes at hand;
> • interrogating texts for the ways in which they constrain interpretation, by excluding alternative ways of documenting experience of the world.
>
> (Freebody 2007: 9)

In practical terms, this means classrooms should both utilize and create a variety of authentic texts, both literary and factual, where their cultural purpose and use is made explicit in classroom discourse. This includes developing talking and listening skills, the teaching of phonics and letter–sound knowledge, teamed with comprehension of meaning, using varied strategies and approaches (Block and Duffy 2008). At the same time, teachers should take opportunities to discuss the purposes that texts serve, such as the range of text types and genres, and develop grammatical knowledge, whilst also providing opportunities for critiquing texts (Christie 2005). Critical literacy has a particularly well developed history in the Australian educational context (Luke 2000).

Reflecting broader concepts of literacy pedagogy, Australian teaching practices generally flow from socio-cultural understandings about language and literacy being connected to authentic texts and contexts (Holliday 2008). The use of quality children's literature is encouraged in classrooms from preschool to Year 12, while the use of factual texts (print and screen) as well as video and interactive multimedia and interactive whiteboards are also common literacy resources (ACARA 2011).

Many literacy classrooms utilize aspects of scaffolded practice for reading, writing, talking and listening. Scaffolding, informed by Vygotsky's work (Vygotsky and Kozulin 1986), starts with a student's actual zone of development, then supports the development of new or more complex skills or knowledge with the help of an enabling teacher or peer, often explicitly teaching and modelling reading and writing skills and concepts (Edwards-Groves and DEST 2003). In the primary (elementary) years, a literacy session will often begin with more teacher regulated practices such as reading to a class, then move to shared or modelled reading and writing, where explicit strategies and features are taught (DEST 2002). This scaffolded support is gradually removed, allowing for more student regulated practices such as guided reading (where a small group of students practice reading together while guided by the teacher) and independent reading and writing. Teachers also utilize a variety of associated literacy activities and strategies in order to best support literacy learners, which include drama, play and ICT-based activities (Louden *et al.* 2005).

Equity has always been an important issue in terms of who has access to effective literacy education (UNESCO 2009). Between 2000 and 2009, Australian 15 year olds performed at a level significantly higher than the OECD average in all three assessment areas of PISA: reading literacy, mathematical literacy and scientific literacy. However, in terms of equity of performance, students from higher socio-economic backgrounds consistently performed above those from lower backgrounds in reading, the difference being the 'equivalent of nearly three years of schooling' (Thomson *et al.* 2009: 21). The results for Indigenous students, as well as students in remote locations, were significantly worse in terms of the equity gap. Literacy, of course, is just one part of the larger picture of equity and education but it continues to play a significant role in student engagement and success at school.

Having presented a broad overview of literacy, the following sections of this chapter analyze the types of literacy practices and associated pedagogies from each case study, in relation to the student engagement framework and pedagogical model. They are grouped around the three broad stages of early years (pre-school to Year 4), middle years (Years 5–8) and later years (Years 9–12).

Early years

Integration

Teachers working in early years classrooms, from pre-school to Year 4, consistently taught literacy in contextually relevant ways. Whether it was viewing and exploring the town map on the electronic whiteboard in Jodie's class or the real life use of literacy in Donna's preschool classroom – where students 'sign in' each day as part of their routine – each classroom worked to connect literacy to meaningful action. This focus on context and meaning not only supports effective literacy practices, outlined in the previous section, but works strongly with the *Fair Go* messages around knowledge being useful and relevant, as well as place, reflecting the value of learning that is connected to student's local community and life experiences.

Text variety

Classrooms that are rich in engaging and interesting texts implicitly model the value and purpose of literacy. In the foyer of Donna's preschool, a daily diary, including text and photos, displays the experiences of the children, sometimes complemented by a slideshow on the computer. There are also brochures and community information for parents and carers, covering topics such as healthy eating, men's support groups and family activities. This not only shows children that text is valuable in sharing with parents what the children have been doing, but also models to children a variety of adult literacy practices. Across every early years classroom, written, visual and electronic texts are used as part of everyday literacy activities, from print texts like big books, book corners and displays of children's written work to electronic texts such as videos, student created animations and slide shows. Literacy research has long encouraged teachers to use a variety of meaningful and relevant texts in the classroom (Healy and Honan 2004) and this is particularly important in terms of student engagement. Varied, well chosen and relevant books and texts used in the classroom send the message that literacy knowledge is in fact worthwhile and useful and that it can connect to place in a student's life. In addition, working successfully with such texts itself offers opportunities to develop literacy skills. It is here that the pedagogy around literacy teaching is important.

Effective practice in reading

The case study data around the teaching of reading in early years classrooms reflected many of the common practices recommended in all early years settings (Louden *et al.* 2005), supporting the multiple reader roles that Freebody and Luke (1990) propose. There were no significantly different literacy strategies utilized from those described in the preceding section, 'Literacy'. While some classrooms worked with a particular literacy program for reading that the school had adopted, teachers adapted these to the needs of the class as well as framing them more broadly with a student engagement focus. While each classroom would organize their day differently, the underlying pedagogy of teaching reading included: reading aloud to students, shared or modelled reading of texts, small group guided reading and independent reading (DEST 2002; Holliday 2008).

All teachers included reading aloud to their class. Reading books together provides enjoyment and builds an extensive repertoire of cultural story knowledge, as well as offering opportunities for young learners to engage meaningfully with narrative (Spencer 1988). The students in Vanessa's Year 2 class talked about the various types of books their teacher read to them, as well as the fact that she sought out topics or books that she knew the children would enjoy. Tammy's all boys Year 2 class were reading well known author Anthony Browne's *Willy and Hugh*, which not only engaged them with the powerful pictures, but also modelled strong themes about making friends, a social skill Tammy was encouraging in her class.

Developing letter–sound relationships

Explicit work on phonics and letter–sound relationships for reading and spelling were evident in all classes, but this appeared to be part of a balanced program, where there was not undue emphasis on one approach (as in commercial phonics programs) at the expense of integrating comprehension, independent reading time or other purposeful literacy activities. This is in contrast to Luke's study of 106 early years classrooms in Queensland (Luke 2010) which found that teachers in low SES schools spent more time on direct alphabetic instruction and drill of grapheme–phoneme generalizations than their middle or high SES counterparts. Luke argues that, far from students in poorer communities lacking 'basic skills', they in fact receive more work on decoding, at the expense of other critical aspects of reading and literacy. The *Fair Go* teachers in the early years' setting appear to integrate 'code breaker' skill development with higher order literacy and learning, in ways that reflect engagement – that is high operative along with high cognitive and high affective.

In Jodie's Year 3/4/5 class, the book for shared reading reflected the Ancient Egypt theme being studied – which itself linked literacy across curriculum areas. The types of reading instruction that occurred in Jodie's class included discussion of various levels of story meanings, visual literacy and comprehension strategies, as well as vocabulary and word level studies – each of which supported both reading and writing. Students commented on the various ways they learned, noting that they learnt 'more and more things' through reading different types of books for information. They also articulated spelling strategies, such as breaking words into syllables. The integration of code breaking skills with higher order thinking complements the work of student engagement, both at the learning experiences level, as well as at the level of classroom messages, particularly around knowledge, ability and control.

Writing

The teaching of writing in early years classrooms reflected aspects of reading pedagogy, in terms of discussion and modelling of various text types and their features, in preparation for joint or independent writing. The pedagogical practices of explicit teaching were evident in different forms in each classroom. Using variations of scaffolding (Christie 2005), a model text was read, structural features and grammar discussed and the class jointly constructed another text with the teacher, before students worked independently writing their own piece of work.

Integrating writing into meaningful contexts or activities supports both 'e'ngagement and 'E'ngagement. At the 'e'ngagement level, writing lessons that provide high cognitive, affective and operative learning by definition require that skills such as spelling, handwriting and grammar also work with high cognitive elements, such as linking writing to purpose and audience, as well as working with affective enjoyment. Students in Vanessa's Year 1/2 class were writing persuasive texts about which animals would make the best pets. Their teacher allowed them to choose any animal they liked as the basis for their persuasive exposition. While there were the usual dogs, cats and fish, one student chose a pterodactyl. Such regular moments of choice support the sharing of control in terms of 'E'ngagement messages. Working in pairs, students made notes on personal whiteboards, discussing ideas together. Returning to the whole class, the teacher used the information from one pair to jointly model exposition writing, using an interactive text type website with text boxes for each stage of the text.

Talking and listening

Talking and listening can be considered in terms of process and performance (Jones 1996). Some classrooms had learning experiences in which the final performance involved talking and listening such as:

- public speaking in Joanne's class on the topic 'My Special Day';
- taking story extracts in Kim's class to create rhythmic chants; or
- the final animations in Vanessa's class, in which students' scripts were voiced by the animation software.

Talk as process is important, not only from the viewpoint of literacy pedagogy, but also from the point of view of giving students voice and sharing control. Every classroom evidenced numerous examples of students being encouraged to talk as they learned, as well as talking about their learning. Whether they were expressing opinions about the story that was read, their views on environmental issues, predicting why a tower they had built as part of a maths topic might stand (or fall), or simply sharing news, talk featured as an active, positive aspect of each classroom.

Middle years

Integration

In our research, classrooms from the middle years straddle the upper end of the primary (elementary) school (Years 5–6 in Australia) to the junior high school years (Years 7–8 in Australia). Thus, some teachers work with their Year 5 or 6 class for the whole day in a primary school, while those with Year 7 or 8 students in high school are generally subject area specialists, such as English or science teachers. Each teacher has particular challenges. Teaching literacy across the curriculum in primary school settings lends itself to the integration of reading and writing with other subject areas. Andrew's primary class were making brochures about the need to clean up the creek in the local area, while Chantal's were scripting and producing a short film about the history of the school. In the junior high context, Ehab teaches science, Rebecca teaches English while Missy teaches Aboriginal language and culture, English and maths. Sue, on the other hand, works with Year 7 students across a number of subject areas. Her class were studying Ancient Egypt at the time of her case study, which allowed Sue to integrate history and English and story writing and historical narratives, as well as incorporating visual literacy in particular texts.

As with the early years, opportunities to connect students' literacy learning to contextually relevant or interesting activities promotes engaging messages around knowledge as worthwhile and meaningful to students' lives. The contextualizing of literacy for students wherever possible was a key feature of all classrooms.

Text variety and visual literacy

The use of a variety of books and multimodal texts in all classrooms signals that teachers were not only aware of the importance of using resources that reflect twenty-first century literacy skills but understood that many of these resources, particularly visual and ICT-based texts, engaged their learners (see Chapter 11). All the middle years' teachers used visual resources in their literacy teaching. Sometimes they were helping students learn *through* visuals, using them to learn about science or discuss a picture book, while at other times they were learning *about* visuals (Callow 1999). Learning about visuals involved developing literacy skills in which teachers explicitly taught about how images were constructed, developing in students a visual grammar or metalanguage (Kress and van Leeuwen 2006). Chantal developed literacy skills around film making, while Dan discussed the use of angles and shot distance when reading a wordless graphic novel with his class. When interviewed, students recalled how Dan explored visual images with 'picture books that teach us more . . . where the pictures show us the meaning'.

Content literacy demands – science focus

Those teachers in the junior high school area taught in areas of English, science or in learning-support roles – the latter where they worked with students across a number of subject areas. While English is seen as the home of literature, including poetry, or of media texts such as film, other texts in other subject areas present different reading and writing demands. Literacy learning in science will look quite different to literacy in an English class, in terms of the types of texts, purpose and vocabulary utilized (Shanahan and Shanahan 2008).

Ehab – particularly aware of the link between literacy and science – used a variety of visual and interactive resources, incorporating technology as a key aspect of his teaching. Ehab believed that 'technology is not a challenge. The real challenge is literacy'. Because scientific concepts are developed through both activities and language, Ehab made sure that there was an emphasis on hands-on teaching and learning, while at the same time including contextual vocabulary development, sentence building and literacy games. He would also 'team teach' with an English as a Second Language (ESL) teacher. In this way, the high cognitive aspects of both science and literacy were supported by high operative activities and the affective elements of engaging learning experiences.

Effective practice in reading

As with the early years, there were consistent examples of middle years teachers using strong scaffolding practices when teaching reading, including: reading aloud to students; modelled reading, and smaller group activities. Although many students have moved from learning to read into a more 'reading to learn' phase in the middle years, many adolescents disengage from reading, whether through lack of interest in reading or underdeveloped decoding and comprehension strategies (Snow and Biancarosa 2003). Teachers in the middle years classrooms engaged students not only in the modelling of reading as purposeful and worthwhile, but also developed reading skills from word level activities through to comprehension and critical literacy, reflecting the 'four roles of the reader' (Freebody and Luke 1990). One of the boys in Chantal's class was a reluctant reader but Chantal persisted in finding books on topics in which he was interested, such as the Holocaust. Far from ignoring the more complex role of 'text analyst' (Freebody and Luke 1990) for her more challenged readers, Chantal believes that 'critical literacy is a point of engagement for boys – you just have to have the right text'. She uses multi-layered picture books to allow students to reflect critically on what they read and to access different levels of meaning in a text.

Writing

The teaching of writing reflected similar pedagogical approaches to that of reading in the middle years classes. Explicit teaching and thorough scaffolding of the writing process was also similar to the early years classes. Writing occurred for a variety of purposes in each classroom, whether working on longer text types such as a persuasive text or narrative, or jointly constructing information and notes together as part of a learning experience. There was strong evidence of explicit teaching of writing at all levels of text, from word and sentence level through to the audience and purpose of a text. Writing in most classrooms linked to the subject area, a local context, a piece of literature being studied or an integrated classroom theme. The diversity of writing tasks was reflected in the contexts in which they were set. Missy's students created a board game for younger students, with instructions written in both English and their local Indigenous language, Ngemba.

In order to motivate very reluctant writers, Missy uses scaffolds and technology to engage them, using the computer to add instructions to their board games. Her valuing of the local language is evident, not only from the tasks which include using both English and Ngemba, but in the way she explains how to move between the two languages. Missy talks about Aboriginal English, which students use. She explains to them that their Indigenous language does not directly translate to Standard Australian English (SAE), so she first translates into Aboriginal English, which is then more easily re-worded into SAE. Engaging students with culturally relevant and powerful knowledge enhances their writing experiences, supporting messages around voice, control and place.

Talking and listening

Teachers in middle years classrooms integrated talk into their classrooms in similar ways to the early years. Provision of classrooms where students are encouraged to share their ideas and thoughts not only allows talking and listening skills to develop but sends a clear message that the students' voice is valuable. While some teachers may consider a quiet classroom as reflecting a disciplined and on-task environment, this belief usually privileges teachers as the authorial voice, controlling what is shared and what is not (Dufficy 2005). Collaborative activities, open-ended discussion and drama activities all require a degree of shared control, if the benefits of such activities are to be realized for students.

Teachers in the middle years classrooms are varied in the ways that they develop student voice and how they share control. Nicole is able to weave a balance between keeping a lesson on focus whilst allowing reflective moments and discussion as a book or video is viewed. In general, she integrates spontaneous discussion, where students simply comment without raising their hands. On the surface, Dan's and Chantal's classrooms look different, one appearing to be a more noisy, spontaneous place, the other apparently more structured and highly organized, but each is careful to provide experiences where all students can share, discuss and give their viewpoints.

Talking and listening as processes are integral parts of literacy practices such as jointly writing a text or discussion around shared reading and collaborative group activities. Talk as performance in middle years classrooms involved activities such as: speeches about Chinese inventions that Kaili's class presented; acting in videos with Chantal's students, or the use of drama activities with Missy, in which one student took on a character's role, while others questioned them about their thoughts and actions. Teacher talk was also critical in this aspect. While there was no detailed linguistic analysis taken of classroom exchanges, there was evidence that teachers were conscious of how talk shaped the classroom. Observations of Nicole's questioning showed that she regularly gave thinking time to students after asking a question. Chantal spoke explicitly to her students about the sharing of responsibility in their class, while Missy's choice of working in both English and the local Indigenous language, showing how to translate one to the other, conveyed messages around knowledge (that local knowledge is important), ability (student language skills were highlighted) and a sense of the importance of place to her students.

Later years

Later years teachers provide opportunities for authentic learning of language and literacy, often drawing on students' funds of knowledge (Moll *et al.* 1992), making connections to their lives and communities and identities. The teachers in this stage worked in a variety of subject areas such as English, history, science and mathematics, as well as working with special needs and multilingual students.

Integration

A variety of strategies are used to integrate literacy into subject areas, as well as to engage their students in learning. Teachers develop appropriate literacy skills that are contextually relevant to the topic, moving between more teacher-regulated practices to more student-regulated practices, reflecting Freebody's call for a range of approaches in the classroom (NCB 2008).

Content literacy: integrating learning of literacies within a subject

Similar to the teachers in the middle years, later years teachers clearly develop the literacies relevant to the topic being studied. Some teachers in the later years explicitly teach grammar and language structures at the sentence, paragraph and whole text level, as well as the key compositional features of multimodal texts in paper and digital media. To varying levels, they introduce students to a metalanguage that can be used to discuss and critique the construction of a text and assist in the creation of their own texts. While some subject areas, such as English and the social sciences, may require more extended reading and writing skills, others such as mathematics still require literacy and vocabulary to be thoughtfully developed. In Mark's mathematics classes, he clearly illustrates mathematical terminology by connecting terms to the experience of their world, 'When the sun goes down we can see it setting on the horizon – horizontal', 'When someone climbs a cliff that's the vertical'.

In Kate's Year 10 girls' science class, she develops the connection between science and scientific language, encouraging her students to see that they are capable of learning complex science at the same time as developing scientific terminology. The learning space is one of shared control with the students. The girls discuss DNA and genetics, guided by Kate's questioning and consolidation of their prior knowledge. She introduces subject-specific language and they practice using the terms during activities, which means understanding a term such as 'deoxyribonucleic acid' and comparing different models of DNA provided through virtual images, printed text, teacher's scaffolds and students' actual experiments. Students work in groups to create a model of DNA using bags of sweets (candy) and toothpicks, referring to a website, their booklets, a wooden model of DNA, and a labelled diagram on the whiteboard. They use laptops to view images and videos, locate information and record notes. The lesson concludes with students giving a spoken explanation of how their model DNA molecule is structured. Kate engages her students with messages around knowledge and ability, emphasizing that learning science is fun and active, as well as integrating both print and digital literacy skills into her lessons.

Text variety – multimodal texts

Just as the early and middle years classrooms utilize a variety of books, texts and resources, so teachers in the later years use multimodal texts to develop content knowledge and multimodal literacies, including video resources for English, history and science lessons. Teachers taught students how to read, view and create a range of multimodal texts, reflecting the importance of developing multiple literacies (ACARA 2011).

In Diane's English classes, she explicitly teaches the skills and language of analysis and critique when working with literary articles, film and images. As well as fostering these literacy skills, she is promoting students' confidence in their own ability to access the ideas in a range of sophisticated texts. Students are encouraged to use metalanguage and to identify features of written and visual texts. Her Year 10 English class worked on a holiday and travel theme, moving towards the design and creation of a travel brochure. She provided opportunities for them to analyze the visual and language features of travel brochures, pointing out the designer's purpose and intended effect on readers. In terms of engagement and message systems, the link to 'everyday' texts and popular culture also built upon students' knowledge as well as encouraging student voice and control by choosing their own travel destinations. Diane had organized for a travel agency to assess the brochures based on industry standards which 'motivated the students to edit and proofread their work even more carefully as it was going to a "real audience"'.

In science, Kate uses a range of semiotic resources to develop literacy and conceptual understandings. She explains that music, imagery and graphics affect communication of scientific information and need to be appropriately used in students' PowerPoint presentations. She expands the substantive conversations about communicating information using PowerPoint by considering how the selection of different modes impacts on meaning: 'Love hearts and flowers! Your powerful messages are lost in the flowers'. In terms of scaffolding their learning, one student commented: '(she) gives us examples and stories. First, does it on the board... asks who knows about the topic... relates worksheets to pictures, explains, uses team explanations, visuals, diagrams, puzzles, videos. Then she lets us do it ourselves'.

Writing

Teaching students to write in the later years includes developing more sophisticated writing styles, as well as continuing to support students who struggle with writing skills. Not every case study included detailed writing lessons. Subjects such as mathematics and drama focus less on extended written texts, while Jennifer in the special education unit worked with shorter texts appropriate for the needs of her students. The later years English teachers such as Eve, Diane, Bronwen and Danny focused on teaching students genres such as reviews and essays, and on developing the particular grammatical and language skills needed to argue, describe and persuade. As with the early and middle years classrooms, writing was always supported with explicit criteria and scaffolded to ensure students developed the skills to improve their writing.

Eve supports her senior classes (high numbers of multilingual learners) by carefully moving them from more defined writing structures and forms to more sophisticated, open-ended writing. In Year 11, a model student essay is presented as a cloze passage for students to fill in, providing a strong scaffold for their own writing. In her Year 12 class, more responsibility is given to students to shape their work and review it. After students have written a short response to a poem, a marking rubric lists the features that they have been studying and that Eve would expect to see in their written work. They peer-assess each other's work, using a highlighter to show where their writing includes specific aspects of the analysis, such as discussing context, technique, effects or a relevant quotation. This strong scaffolding of writing is combined with critical thinking, which is reflected in the high levels of engagement, higher order questions and comments during pair work, group work and general class discussion.

Talking and listening

In the later years, talking and listening continue to play as important a role as in the early and middle years. Classrooms where knowledge and voice are shared are necessarily talkative, allowing meaning to be negotiated between teachers and students, as well as between students. This is important in building respect and creating a positive, high affective learning environment. Teacher talk can have a powerful impact. The way in which Danny speaks to his students instils a sense of mutual respect, always addressing each student by name. He brings his cultural knowledge and sensitivity about Aboriginal learning styles to his classroom, particularly in the way he communicates in lessons.

The role of questioning reflects the importance of talking and listening in all subject area learning. Questioning is used to develop higher order and critical thinking, to encourage students to go beyond the concrete or literal to the interpretive. Eve uses higher order questions and comments in pair work, group work and general class discussion, representing high cognitive and high affective learning. She represents class discussion to the students as 'big-group-work'. Through questioning, effective listening and responding she is in constant dialogue with the students. Use of peer marking has students discuss the nature of one student's response to another student's piece of writing, with a lot of talk around justifying grades, clarifying thinking and reflection.

Conclusion

Literacy data from all classrooms shows evidence that the *Fair Go* teachers integrated literacy purposefully and effectively across a range of classrooms and subject areas. This is significant for low SES students, given that literacy plays such a key role in students' current and future educational and life opportunities. Not only were a range of appropriate pedagogical practices observed in classrooms, but these practices complemented and developed both 'e'ngagement and 'E'ngagement. Explicit language teaching and scaffolding of literacy skills in supportive and cognitively challenging contexts reflected the importance teachers placed on literacy at each stage. Literacy not only opens up curriculum knowledge and learning, but, as the opening quote by Matsuura acknowledges, it is also about empowerment, self-confidence and self-esteem. This is captured in the conclusion of Nicole's lesson about Uncle Bob at the beginning of this chapter. At the end of this session, after much discussion, one quite shy nine-year-old has a 'light bulb' moment, which Nicole affirms as clearly articulating the intent of the book they have been reading. Nicole writes a paraphrase of the student's words for the class to read: 'By sharing Aboriginal culture with everyone, we can learn from each other and be joined together.'

10 Imagination, creativity and intellectual quality

Bronwyn Cole, Mary Mooney and Anne Power

> Education . . . is a process that awakens individuals to a kind of thought that enables them (students) to imagine conditions other than those that exist or that have existed.
>
> (Egan 2007: 43)

The opening quote by Kieran Egan, a Director of The Imaginative Education Research Group, reminds us that the purpose of education is more than the accumulation and reproduction of knowledge. Rather, education is a process through which students journey to new horizons in thinking, doing and valuing, and from which they can construct hopes and possibilities beyond those of their immediate surrounds and circumstances. Students' journeys are influenced by the experiences and encounters that teachers plan and the ways in which teachers help students make connections in knowledge, construct new understandings and adjust and develop skills and values (Bruner 1986; Egan 2007).

Classrooms in the *Teachers for a Fair Go* project (*TFG*) abound with displays of students' work and a variety of resources readily accessible to students: some of these are technological tools for learning, models, scientific or manipulative equipment, paper-based charts, graphs, maps, representations and books – and some are live displays or artifacts. *Fair Go* teachers facilitate high learning expectations and active learning amongst students. Students are aware of a constant focus on learning and frequently shift from working independently to participating in teams, or as a class. The classrooms are learning spaces deliberately planned by the teachers and shared with the students, in which high cognition and content that matters are explored in-depth and where students are encouraged to employ their imaginations, investigate and use novel thought and express learning in creative ways. These stimulating environments awaken students to learning that makes a difference to them, their futures and that of others. These are classrooms often denied to students in schools in low socio-economic areas in which challenging behaviours can be frequent and where the pedagogical emphases can be on management and instruction in the basics rather than stimulating, meaningful learning (Haberman 2005; Luke 2010).

Many of the teachers in *TFG* consciously planned and implemented peda-gogical practices that actively encouraged students to employ imagination and creativity in their learning. They deliberately looked for and organized spaces, in classrooms and outdoors, in which students could engage with intellectually challenging tasks and think and perform in meaningful, imagi-native ways. In this chapter we explore the links between imagination, creativity and learning, then describe some of the planning and practices of the teachers and students' responses to these. In particular, we describe ways teachers in the *TFG* project:

• consciously plan creatively, making space for students to engage in creative activity;
• facilitate the use of students' imaginations;
• elicit and support imaginative and creative activity amongst *all* students in their classrooms; and
• constantly expect high intellectual quality in students' achievements.

Within these headers, the stories of nine teachers, representative of the three stages of the project – early, middle and later years – and contexts of the study -- urban, suburban, housing estate and rural-remote – are drawn upon as exemplars for the pedagogical practices described in this chapter. While all nine teachers regularly employ many of the practices in differing ways and to varying extents, their case studies are selectively used to exemplify just one practice. Through the nine stories we explore the question, 'How do exem-plary teachers encourage imagination and creativity in learning, build intellectual quality and achievement and help close the equity gap for students in schools in low socio-economic communities?'

Imagination, creativity and learning

Imagination is likened to a preamble to identifying and exploring a problem, or a heightened consciousness that enables humans to process what is outside their lived experience. It makes the strange become familiar and allows ques-tions such as, 'How might?' or 'What if?' Creativity, by contrast, is taking something that is familiar and seeing it in a new way. Both imagination and creativity can be considered as mental maps that find relationships between the familiar and the strange and are important abilities and tools for new learning (Thomas and Brown 2011).

Definitions of creativity encompass notions of the mind being open to ideas and working to create something that is new, different and of value (NACCCE 1999; Robinson 2001; Safran 2001). While often associated with creative arts subjects such as music, visual art, drama or dance, creativity can be demonstrated in any subject at school, or in any aspect of life (Boden 2001; Lucas 2001). It can result in new thinking or ideas for an individual in their everyday life or an outstanding innovation that could be of benefit to all humankind (Craft 2001; 2010). Teachers can see students demonstrating creativity through working scientifically, symbolically or metaphorically. Teachers can see students demonstrating creativity in the ways in which they solve mathematics problems, resolve complications in groups, create poems, musical compositions or new 'apps' for technology, or think critically about global human experiences. Associated with creativity is imagination, the human capacity to be able to form mental images and perceptions of concepts and ideas that are not within our immediate senses, such as 'seeing' through an author's eyes, 'picturing' the historical past, 'listening' to raindrop sounds created through music, or 'viewing' possible futures, outcomes or creations (Robinson 2006). Distinct from dreaming or fantasizing, imagination involves conscious mental activity and deliberate flexibility of the mind in which people draw on perceptions, memories, emotions, thoughts, experiences and metaphors, in order to see and think of things in less constrained ways (Egan 2007). Imagination is a joining of human cognitive and affective processes. When teachers encourage students to use their imaginations they are asking them to consciously draw on knowledge, skills, perceptions and emotions acquired through experiences, to respond to new experiences and answer questions such as, 'What if...?' 'How could...?' 'What do you think...?' (Egan 2007). Exhorting students to be imaginative and creative during classroom experiences of intellectual rigour distinguished many of the *Fair Go* teachers. Students see the classrooms of these teachers as exciting places in which to be and to learn.

Planning creatively and making space for creative activity

'Teachers plan hard and teach easy'. These are the words of Dan, a middle years teacher working in a highly diverse urban school with significant numbers of multilingual learners. Dan's Year 6 classroom is characterized by spontaneity and surprise, the development of curiosity, imaginative thought and problem exploration, provisions for student choice and joint construction of knowledge. Spontaneity and surprise are often used to initiate learning activities: 'Which of these tennis balls will be best for handball?' questions Dan as he releases tennis balls from a height onto the classroom floor. Students laugh and scramble for the balls. The surprise encounter with real props motivates the students to think about and design performance tests and criteria for a science investigation. Similarly, another of Dan's lessons commences with a square of butchers' paper floating onto the floor and Dan painting a large pink square upon it with an aerosol can. He asks, 'How could these tools (the paper, spray can and trundle wheel) be used in the playground to help us learn about and calculate area?' The students have another unexpected challenge to solve and permission to work creatively and mathematically outdoors, with real props and tools.

Students in Dan's class see these as fun activities to be explored and solved, but Dan has spent much time and intellectual energy planning how he will capture students' interests and maintain engagement with significant stage-based subject matter. Such planning for effective surprise and engagement is common amongst a number of the teachers in our project. Lessons are initiated affectively through spontaneous acts, imaginative stories or by using props or games to elicit fun in posing problems. The lessons that follow are neither trivial nor fanciful. They involve content prescribed in syllabus documents but introduced in challenging ways, connecting to students' real life contexts. In Dan's classroom, the surprise of the pink square sparks students' curiosity and Dan's pedagogy quickly transfers to preparing them with explicit, yet negotiated, criteria for investigating big ideas about area.

The students move outside in groups with their equipment and group member roles clarified as 'Calculator, Measurer or Recorder'. Each group is aware of the time frame for the task, criteria for achievement and the parameters and constraints of group behaviour in an outdoor setting. Each group 'paints' a section of the nearby paddock and explores the problem of calculating the area bounded by the paint. Dan monitors and questions groups about how they are dealing with irregularity of shape and whether ground undulations are affecting their calculations. When the time is up, groups report their strategies and findings. Dan questions further, 'Can someone tell me why this strategy was used to complete the task?' He probes, clarifies and checks that all students are jointly attaining common understandings about the calculation of area.

These lessons share many pedagogical features with a typical mathematical lesson in Sarah's Year 6 classroom in an outer urban school. Sarah stimulates students' imaginations as she reveals a bright purple, glitter-covered top hat with the name Darcy clearly displayed on the front. This is the hat of *Darcy the Decimal*, to be worn proudly by a student who will carry a card with a large black dot, while role-playing a shifting decimal point amongst a row of integers created by a line of fellow students holding number cards. Darcy's movements create excitement as the class reads increasingly longer decimal numbers, then takes up the challenge of predicting Darcy's movements left or right, one, two or three places, when numbers are multiplied and divided by tens, hundreds and thousands. Sarah questions and promotes fun with, 'So who's the winner? Which number is bigger?' She assists students to jointly construct the pattern, meaning and rules for decimal calculations before her pedagogy moves to whole-class guided examples, colourfully presented using a Darcy simulation on the interactive whiteboard. The examples are planned to gradually progress in difficulty and Sarah constantly checks for understanding, requesting, 'Hands up if you are still a little bit confused. How?' When most students demonstrate understanding she sets independent work, negotiates timeframes and gives individual attention as needed. When time is up, the independent work is checked, clarified and acknowledged as a class. Sarah intentionally builds a whole class sense of achievement and excitement. She then poses group 'challenges' that are real life tasks involving decimal calculations. Groups move around the classroom space helping each other to solve the problems.

Dan and Sarah 'plan hard'. They have clear goals for what they want students to achieve in lessons and these goals are inextricably linked to deliberately planned pedagogies. They create spontaneity and fun in learning environments that are intellectually challenging, yet highly supportive, and where additional behaviour management is rarely required – but they employ quite different lesson structures. Dan commences with open challenges, allowing students to explore creatively, before bringing them together to develop common understandings. Sarah begins with explicit instruction, building students' understanding then guiding them to take up creative challenges. In both classrooms, the creative spaces are intentionally designed, engaging students affectively through spontaneity, surprise and fun, operatively through movement in, out or around the classroom, and cognitively through investigating the subject matter in depth. Students in both classrooms are supported in exploring knowledge, searching for meaning and feeling and expressing new understandings and imaginings, openly and creatively. These teachers acknowledge the strong relationship between teaching and learning. They work as 'educational artists' (Eisner 2005) or 'conductors' (Bransford *et al.* 2007) moving beyond technical implementation of single standard lesson formats to design sequenced experiences that promote deep, meaningful learning. These teachers plan and organize learning such that it gives students positive messages that knowledge is shared and that all students have ability to jointly construct knowledge.

Facilitating the use of imagination

In Chantal's Years 5 and 6 classroom in a diverse urban school, students are frequently and consciously encouraged to employ their imaginations during the learning process. Her classroom models education as a process that facilitates meaning-making and the mental freedom associated with composing and constructing new understandings and imaginations (Bruner as cited in Egan 2007).

Chantal often uses a jointly-constructed narrative to sustain a class simulation that connects learning experiences for the students and helps them make meaning and move towards higher levels of thinking and problem-solving. During our observations, the students accept an imaginary invitation to become workers in a rainforest reserve as a way of introducing a society and environment unit of work, taught as a Storypath.[1] They think deeply about their new roles and develop questions about rainforests before listening to a detailed description of the environment in which they will work. Chantal invokes students' imaginations by asking, 'What can you see in the layers of the rainforest? What colours might there be on the forest floor...in the understory...in the canopy? What else might you find?' No pictures are shown. Rather, Chantal encourages the students to create mental images from the discussion and while listening to sounds of rainforest birds. The students move into groups to plan a section of the rainforest frieze or mural for the classroom, to be the setting for the rest of the rainforest narrative. In these lessons students tread a line between imagination and reality as they explore rainforest ecosystems and solve problems, such as the potential sale of the rainforest to a lumber company, whilst in their character roles of rainforest workers.

Chantal integrates critical literacy by linking the students' imaginings of the rainforest reserve to the picture book, *Where the forest meets the sea*. She guides them in analyzing images from various viewpoints and through different themes. She models thinking associated with each of de Bono's 'Six Thinking Hats' (de Bono 1985) then asks groups to don a hat to discuss key environmental issues emerging from the book. The students rotate around tables discussing the issues within the thinking hat roles. Chantal joins groups, probes, and comments on thinking. 'If you lived in this community what would your next step be? ... Justify your thoughts.' The lesson ends with the students coming together to debrief their thinking about issues such as deforestation, progress and tourism.

In these lessons the use of narrative, characterization and imagination is highly affective, engaging students' attention and participation. The joint construction of questions about the rainforest, the frieze and characters creates ownership and purpose for learning amongst the students. In this learning environment students are given freedom to take risks in thinking, to explore issues and problems. Chantal challenges them to think about 'What if?', 'What could be?' and 'What should be ... in the rainforest environments?' She steps forward at the commencement of lessons to establish the affective and cognitive stimuli, then moves to the background as the lesson progresses and students take more control of the learning space. Chantal probes and guides students to deeper knowledge levels before she deliberately steps forward again to consolidate and reflect on the learning process.

Imagination and characterization also feature in Josephine's drama classroom in an outer suburban secondary school. In a Year 11 class, Josephine encourages the refining of characterization through improvised action and dialogue to inspire students' imaginations. The students work with theatre masks of the *commedia dell 'arte* tradition of Italian comedy creating their own interpretation of a scenario – the action and dialogue.

The students work in pairs, donning their self-made half-masks of one of the commedia characters, such as, Pantalone, Il Capitano, Pulcinella and Arlecchino. In the open space of the drama room and within the defined structure of the lesson, the 'masked' students imaginatively experiment with hand gestures, body language and dialogue to enhance the narrative of the scenario and the comic intent of the Lazzi, a physical interlude by one of the characters. In pairs, they negotiate decisions about comedy, masked drama, commedia themes of dominance and subservience (masters and servants) and performative elements such as mimicry of gestures, proximity of characters and refining the dialogue. Josephine facilitates social and operative learning through these active, oral and research strategies and encourages the students to make metaphoric connections to their own lives. Students experiment with a range of imagined possibilities as they represent the interactions of comic characters, physically testing what would happen with the inclusion of different gestures or metalanguage. They play, collaborate creatively and experiment in this safe drama learning space. Josephine works the room informally as a mobile resource, extending students' understanding and application through open-ended questions.

Josephine explicitly communicates high cognitive expectations for learning and performance through focused questions about learning processes. In this culture of reflective practice, a question to the whole class is, 'How do you know when you are within your comfort zone or not?' prompting the students to reflect on their actions in the risk-taking environment of the drama classroom and challenging them to explore and imagine concepts beyond their existing dramatic interpretations. Constructive feedback, peer–peer and teacher–student, is a path to further learning. Through this process, Josephine lets her students know they are not alone, that she cares for and respects them. She provides opportunities for the students to embody their imagination through improvised responses and to conceptually and physically shape and practice ideas before they share them with the whole class. This rehearsal approach is a familiar strategy of the drama teacher. Towards the end of the lesson, the students have the opportunity to reflect on their practice with guiding questions from Josephine, such as: 'What did I find challenging? What do I need more practice in? Where do I need more help?' Out of this role-play, discussion of possibilities, embodied learning and laughter, the students perform their commedia scenarios to each other. Their performative interpretations prove to be novel and comic, embellishing both the historical and metaphorical demands of the Italian masked-theatre style. Joyously surprised by each group's dramatic control of the narrative, character interactions and comic theatre, the students display a sense of having achieved something great, beyond their imaginings.

Josephine's reflective classroom environment is manifest by mutual reciprocity of exchange about drama learning processes and the opening of spaces for in-depth learning through intellectual and imaginative exchange. Josephine reflects that, 'I play as well as the students in the classroom, and enjoy being in the classroom'. New imaginings and creativity emerge in the classroom when Josephine designs and facilitates recurring reflective practice as a way for learners to articulate their learning and connect experiences and knowledge with their lived experience.

Narrative and role-play are creatively used by both Chantal and Josephine to facilitate students' imaginations beyond their everyday experiences and understandings. They deliberately design high cognitive, affective and operative learning spaces and experiences to shift and extend students' understandings. In role and play the students are invited as social and active agents to collaboratively share control of learning. They do this at the invitation of their teachers by reflecting, imagining, taking risks and testing the limits of their lived experiences.

Eliciting and supporting creative and imaginative activity amongst all students

Sonia teaches in a remote rural town in New South Wales. She encourages her Year 2, 3 and 4 students to use a creative approach with technology to express their ideas about the feelings of the Indigenous people at the historical arrival of Phillip and the First Fleet of convicts, soldiers and settlers to colonize Australia. In a classroom with both Indigenous and non-Indigenous students, she encourages all learners to use *Mixcraft*, a music software program, to depict the emotions of puzzlement, sorrow and rage. She encourages students to think about how people in the First Fleet might have felt, linking ideas to what it might be like to arrive on Mars, the strangeness and uncertainty of it. The use of metaphor is a creative strategy that Sonia uses to provide language to frame new experiences in imaginative ways. It allows the students greater freedom to express complex ideas and emotions.

To support the creative *Mixcraft* activity, Sonia models a soundscape (musical collage) so that students know how to bring different downloads of music together. Her modelling enables students to understand the nature of their creative task and the group roles through which they will accomplish it. The students work collaboratively, discovering specific information for their topic. To show the emotions of the Indigenous people, students choose country music blues for sadness and drumming patterns to represent hearts pounding. These music choices come out of the students' lived and familiar experiences. For the First Fleet of colonizers, they choose eighteenth-century classical music from Haydn and Mozart, from the same era as the First Fleeters. They aim to create an expression of sadness, arising from different causes but linking to the sadness of the Indigenous people. The students use music that sounds like rain to represent people crying. Through such symbols and metaphors, the students imaginatively reach a solution to the challenges of multiple contexts. Their creativity is encouraged by Sonia's continuing demonstration of the technology, use of imaginative language and modelled reflection. Throughout the lessons, she consistently provides all students with positive messages about their ability and the control they have in their learning. The students extend their learning by positioning themselves in the shoes of the 'other' and express their feelings about the impact of the historic arrival of the Fleet. Through their musical choices they supplement and enrich their responses in ways that go beyond words.

Similarly, in Nancy's classroom all students are helped to make connections between different applications of learning. When such connections are made, there is a sense of moving from the known to the unknown, embarking on the journey of learning. Nancy's lessons are underpinned by the belief that, if key principles are in place, students will take responsibility and explore different ways of thinking. She provides all students with the opportunity to self-assess and peer-assess performances, discussing strengths as well as areas for improvement. Nancy talks about connections in learning for Year 12 students in music: 'The key thing is connecting what they know with what I'm going to teach them.' She is a committed proponent of the micro lesson to refresh information, extend the intellectual quality of the experience and deepen understanding. She explains,

> When students learn about the ground bass (a repetitive bass line over which different melodies are spun) in the Baroque period, they begin to understand a sense of pattern that exists in the past. When we study contemporary popular music and we're looking at bass lines, I can say, 'What was happening in the Baroque period which is clearly very similar to this?' and they will tell me because, not only did they listen to musical examples and recognize the ground bass, they also played the ground bass, they created their own piece of music over a ground so they have actually experienced it and I really do think they understand it.

This is high operative learning. The students reach the stage where they articulate the process of the ground bass through internalizing it in their own listening, performing and creating. Nancy demonstrates to students that she respects their ideas, listening to them carefully and always challenging them to deepen their knowledge. Her talk is of 'we' not 'I' and is peppered with 'Now you're extending that answer,' 'Now we're getting more information.' In Nancy's classroom, too, students' success is prepared and elicited by her deliberative, creative planning, providing a range of experiences that will ultimately lead them to deeper learning.

In Georgia's classroom creativity and high expectations are manifest when she plans and provides positive challenges for students and gives them freedom to explore their responses. Georgia believes that learning is about risk-taking and that students should be encouraged to make decisions for themselves. In an observed lesson, students are asked to make 3D models of buildings using cardboard materials. After setting the challenge, Georgia asks the class to think about the construction process and the sorts of things that might happen to their models. She asks, 'If it is floppy in the middle, how will you solve that problem?' 'If the stairs are too big for the building, what can you do?' She does not provide students with solutions, but through probing, ensures they all have an understanding of the nature of different dimensional shapes. Her philosophy is that exploration will bring out independent learning. Her ways of giving control of learning to students are varied. She might say, 'What should you be thinking about now?' If needed, she will ask, 'Do you want me to give you some ideas?', but her scaffolding of learning mostly involves probes that redirect students' foci to creative solutions of problems. Georgia models positive reactions to students' solutions, explaining that 'You try to change their story' by ensuring students benefit from a positive learning environment. She gives her students strong messages about knowledge and their control and ability in learning as she believes firmly that students collaborate to make learning better. Georgia uses the word 'challenge' with the students to imply that a solution can be found, and she gives students time to reflect, rethink, and refocus on their challenges.

The three teachers just described differ from each other in many ways. They teach students at different stages in learning, their local school contexts vary considerably and their lived experiences are different. What unites them is a focus on setting up challenges and promoting imaginative and creative responses to these from all students in their classrooms. They do this by assisting students to be reflective about past learning, helping them to recall what they already know and how this might connect with their new project, before explicitly questioning students or modelling new skills, strategies and techniques and encouraging imaginative and creative responses. In their learning projects, these teachers engage their students in substantive and reflective conversations about learning and challenge their creative responses. They constantly affirm the learning of all students with positive messages about their successful knowledge acquisition, ability and application of learning.

Expecting high intellectual quality in the students' achievements

Eve is a dynamic secondary English teacher, teaching mostly multilingual learners, whose pedagogy promotes high intellectual quality in students' creative and imaginative achievements. The high cognitive environment of Eve's classroom is demonstrated through the ways she promotes critical thinking, uses meta-language and higher order questioning, creates emotional connections with the area of study and provides opportunities for student learning choices. Her typical teaching style involves considerable individual interaction with students. High-level student engagement is a key outcome of Eve's approach.

In building a scholarly relationship with the students, Eve conveys high expectations of intellectual quality. A distinctive pedagogical practice observed in her classroom is the explicit teaching of metacognitive strategies, which go well beyond encouraging students to use appropriate technical language. For example, when Eve teaches the linguistic techniques of the poem, '10 Mary Street' (Peter Skrzynecki from *Immigrant Chronicles*), the effects of these techniques, the poem's vocabulary and sentence structure, students delve deeper into the textual meaning using meta-language. Eve deliberately sequences lessons to bring meta-level representations in the text to a level of consciousness for the students, and provides space for high cognitive learning experiences about representations of knowledge and knowing.

Emotional connections are elicited early in the textual study in order to have students 'buy in' to the learning. These affective and metaphorical connections to the text are shaped through open-ended, personalizing questions posed for the students to discuss in partners or small groups: 'What do you remember about the home where you grew up? Tell the person next to you about this home and a memory you have of it.' Such dialogue is continually encouraged between students and with the teacher, and gradually shifts to higher-order questioning and critical and metaphoric discussion across the whole class so that imagined possibilities are reached and textual links are made. Students are provided with many opportunities for choices about their own learning as they write, converse and extend what they know about the poem. When they write about the themes of the poem and the effect of the language, Eve encourages the students to analyze each other's work using a colour-coded system to highlight features such as the context, techniques, quotes and effects of the poetic language. The intellectual level of the classroom, sophisticated language use and critical thinking are lifted when the students engage in this peer–peer feedback. This is a dynamic environment where Eve promotes student enjoyment of learning.

Eve views the call to engage as an intellectual and creative challenge for herself as an educator. She, like the other teachers in this chapter, 'plans hard' by making the English syllabus and a prescribed text relevant to the students' context and creating something new with high cognitive demands and personal significance. 'How can I do this?' becomes both an intellectual and creative question for Eve as she plans. She takes what is complex, analyses it to create teachable parts, then re-synthesizes it as she teaches, so that students see the product as a complex whole, not just as parts. Creativity in this environment emerges as a logical, focused and intelligent process rather than something that is nebulous. It is open-ended with diverse outcomes for the learners. Messages of high expectations and intellectual quality characterize Eve's teaching practice.

In Sue's classroom in an outer urban secondary school in the heart of a housing estate, students work on problem-based cooperative learning projects that are intellectually demanding and open-ended, so that every student can achieve their personal best. Sue conveys expectations of high intellectual and creative achievement in these projects and artfully supports all students in a learning environment that models inquiry and persistence and encourages risk taking. She believes that students are *producers* of knowledge not *reproducers*, and responds to the *call to engage* by creatively planning and carefully integrating English, mathematics, social science and visual arts subject matter with topics that will bring relevance and meaning to students' learning. Topics are often introduced with elements of surprise, imagination or fun, but students are given clear purpose and expectations for the learning that will evolve. They each have workbooks created by Sue, in which activities are detailed, learning outcomes are listed and pages are devoted to a reflective journal in which students regularly write their thoughts about what they are learning, how they are learning and how they feel about their learning.

'Don't take the magic necklet off because the people of the underworld are looking', she tells the class after they have constructed symbolic necklets to gain permission to enter the world of Ancient Egypt in which they will learn about absolute power, hierarchical organization, ritual and the science of embalming and mummification. Students' curiosities are aroused as Sue takes a potato, orange and skewers and describes each to link the new vocabulary with each object, then models how to create a 'fruity' pharaoh. She focuses on the orange, cuts it open and explains that she is about to remove the organs (the orange flesh) from the pharaoh's torso. The organs will be kept in a canopic jar that the students will sculpt in another lesson, and the body is embalmed in natron and placed in a coffin (a plastic tray) to mummify. Sue captivates the students as she explains the 'scientific' instructions in a narrative, and refers students to the procedural instructions in their workbooks. Students work through their group task. When they are unsure and ask, 'What do we do next?' Sue replies, 'Read your instructions', focusing them on their responsibility for learning and her expectation that all students can and will achieve. She monitors the activity of each group, maintaining the narrative as she checks for success. 'Everyone should have a pharaoh in a tomb – Yes! Everyone should have a set of organs mummified – Yes! Remove your magic necklets which have protected you'.

In the lesson follow-up Sue foreshadows an English task in which the students will write a narrative explaining why their pharaoh has no limbs. 'Pyramid raiders!' may be the title. There is no down time from learning. Linking tasks, plus systematic planning and mapping of tasks, are learning tools that Sue teaches to students to encourage their ownership and direction of learning and achievement. They are also Sue's strategies for ensuring students feel 'safe' to explore their ideas, take risks, make mistakes, adjust plans, create new possibilities and learn.

Eve similarly has a constant focus on learning and achievement, clearly evident from her high level of planning and classroom expectations. She also provides a safe environment in which all students critique each others' work, respond to high intellectual demand, share ideas and use meta-levels of language. Both Eve and Sue plan units of work that are meaningful to students, with manageable tasks that enable all students to take risks, make links and create new possibilities. They introduce learning in creative ways, often encouraging imagination and creative thinking and performing. They teach and embed learning strategies that focus all students on analyzing work quality and achievement. And, they involve students in substantive conversations and reflections about learning, acknowledging students' voices and providing them with positive messages about their ability and shared responsibility for learning and control of the learning space. They share much in common with Dan, Sarah, Chantal, Josephine, Sonia, Nancy and Georgia.

Conclusion

All the teachers in this chapter have an in-depth knowledge of their subject matter that enables them to 'plan hard' for imaginative and creative lessons with high intellectual quality. These teachers do not stifle imagination and creativity. Rather they value, plan for and promote these abilities as essential tools for high intellectual learning. Students in the classrooms described in this chapter value the imaginative and creative experiences provided, as voiced by one of Dan's students who excitedly reflected, 'My teacher says, "In this class you can imagine."' These *Fair Go* teachers create learning spaces that provide opportunities for students to imagine outside of their everyday experience and respond creatively. They work to transcend the education gap for the students who live in poverty by encouraging them to imagine lives and perspectives beyond their own. These imaginings emerge in the musical creativity that is inherent in Sonia's and Nancy's classrooms, in the characterization and role-plays evident in the classes taught by Josephine, Sarah, Chantal and Sue and the permissions for students to explore and create in the classrooms of Dan, Georgia and Eve. In sharing classroom time and space in these imaginative ways, students across the early, middle and later years of schooling are confidently engaging in activities, explorations and conversations in order to learn, developing ownership and control of their learning and using a reflective voice to improve their learning. The high intellectual expectations and support of the teachers lead to students continually surprising themselves with new understandings, abilities and experiences that are sometimes individual achievements, and sometimes a collaborative group practice. The teachers' pedagogical practices described in this chapter portray professionals who 'plan hard' and work dynamically and creatively in an emergent, and, simultaneously, structured learning space. These teachers respond to the call to engage diverse student groups by planning, implementing and fostering inclusive, imaginative and creative learning experiences of high intellectual quality.

Note

1   Storypath units organize and sequence learning as a narrative. Students take on the roles, or characters, in a time and place and investigate a topic and issue in depth.

11 Engaging teaching practices with ICT in low SES schools

Joanne Orlando

Technology in schools...the key to America once again having the highest proportion of college graduates in the world.

(President Barack Obama 2009)

Technology is crucial to our drive to raise standards.
(UK Secretary of State for Education and Skills, Ruth Kelly 2005)

Computers will enhance the learning experiences of every high school student in the country.

(Australian Prime Minister Kevin Rudd 2007)

Information technology offers young African learners the opportunity to have access to the internet, to have a means of gaining knowledge, to become educationally competent, and to grow in conditions comparable to those of schoolchildren in developed countries.
(President of the NGO SchoolsNet Africa Professor Babacar Fall 2007)

The foregrounding of the term 'exemplary' in this project has been important for understanding teaching practices with technology that engage students in low SES schools. First, it enables us to position exemplary practice as the starting point and primary focus of analysis of teachers' uses of technology. This is different from much of the research on teaching practice with technology that places the technology as the central focus. We know that teaching practice is complex and the decisions teachers make are influenced by myriad factors. However, there is little information about why they make the choices they do in their uses of technology. Our focus in *Teachers for a Fair Go* was to understand how technology can be used to support progressive interventions in education that attempt to redistribute resources, power and prestige, and therefore seek to achieve equality of opportunity and outcomes.

Our interest in technology is directly informed by the intense interest of governments and educational organizations across the globe, convinced that they must aspire to capitalize on the potential of these resources to affect entrenched social justice issues in education. The quotes that open this chapter are drawn from government policies on education and technology. A common belief communicated in such policies is that technology will: increase the range of learning experiences available, thereby engaging with learners who are challenged by more traditional approaches; increase the learners' control of their education, and lower the barriers that may otherwise prevent individuals from participating in education, for example, physical costs, geographical isolation, and the need to learn at a slower or faster pace (Selwyn, 2011). The quote from President Obama is part of his address to Congress on the 'Transforming American Education' initiative. In this policy, many of the failings of the nation's education system are linked to the inability of educators to engage the 'hearts and minds of students'. Technology is positioned as the solution for winning over all students, 'especially those in underserved populations, low-income and minority students, students with disabilities, English language learners, preschool-aged children, and others'. It is anticipated that technology will provide all groups of students with

> ...engaging and powerful learning content, resources, and experiences and assessment systems...With technology we can improve student learning and generate data that can be used to continuously improve the education system at all levels. With technology, we can execute collaborative teaching strategies combined with professional learning strategies that better prepare and enhance educators' competencies and expertise over the course of their careers. With technology, we can redesign and implement processes to produce better outcomes while achieving ever higher levels of productivity and efficiency across the education system.

The transformational qualities of technology to resolve many of the imbalances and inadequacies of current educational provision are clearly attractive to all participants. However, as stated in Chapter 1, despite efforts to engineer change, many education systems end up favouring those who are already in a position of advantage, with little genuine improvement to those who are less well off. The position of the *Fair Go* Team is that digital technologies on their own can do little to alter the social complexities of people's lives that are impacted by poverty, social isolation and the reproduction of inequalities from generation to generation. As Selinger (2009: 206) states:

> Technology is not a panacea for education, but it is a powerful tool that when implemented appropriately can catalyze and accelerate education reform and development...

In this chapter we present locally informed, articulated examples of how teachers use technology to support learning in low SES locations. These examples shed light on what successful experiences with technology look like in these schools, and how teachers may be supported to develop practices with technology that genuinely engage students. The illustrations of successful practice in the schools in this project will also assist in moving beyond deficit notions of technology that dominate discussion of technology and poverty (the 'digital divide'), to the understanding that exciting and meaningful technology practice can take place in these locations. Commonly the digital divide is defined as the gap between those who have the opportunity to fully utilize technology and those who do not (van Dijk 2005). The digital divide is a very real notion in low SES locations. While our schools had access to technology funded by Australian state and national governments, many students who participated in our study had limited or no physical access to technology at home, nor the social and cultural resources needed to use it productively for learning. We argue that a sole focus on the technological resources students do not have can be an excuse for not engaging with, and examining, good practice with technology that can make a difference to student learning. The localized, engaging practices illustrated in this chapter also, importantly, provide meaningful, forward-thinking input to governments and policy makers for re-conceptualizing educational technology for students in poverty.

Teachers' engaging practices with technology

In the *Teachers for a Fair Go* project, we did not define exemplary teaching in terms of technology use or expertise. We were interested in the repertoire of approaches teachers used and their different strengths and interests. As can be expected, technology was more prominent in the practices of some teachers, and it is their practices that provide the majority of input for this chapter.

Teachers use technology in a variety of ways in their teaching. For example, the range of technology-mediated learning experiences used by Bronwen, a secondary school English teacher in a regional secondary school, included: multimedia/digital storytelling, modelling procedures on the interactive white board (IWB), storyboarding on laptops, researching on the internet, viewing different interpretations of a particular speech on *YouTube*, creating a live performance (researching on the internet, script writing, background music and editing), linking to mentors in another state via IWB and developing ideas as a class using IWB. What was important about this teacher's practices with technology was not her frequent use of, or her high-end knowledge of, technology but the strategies she integrated into the uses of technology that supported student engagement.

Data analysis involved mapping the teachers' practices with technology against two frameworks:

1   the MeE learning experiences: high cognitive, high affective and high operative; and

2   contemporary, empirically-based analysis of teaching practices with technology in schools (see Selwyn 2011; van Dijk 2005; Warschauer and Matuchniak 2010).

A significant finding using this method was that even though the teachers used technology in distinct ways, taught in different contexts and with different levels of technological expertise, there were particular strategies underpinning all their practices with technology that facilitated student engagement. These are outlined below. The strategies are technology-specific, but are also reflective of the *Fair Go* teachers' overall approach to teaching (see Chapter 8). As is evident from the bullet list below, the teachers used technology as a resource to facilitate engagement: to drive the learning of curriculum content, nurture the class as a learning community and scaffold learning. An important observation was that their uses of technology were often influenced by more than one MeE process at a time. For example, a teacher's high cognitive strategy may be underpinned by a high operative strategy. This is explained in greater detail later in this chapter. The ways in which the teachers used high cognitive, high operative and high affective strategies with technology are expanded below.

High cognitive (driving the learning of curriculum content)

- provides impetus and support for using technology which takes it beyond 'use' to 'learning';
- synergises screen-based and face-to-face teaching to support learning;
- uses technology to shift students beyond passive physical presence in the classroom to intellectual engagement in lesson.

High affective (nurturing the class as a learning community)

- uses technology to empower students;
- builds student agency using technology;
- uses technology to build classroom community.

High operative (scaffolding learning)

- uses technology to build on students' funds of knowledge;
- uses technology as learning scaffold;
- uses technology to increase the range of learning experiences available.

High cognitive strategies

As indicated in the breakdown above, high cognitive strategies were the ways teachers used technology to support and deepen students' knowledge of curriculum content. In the classroom, teachers were observed to use technology in the following ways:

- to access new information;
- to provide a range of vantage points from which students could think about, discover and work with ideas;
- as a platform to which they brought their own expertise in pedagogy and curriculum to build student learning. For example, teachers modelled new processes using the screen-based content with which students worked and also provided a more 'knowledgeable' other for students by questioning, making links and building vocabulary when technology was being used.

The teachers carefully orchestrated high cognitive strategies to mediate a greater connection to the lesson content and to deal with challenging class-room behaviours that took students away from learning. The coordination of these strategies also minimized students being distracted in their use of tech-nology, or merely using technology without intellectually engaging in the lesson.

For example, Ehab's strategy was not to react to any student resistance, but instead to listen to what this might signal and think about how his prac-tice could be shaped accordingly. He stated that he used high cognitive strategies with technology to make learning more interesting for those of his students who might lack self-direction and regulation.

The learning outcome of one of Ehab's Year 10 (14–16 years) science lessons during his case study was for students to understand the structure and functions of the heart and also to work cooperatively on scientific and liter-acy knowledge. He brought to the class four different film and interactive media sequences, content summaries on worksheets, 20 sheep hearts acquired from the local butcher, gloves, scalpels and tweezers for groups of students. He wanted all students to work in groups of three and stay on task, so his planning included the organization of group roles, framing discussion and probing questions. Ehab's philosophy is that he is always prepared with multiple resources so that he can shift his teaching during the lesson to ensure all students stay on 'learning'.

Ehab began the lesson by revising prior knowledge, which involved view-ing the dissection of a frog's heart. Content specific vocabulary (for example 'ventricle', 'alveoli') was also reviewed for spelling, meaning and key concepts. He then showed a short film of the dissection of a pig's heart to demonstrate blood flow and how dissection tools were to be used. Safety parameters were set and explicit instructions given to students regarding protocols and group member tasks. The introduction provided the necessary knowledge for students to ably collaborate in groups to examine their sheep's heart. When students were doing this, Ehab moved twice among all groups. At first he questioned students about what they found and understood about the different sections of the heart. On his second visit to each group he clarified that they had identified accurate information and all group members had fulfilled their roles using the different tools to examine the heart.

Students were highly engaged, cooperated well, compared dissecting techniques with the film model and enjoyed comparing similarities and differences among the hearts of frogs and sheep (and humans). Ehab successfully modulated behaviour, sometimes insisting that students re-focus. Individual students, unable to self-regulate for the lesson duration, were asked to remain after class to re-negotiate behaviour in future practical lessons.

After this practical lesson, Ehab showed a short film depicting the relationship of the heart to the rest of the body. Feedback from students generated many thoughtful questions and sustained discussion about the learning. Ehab informed students that they would be sitting for a quiz on the concepts learnt in this lesson. He assured the students they would be well prepared if they listened to the discussion, completed associated work sheets and attended to the 'drag and drop' computer assembling of the heart undertaken by several of them. He concluded the lesson with a debriefing that aimed to review the purpose and content of the lesson: 'What have we done? What have we learnt? How does it connect with our own bodies?'

As the description shows, this teacher used the synergy between face-to-face teaching and teaching with technology to drive learning in this lesson. The range of resources he used and the explicit planning around those resources provided the students with the content and processes they needed to intellectually engage with the task and the longer-term learning outcomes. He does not use technology as a one-off solution to address disengagement. Instead, his use of technology is reflective of a more holistic approach to student engagement which he had developed over time.

High affective strategies

High affective strategies here refers to the ways teachers use technology to nurture the class as a learning community. A particular approach teachers used was to position students and teachers as equally important users of technology in the classroom. This did not mean that students had free rein – the establishment of clear and consistent boundaries for choice always underpinned technology use. Instead this approach with technology was used to:

- promote shared decision making. For example, teachers would ask, 'Which mathematics game are we going to choose today?' 'Whose turn is it to . . . ?', 'What is a good way to display this information on the screen?'
- facilitate pro-social relationships. At times, this was the reason for the use of technology, and other times, it was the practices teachers established around technology use which promoted respect and community building.

- establish an environment of trust and respect. Students were entrusted to use the technology with care and teachers also used the technology to initiate and develop respectful behaviours at the whole class level, as well as nurturing respect for individual students.

Harmonie's teaching described below illustrates how she used high affective strategies with the IWB to nurture belonging, security, independence and success in the class. She taught Years 1 and 2 (6–8 years) in a coastal rural area of NSW and had been teaching at the school for 18 months. The school had experienced transient teaching staff, which had contributed to serious struggles around school stability. Harmonie told us that one of the first questions the students asked her when she arrived at the school was, 'How long are you here for?' It was a common occurrence for students at the school to have a succession of three or four teachers in one year. Harmonie believes that in this context it is important to build positive relationships between students and teacher, and students and students, and she develops such routines across the day using technology for this purpose.

To empower students and build relationships Harmonie, each day, selects a student as her teacher helper. The selection process is an equitable one, with the names of all students who have not yet been a helper placed in a cup and one randomly selected. The responsibilities of the helper are well-rehearsed and mainly centre on administrative tasks using the IWB. Without instruction from the teacher, the helper firstly downloads a class list, which tables those students who have been a helper and those still to have their turn and marks his/her own name off the list. He/she then downloads the class roll onto the IWB. On one particular day during the case study week, the teacher helper did not know how to read all the names. Harmonie built in the opportunity for the teacher helper to choose a classmate to assist them in their duties. The teacher helper selected a student (whom the teacher later explained was known by the children as the best reader in the class) to assist her in reading the names on the screen. This is accepted by the class as a regular part of the process. The helper then busily uses the IWB to help the teacher throughout the day, for example by downloading files, pointing to important information on the IWB and selecting students to choose online games to play.

The particular student who sought help reading class names had been selected as teacher helper on the Monday of the case study week and in the week of observations that followed we did not observe that student speak again during class time. Harmonie explained that she was a young Indigenous girl who was extremely shy and quiet and who had very poor literacy and numeracy skills. She stated that disengagement was a constant issue with that student – apart from when she was a teacher helper. The use of technology in this routine made the role less threatening for the student, thereby providing her with the opportunity to engage in the class in ways she would not have otherwise.

As the description shows, this teacher used the IWB to empower students and build a secure classroom environment. Taking charge of the IWB is a role many students would find appealing. However it was the organizational structures which the teacher implemented around the role of teacher helper which facilitated high affective use of technology. Such structures provide a space in which reluctant students can feel secure in undertaking a leadership role.

High operative strategies

High operative strategies refers to the ways teachers used technology to scaffold learning and includes the:

- presentation of content and/or instructions in multiple ways using various computer and IWB applications;
- provision of screen-based technologies as resources students could select to work with and present ideas.

Many students in Georgia's class had, like many of the *Fair Go* students, experienced failure in their previous school learning. Georgia explicitly and implicitly (yet continuously) used high operative strategies through the use of technology to build confidence and independence in learning so that students could succeed.

In the year of the case study, Georgia taught a Year 4 class (8–10 years) in a multicultural suburban school in Sydney. The student cohort in her school represented over 40 cultural backgrounds with 99 per cent of the students coming from non-English-speaking backgrounds. Georgia explained that she began the school year with a series of lessons that explicitly taught students: how to use some of the technologies (for example IWB, digital camera, video camera, computers); their applications (for example sound recording, Photoshop, editing, publishing) and the purposes for which they could be used (animations, game-making, movie-making, desktop publishing, multimedia presentations). She explained that this explicit teaching always linked to a meaningful purpose. For example, in learning how to use the animation and hyperlink features of PowerPoint, the students were required to make a presentation using these functions to introduce themselves to their new class. Content from these lessons was then reinforced by classroom displays and discussion and questions in subsequent lessons over the school year. As the following illustration shows, Georgia used this explicit layering of information to facilitate funds of knowledge and more choice in what students learnt, how they learnt, and the type of support she provided throughout the year.

The aim of one lesson was for students to design a lesson about animal habitats to teach to Year 2 (7–8 years) students in the school. The lesson began with a whole class brainstorming session to establish what the students already knew about animals and their environments. From this discussion, five environments (for example, Rainforest, Great Barrier Reef) were identified on which students could base their lesson. Students moved into groups based on the environment with which they wanted to work.

Georgia scaffolded the groups using a number of high operative strategies. She firstly worked on overall organization, stating that each group would need to consider three questions: 'What do you already know about that environment? What do you need to find out? How will you present this information to Year 2 students?' She then moved around the classroom talking with groups about how they would find further information and how they would present it. She did this by assisting students to make connections between successful learning experiences of which they had been part and the requirements of the task at hand. For example she asked, 'Remember when we used PowerPoint to make..., how did we start?' 'Remember when John made that film using...for science work, remember it was great because it...How might you...?' She also referred to charts on the walls which showed step-by-step processes students had documented in previous lessons, for example, how they had developed a multimedia presentation or a brochure.

One group was developing a computer game using PowerPoint and hyperlinks for their lesson. When they had been working on it for a while, one student approached Georgia and explained that while he was working on the PowerPoint he found an internet tool which could create multiple-choice questions and he decided to make a website using that tool to incorporate into the lesson. Georgia explained in a later interview that while she did not necessarily value multiple-choice testing, his initiative in finding this website and incorporating it into his group's lesson was commendable: '...his purpose was the most important thing'. Groups completed their lessons over a number of days and then taught them to Year 2.

This lesson illustrates how technology was offered to genuinely extend options for students in their learning. Students had choice about whether to use it or not, but also, importantly, they had been given meaningful and focused opportunities to develop expertise in various technologies and applications. The inclusion of technology into the lesson was an important aspect to the scaffolding this teacher was providing.

Continuous shift between cognitive, operative and affective processes with technology

The strategies teachers used with technology have been separated above to facilitate the discussion. However, in the classrooms, there was continuous shifting backwards and forwards between high cognitive, affective and operative strategies with technology and also a layering of strategies, with more than one strategy used at the same time. The movement was not *ad hoc*, nor were strategies used equally within each lesson. Rather, particular strategies were selected as the lesson progressed, to fulfil different needs for student engagement. An example of the quick and continuous shift between strategies is illustrated below in a mathematics lesson we observed in one of our primary schools in a remote Indigenous location. The strategies are in bold font to assist tracing the shift.

In the case study year, Jodie taught Years 3, 4 and 5 (8–11 years) in a primary school in a far western rural town in NSW. Over 75 per cent of the students in the school are Indigenous. In the weeks immediately before the case study, mathematics learning in the class had focused on 'position' and 'direction' and the lesson discussed here began by recapping the language for these concepts learnt in previous lessons, for example 'right', 'left', 'backwards', 'forward'. Jodie then asked students about other words they could use to give directions. Jodie had a compass around her neck and asked the class if they liked her 'new necklace'. She discussed the purpose of a compass then asked students to move into a circle. The compass was placed in the middle of the circle and students were asked to recount what they observed: for example, numbers, directions, red and white needles. Jodie explained that the compass always pointed north and that if you knew where north was you could find the directions south, east or west. Jodie used the compass to find north in the classroom and marked it with a sign. She asked, 'If you know where north is, point to south.' Jodie sought clarification from the students as to where the sun rose and set and reinforced that north is always constant. The students appeared to enjoy exploring the positions on the compass.

Jodie then **synergised online and face-to-face teaching** and used technology to motivate students to intellectually engage at a deeper level. Aerial and street maps of their town were displayed on the IWB to empower students to transfer their knowledge about their town to the abstract knowledge required for reading and engaging in a discussion about the maps. The teacher **scaffolded learning** by asking questions, building on answers and encouraging further explanation.

Jodie then displayed on the IWB digital footage of her own journey around town. On the weekend, Jodie had driven around the town and recorded her journey on the school video camera, now uploaded onto the IWB for the class to view. This use of technology can be understood as another move toward intellectual engagement. There was consistent and excited talk by the students as they built on their funds of knowledge to comment on the different scenes in the town to which they related: 'That's my street', or 'My aunty lives in that street'. Jodie **scaffolded the learning** by asking, 'What am I travelling past now? What will I get to next?' Jodie then displayed the street map of the town and traced and explained where she had driven.

Students viewed the journey a second time, and this time were asked to recount the route using the acquired field knowledge which had been the focus of previous lessons: for example, 'turned left and headed east then turned right'. The teacher **scaffolded learning** by encouraging the student responses: 'That is a good start. Can we keep going? Someone build on that'.

Jodie facilitated further **synergy between on-screen and face-to-face learning,** by giving a printout of the street map of the town to some students. Students were then asked to form small groups and, using a white-board marker, to locate various places on the map. For example, students were asked to identify the golf club. Students were asked to identify north, south, east and west to plot directions from the golf course to their homes. The aerial map continued to be displayed on the IWB to assist students and they referred to it individually when needed as they worked in groups with the paper maps.

Jodie explained that there were behaviour issues that could have potentially arisen if, for example, they had walked into town as part of their mathematics learning. In this context, technology provided an authentic and engaging learning experience that would otherwise not have been available to the students.

Using technology to enhance the engagement of students from low SES backgrounds

Most technology-enhanced gains in learning primarily occur because teachers have designed new contexts as well as new learning processes to support learning with digital technology (Reynolds *et al.* 2003; Muller *et al.* 2006). What our analysis shows is that the learning contexts the teachers designed were underpinned by the inclusion of three experiences important to student engagement: high cognitive, high affective and high operative. They adapted and moulded these processes around the opportunities for learning provided by technology.

An important element of the learning environment the teachers designed was positioning themselves as the 'knowledgeable other' when technology was being used in the classroom. Many argue that technology-based learning without the accompaniment of a teacher will only produce skills and competence – expertise and practical wisdom will be out of reach (Dreyfus 2001; McWilliams and Taylor 1998). This is particularly pertinent for students from poor backgrounds, who often come from homes in which parents, for a wide variety of reasons, are not able to support school success (Kozma 2003). The *Fair Go* teachers' practices show the importance of the teacher in: selecting the content and processes with which the students are working; identifying which technologies can be used for which purposes, and applying multiple scaffolding techniques in conjunction with the technology. In addition, while students could easily be distracted in their learning when using technology, another important element of the teachers' practices was clear expectations for high standards of learning when using technology. For example, Ehab made extensive efforts in his planning to ensure learning remained the focus of classroom activity. In this sense, teachers' practices with technology play an important role in supporting whole class and student self-directed activities. This is different to research and policies which expect the act of simply placing technologies in schools to make the difference to student learning.

Equally important was that the teachers used technology to facilitate the social engagement of students with learning. The teachers in this *Fair Go* project were teaching in challenging contexts, often experiencing students with motivational or behavioural problems that work against engagement. Harmonie's high affective strategies, mainly in her use of the IWB, were successful, and at the time of collecting data in her class, which was four months into the school year, she had perfect student attendance on most days. Other teachers made similar high affective uses of technology, particularly in their uses of the IWB. This raises two points:

1   that producing engaging practices with technology involves addressing social issues of engagement;
2   that particular technologies are well suited to addressing particular aspects of student engagement.

While IWBs have been critiqued as more successful for business than education (Selwyn 2011; Ball 2007), the use of IWBs by some teachers in this project suggests that they may be particularly well suited to addressing the social aspects of student engagement. This may also alleviate concerns that while the hundreds of thousands of IWBs placed in classrooms around the world are not being used in the ways funding bodies expected them to be used, teachers are drawing on their own pedagogical expertise to find meaningful ways of using them.

The *Fair Go* teachers were able to use technology to create a successful learning environment because they used their reflections on the learning needs of their students to guide them. As stated in earlier chapters, the teachers were consistent and careful observers of their students' actions and interactions and of their teaching contexts. They drew on their observations, as well as their knowledge of learning, to find gaps in student engagement and asked how technology could be used to address these. Kemmis (2005) refers to such an approach as 'searching for saliences'. He explains that

> The teacher cannot rely on prior professional knowledge alone, but must also 'search for saliences': that is search for knowledge in and through practice to correct and amend practice in light of the changing circumstances and new perspectives.
>
> (Kemmis 2005: 421)

In this respect, teachers drew on a range of resources to make judgements about which technology and which strategies required priority at the time in the given context. Ehab, for example, made extensive use of cognitive and operative strategies because he identified that his students needed support developing greater self-regulation in learning. Georgia was aware of the history of failure of many of her students and wanted them to succeed. Other teachers addressed different priorities and needs. In this respect, engaging teaching with technology is not technology-driven but a reflective and informed process which is needs-driven. Technology is often presented in the literature as a ready-made remedy for pre-existing barriers and impediments to learning. However, because the use of technology is often shaped by an individual's existing behaviours and life (Castells 1996), generic or limited approaches to educational uses of technology tend to reinforce existing social structures and inequities (Bozionelos 2004: Kent and Facer 2004).

The *Fair Go* teachers did not see technology as a fix-it solution, (some did not use ICT at all), but, when using technology, did so whilst acknowledging the deeply complex social nature of challenges for students from low SES backgrounds. The uses of technology by the *Fair Go* teachers show that teaching strategies based on localized, meaningful reflection about student engagement can contribute to addressing social justice issues in schools.

12 Culturally responsive pedagogical practices

Leonie Arthur and Margery Hertzberg

Introduction

The novel, *Soraya the story teller* (Hawke 2004), tells the story of a 12-year-old Afghani girl who is living in poor circumstances on a temporary refugee visa in Australia. Soraya writes stories that not only narrate her experiences for others, but also assist her in coping with the difficulties of both her past and present life. She states, 'I think if I couldn't write stories I'd need an oxygen mask. But surely I wouldn't be able to write stories as well as Australian students' (p. 66). One dominant theme in the novel is the support Soraya receives from a teacher who encourages her storytelling gift and suggests she enter a story writing competition as the prize is a much wanted computer. Soraya is not convinced of her literary talent because of her current difficulties with English spelling and grammar. The teacher responds (p. 67):

> That doesn't matter at all, Soraya . . . It's your story that matters and the way you tell it. You have a go . . . Besides you can bring your draft to school and I can show you how the computer can help you fix the spelling. Would you like that?
>
> I nod – I am sure my eyes are smiling.

In any classroom there is a diversity of learners – cultural, social and/or linguistic. Effective teachers capitalise on this diversity and program to build on all learners' capabilities. The episode above captures one teacher's culturally responsive practice with respect to one student's abilities. This chapter examines how teachers in low SES communities acknowledge and use the diversity of all learners in their classrooms as a genuine and essential resource, and at the same time extend learning to enable all students to access the language and culture of power. With respect to Chapter 3's discussion about diverse learners, this chapter specifically addresses the diversity within this diversity. Much of this chapter's discussion about culturally responsive pedagogies addresses the specific needs of students who are either bilingual or multilingual speakers of language/s and/or dialect/s.

Many developed countries with high levels of migration (and/or Indigenous populations) face similar challenges of providing a curriculum that gives all students access to powerful language and knowledge (in this case, academic English proficiency), while also demonstrating respect for diversity. Exemplary teachers take up this challenge in two ways. The first is to recognize the importance of cultural and linguistic knowledge for identity, wellbeing and family and community relationships. The second is to plan programs across all curriculum areas that incorporate prior cultural and linguistic experiences because these pedagogies enhance rather than hinder academic achievement (Au 2006; Cummins 2001; Cummins *et al.* 2006; Delpit 2006). This chapter will first highlight the underpinning principles of culturally responsive pedagogies and practices before showing how *Fair Go* teachers follow these principles in their teaching.

What are the underpinning principles that inform culturally responsive pedagogical practices?

Engaging students from diverse backgrounds requires teachers to pay particular attention to the principles that inform effective pedagogical practices. These principles have been drawn from both the research literature and the *Teachers for a Fair Go* (*TFG*) research:

- congruence between home and community contexts and school;
- high expectations and intellectual challenge in a supportive environment;
- authentic assessment;
- purposeful planning;
- a thoughtful and dynamic repertoire of practices.

Congruence between home and community contexts and school

All the teachers that we discuss in this chapter have a philosophical stance that recognizes and builds on learners' 'funds of knowledge' (Moll *et al.* 1992) to establish congruence between home and the community and school. This links to the *Fair Go Program* framing around engaging messages of knowledge, ability and place. Furthermore, they believe that each learner's prior experiences are not only rich for affective and emotional reasons but also provide a firm foundation of cognitive resources for extending academic learning. Socio-cultural theory provides a useful explanatory framework for the issue of home–school congruence. It highlights the ways that children learn in the context of their families and communities and are socialised by members of their family and community into particular cultural practices. These include 'ways of using language(s) and ways of using artifacts that become the "tools for thinking" through which we interact with our social worlds' (Gonzalez *et al.* 2005:18). Luis Moll and his colleagues (1992) use the term 'funds of knowledge' in recognition of the many assets within families and communities. All children's homes are 'rich in funds of knowledge' (p. 139), that include cultural and cognitive resources with great potential for use in classroom instruction. This view contrasts with the dominant perception of working-class families as 'disorganized socially and deficient intellectually' (p. 134). Similarly Thomson (2002) uses the term 'virtual school bags' to explain funds of knowledge as 'roughly equal but different knowledges, narratives and interests' that students have 'already learned at home, with their friends, and in and from the world in which they live' (Thomson 2002: 1). She argues that these virtual school bags can be 'opened, mediated or ignored' (p. 9) by teachers.

Research shows that effective teachers build partnerships with their students' families in order to find out about the 'lived experiences of children' (Gonzalez *et al.* 2005: 11), and the 'ample and positive resources families possess' (p. 18) that are 'ripe with potential for children's formation of knowledge' (p. 13). When teachers are knowledgeable about their students' everyday lives they are able to help students connect classroom learning with their family and community experiences. In this way the teacher is 'the bridge between the students' world, theirs and their family's funds of knowledge, and the classroom experience' (Gonzalez *et al.* 2005: 37), rather than leaving it up to the student to try to find connections. Effective schools link students to the world outside (Martin 2002), by working towards 'bringing the outside in' or vice versa (Alloway and Gilbert 2002: 204). When teachers bring the students' world into the classroom and also take the students out into the local community, students receive engaging messages around knowledge, place and voice.

In order for every learner to have opportunities to build on their funds of knowledge and have a positive self-identity, teachers must 'find, use and value each child's particular configurations of knowledges, narratives and interests . . . (and) have a repertoire of pedagogical practices that will connect these to the knowledges of power' (Thomson 2002: 8). Many of the *Fair Go* teachers welcome the 'virtual school bags' of their students and provide a curriculum that connects to students' existing knowledge. In so doing, they challenge the hegemonic discourse of 'poor, underprivileged kids' coming to school as empty vessels with no hope of achieving academic success. They affirm a respect for each student's linguistic and cultural identity, supporting research which confirms that a positive self-identity is critical for learning (for example, Delpit 2006; Cummins 2001).

High expectations and intellectual challenge in a supportive context

Research (for example 'authentic' instruction, Newmann and Associates 1996; Productive Pedagogies, Hayes *et al.* 2006) demonstrates that effective pedagogy includes high expectations and intellectual challenge in a supportive classroom environment, respect for difference, and connectedness between home and school. The *Fair Go* student engagement framework (see

Chapter 2) draws on this research, and examines how teachers help students to engage in the learning process. Experiences that are high cognitive, high affective and high operative provide this level of engagement. Similarly, researchers (for example Cummins 2001, 2000; Gibbons 2009; Mariani 1997) in the area of English as an additional language highlight the importance of intellectually challenging tasks, with appropriate supporting cognitive and affective structures. In addition, writers emphasize the importance of challenging tasks for students with additional learning needs (see, for example, Loreman 2007). The *Fair Go* teachers have high expectations for all students' achievement and provide appropriate levels of intellectual challenge in a safe environment with teacher support, based on a thorough understanding of the subject matter.

The *Fair Go* project's emphasis on high cognitive, high affective and high operative learning experiences and 'insider' classroom processes supports students so that they come to view themselves as an important part of a reflective learning community. In combination, the experiences and processes send engaging messages to students that both validate and respect the students' role in the pedagogical process (see Chapter 2).

However, a challenging program that expects students to be producers of knowledge, in itself, is arguably not enough. Unless appropriate structures are put in place, 'producing' rather than 'reproducing' ideas can be very threatening for many students. High cognitive learning requires dispositions/habits of mind such as curiosity, creativity and persistence (Costa and Kallick 2000; Katz and Chard 2000) and these are fostered in a supportive environment where learners feel safe to take risks. As outlined in Chapters 2 and 3, risk-taking and challenging tasks are often avoided by students from low SES areas. In the *TFG* classrooms, safe and supportive environments are established so that students feel confident to take risks when presented with challenging tasks. In these environments teachers convey engaging messages that promote imaginative and creative thinking and the exploration of multiple possibilities.

One important way towards a supportive environment is through play. 'Play' is a common term in early childhood, but the concept is not confined to learning in the early years. Play is active, 'hands-on' participation in learning, where learners construct understandings as they interact with materials and people. It provides learners with confidence to try out new ideas and operate at the upper end of their zone of proximal development (Vygotsky 1978). The *Fair Go* teachers in primary and secondary contexts use terms such as 'active' and 'participatory' to reflect the same learning principles. Active, 'hands-on' learning with challenging and open-ended resources is a key feature of the *TFG* classrooms from pre-school to the final year of secondary school. Play-based/active/participatory learning is constructed in a language-rich environment and encourages students to explore, experiment, try out different hypotheses, investigate and solve problems. Through these operative processes students construct their own learning and are active producers rather than reproducers of knowledge (Hayes *et al.* 2006).

Fair Go teachers also create a supportive learning environment by providing multiple resources for students to use as they investigate knowledge, share ideas and then represent new learnings. Students in the research classrooms are provided with a range of paper-based and computer-based resources as well as concrete objects to use to investigate ideas. They depict their new understandings using multiple communication modes, including dance, drama, painting, three dimensional constructions, and still and moving images as well as writing, or a combination of any of these, to create multimodal texts. These multiple modes of representation provide teachers with rich evidence for use in authentic assessment.

Authentic assessment

Authentic assessment processes give engaging messages to students that their voices are valued, and provide rich data that teachers can use to inform future planning. They are a feature of *Fair Go* teachers' classrooms. Authentic assessment occurs when students are involved in 'tasks that are worthwhile, significant and meaningful' (Hart 1994 in Fleet and Torr 2007: 186). That is, authentic assessment (formative and/or summative) is embedded within everyday learning experiences in familiar contexts and is not something that occurs in isolation. Furthermore, authentic assessment is not standardized assessment in the form of checklists and tests, and it is more than just assessing the end product and content knowledge. It also involves assessing learning processes (such as problem-solving) and dispositions (such as the propensity to employ imaginative thinking), and employs a variety of methods of documentation that 'value depth and context' and 'acknowledge cultural and linguistic diversity' (Pacini-Ketchabaw and Pence 2011: 4). This information is collected over time and importantly includes learner self-reflections and self-assessments of their progress towards meeting content outcomes, their learning processes and dispositions.

Substantive engaging tasks that integrate high cognitive, affective and operative domains provide an ideal context for authentic formative and/or summative assessment. Teaching and learning sequences such as these provide the context for all students to demonstrate their capabilities within their zone of proximal development and focus on future potential as well as current understandings (DEEWR 2009). This not only affirms and sends engaging messages to students that they have knowledge, ability, control and voice, but also provides rich and in-depth information for future planning.

Purposeful planning

Effective planning allows for flexibility and negotiated pathways of learning so that learners can make decisions about the ways they will progress towards meeting mandatory learning outcomes. Importantly though, such open-ended tasks also allow for achievement of unexpected outcomes, which are equally important for lifelong learning. The *Fair Go* teachers plan open-ended in-depth experiences and easy access to a range of authentic resources to enable student choice in how they investigate ideas and represent learning. This differentiated approach, along with considered decisions about length of time, grouping methods and a thoughtful and dynamic repertoire of practices, provides the scaffolding necessary for students to feel confident to take the sorts of risks required for meaningful learning, thus sending messages of, in particular, knowledge, ability and control.

To facilitate successful deep learning, teachers purposefully plan programs that take into consideration the importance of challenge and do not 'dumb down' the curriculum. Such purposeful planning develops structures that scaffold learning to enable students to achieve within their zone of proximal development. Wood *et al.* (1976) used the term 'scaffolding' to mean carefully constructed steps that teachers plan explicitly, so that learners can complete tasks in manageable chunks. To scaffold learning, teachers need a thorough understanding of the subject content, students' family and community contexts, and students' current understandings drawn from recent assessments. Using these three sources of information, they plan integrated, contextually relevant and intellectually challenging experiences.

A thoughtful and dynamic repertoire of teaching practices

Using the information gained from authentic assessment (including student reflection on their learning) *Fair Go* teachers select teaching strategies to accommodate the different ways that individual students learn, the specific content that is being taught, and the degree of guidance needed. They use their observations to make strategic decisions about the extent of their involvement as students engage in individual and small group experiences. This involves knowing: when it is appropriate to participate in inclusive conversations that guide learning; when it is useful to provide a specific demonstration or directions; and when it is appropriate to take more of a backward step and provide encouragement from the sidelines. These teachers constantly monitor the situation and intervene when necessary to support students to feel confident enough to persist with what they are doing, to take risks and to share their thinking with others and, critically, to extend their learning.

Siraj-Blatchford and Sylva's (2004) seminal study of pre-school education in England found that effective early childhood teachers draw on a repertoire of teaching practices in order to extend learning. As Comber (2001) has argued, it is essential that teachers question the effects of different pedagogical practices for different groups of students and select those that are most appropriate. Of particular importance for students' learning are conversations that support 'sustained shared thinking' (Siraj-Blatchford 2009) between students and teachers and amongst students. Sustained shared thinking involves teachers listening carefully, engaging in respectful interactions that invite students to elaborate and extend on their ideas, and asking questions and offering ideas that extend students' thinking. In this process, teachers also model vocabulary and sentence structure with the aim of further enhancing students' academic English. These are key dimensions of the *TFG* project *insider classroom* framework that in particular send engaging messages about ability.

To summarise thus far, a number of principles have been established that underpin culturally responsive pedagogical practices. These principles have been drawn from analyses of data from the *Teachers for a Fair Go* project and the international research literature. Within each of these principles links have been made with the *Fair Go* student engagement framework. The next section provides details of the ways these principles are reflected in the pedagogies employed in the research classrooms.

How do *Fair Go* teachers' pedagogical practices reflect these principles?

The *Fair Go* teachers' pedagogies reflect the principles outlined above, and these pedagogies include:

- partnerships with families and communities;
- contextually relevant experiences;
- purposefully planned, intellectually challenging integrated sequences of learning;
- negotiated pathways of learning to progress towards prescribed curriculum outcomes;
- a range of grouping methods;
- a range of teaching strategies to scaffold learning.

Partnerships with families and communities

The data showed that *Fair Go* teachers emphasize the importance of genuinely getting to know families and finding strengths rather than making deficit assumptions. Many teachers in the research familiarize themselves with the local community to see how families really live, rather than making assumptions that could well be inaccurate. They initiate opportunities for genuine two-way conversations with families about students' family and community experiences and funds of knowledge, family expectations and values, and student learning, thus sending engaging messages about place. At schools where there is a high percentage of multilingual speakers, interpreters and translators are used to facilitate these conversations with families.

Learning about community is often a complex process. Chantal confirms that when teachers know the community well they 'see the difficulties but also see the strengths in the community'. Bronwen reminds us 'knowing well does not necessarily mean agreeing with everything, but being open to discussion and debate'. These quotes show that disagreements between teachers and family members may not necessarily be a problem, but rather acknowledge the complexity of issues and enable different perspectives to be shared and new questions asked (MacNaughton and Hughes 2003).

Teachers use a range of strategies to build partnerships with families and the local community and to bring family and community funds of knowledge into the school. These strategies vary across age groups and include regular conversations with families and students, surveys, parent–teacher interviews and family and community meetings and events that transcend multicultural or harmony days. Two varied examples of family and community partnerships follow. Nicole is the coordinator of the local Aboriginal Community Committee, and believes in 'working closely with the Aboriginal community to make things work for students'. She organizes a range of events, such as young Aboriginal men coming to school at lunch-time to play football with the students, while at the same time mentoring these students on the value of school education. In quite a different context, Jennifer shows the importance of including families and community members in decision-making at the classroom level. She is in constant dialogue with other teachers, parents, individuals and groups within the community as she negotiates individual education programs for her students with special needs.

Contextually relevant experiences

The *Fair Go* teachers use their knowledge of children's family and community experiences and funds of knowledge to provide contextually relevant experiences that value difference and build on existing knowledge to then extend learning. Teachers' respect for learners' family and community contexts builds a strong and positive feeling of identity amongst their students and sends engaging messages about place and belonging. Different kinds of contextual experiences are shown in the following illustrations. Kim, a kindergarten teacher, provides resources from the local Vietnamese community in the dramatic play area. In the pre-school, Donna includes puzzles and books as well as dramatic play resources that reflect the local Indigenous cultures. She works closely with local Indigenous organizations to incorporate words and songs from the local Indigenous language. In a rural secondary context Missy uses local Indigenous language and traditional knowledge of the town's river to teach literacy. In an urban secondary context when learning about different climatic conditions in geography, Sue displays an information poster depicting the local Indigenous seasons to acknowledge the cultural background of some of the students in the class.

Intellectually challenging integrated sequences of learning

Usually with support from an executive, many *Fair Go* teachers are able to resist the trend for isolated, skills-based, de-contextualized instruction, at times fuelled by national literacy and numeracy testing (see also Chapter 3).

Instead, they plan intellectually challenging integrated sequences of learning that focus on conceptual understandings. These learning sequences (often sustained over several lessons or weeks) promote deep, authentic, contextualized learning and reflect the connected nature of concepts. Integrated sequences of learning enable teachers and students to focus on challenging, inclusive and dynamic content and 'big ideas' (Hamston and Murdoch 1996/2004). This authentic curriculum enables students to see how different subject areas connect in the real world where concepts are complex and multi-disciplinary. Integrated sequences with their focus on creative and imaginative thinking also support the flexibility, curiosity and problem solving (Wilson and Murdoch 2008) necessary for learning in a rapidly changing world.

Authentic curriculum is demonstrated in Nicole's Years 3, 4 and 5 primary class where the concept of neighbourhood is explored, integrating social studies, design and technology and English. Small groups plan, design and construct a model of an imagined local neighbourhood. As part of the assessment process they present an oral report to explain their learning and the processes involved to achieve this learning to their Year 2 'buddy class'. In Sue's Year 7 class, small groups construct board games using the Egyptian numbering system. This open-ended integrated task consolidates students' understandings of several other concepts, including the net properties of a cube, the writing of a procedural text (instructions for the game) and the design principles for board games.

Even within the constraints of the timetable in many of the *Fair Go* secondary schools, teachers negotiate with others and work collaboratively to provide integrated sequences of learning. For example, Diane negotiates and collaboratively plans with the visual arts teacher to integrate English and visual arts in a shared unit of work.

Negotiated pathways of learning to progress towards prescribed curriculum outcomes

The *Fair Go* teachers' planning typically includes multiple pathways for students to achieve curriculum outcomes, and quite often incorporates students' suggestions for experiences and resources. Again, this sends engaging messages around ability, control and voice. Chantal includes students' questions about what to investigate in her planning of a unit of work on rainforests. Jo invites students to reflect on what they feel confident with and aspects they need help with, and then plans accordingly. In Georgia's classroom, groups of students are able to choose experiences and the relevant resources to enable them to achieve curriculum outcomes. Sonia also provides a flexible curriculum that includes the negotiation of individual contracts. These contracts enable students to both choose from a range of experiences and plan when they will complete these during the week.

This same amount of flexibility is more difficult with the constraints of a more prescribed curriculum content in secondary schools. However, teachers still provide students with choices. Secondary students are encouraged to talk about their learning and negotiate the best pathway to achieve these outcomes. In Sue's classroom, the maths text book section on the Egyptian number system, with its emphasis on true and false exercises, is changed to a group task of designing and constructing a board game using the Egyptian number system for the local Year 4 primary class. To ensure that this authentic task has rigour, students are required to write a plan to include the framework for the game and resources needed in its construction and their plans needed to be negotiated with Sue ('the plan man') before construction begins.

A range of grouping methods

Most *Fair Go* teachers plan for a range of grouping strategies. Decisions about the composition of small groups and pairs are based on similarities or differences in language, age, ability, gender, friendships or interests. Both teachers and students make these decisions, dependent on the learning experience and its purpose. Such flexibility sends engaging messages about voice and control.

For many *Fair Go* teachers, pair or small group work is preferred to individual work because pairs and small groups promote the sharing of ideas necessary for deep, meaningful learning. Chantal's Year 5 and 6 class know the importance of this, explaining Chantal's slogan 'chatter matters' in an interview. Chantal uses a range of grouping strategies to promote substantive conversations. One of the strategies she uses in small groups is the de Bono (1985) problem solving 'six thinking hats', when for instance discussing critically a novel's key themes. Similarly, Nicole encourages talk. Although there may be enough computers for each student, they work at computers in pairs so they can talk about their learning. She also uses mixed age groups in her integrated learning sequences to facilitate peer scaffolding of concepts and to develop social skills of negotiation and collaboration. But at other times she uses ability grouping to enable her to target her teaching to the students' zone of proximal development. In many classes, talk is not necessarily only in English, especially for newly arrived bilingual students. Georgia pairs a newly arrived Urdu-speaking child with a more proficient Urdu-English bilingual child during the construction of 3D shapes to enable the newly arrived child to participate fully and acquire these mathematical concepts. Sue's students usually choose to work in friendship groups and Sue sanctions this because these normally very resistant students work cooperatively and stay on task if they are able to work with their friends. Nevertheless, Sue also encourages the students to consider the different skill sets they need for group experiences and this process results in students varying their groups accordingly. As an example, during maths, the child with autism nicknamed 'the maths king' is always in high demand.

A range of teaching strategies to scaffold learning

The research revealed that the teachers use a range of strategies to scaffold learning. Scaffolding is a specialised type of assistance or help. 'It is important to understand that scaffolding is not just any type of help. It is carefully constructed support provided by teachers to facilitate students' learning in tasks that will extend and challenge them' (Hertzberg 2012: 38). Scaffolding can occur at two levels – micro and macro (Dansie 2001). 'Macro' scaffolding refers to strategies and supports used at the programming stage, while 'micro' scaffolding refers to more spontaneous interactions that occur between the teacher and individuals or small groups of students as an experience unfolds.

Macro scaffolding

For the teachers in the *Fair Go* project, macro scaffolding involves purposeful planning of experiences and integrated sequences of learning. This planning includes careful consideration of strategies to support students to meet the intended learning outcomes. In their planning, teachers identify the:

- purpose of the experience or sequence of learning;
- experiences they will provide to build students' knowledge of the topic;
- ways in which they will demonstrate and model processes and concepts to support the continuum from guided to independent learning;
- resources they will use to enable students to engage in processes that enable them to investigate concepts;
- grouping methods that will promote peer scaffolding and collaborative learning;
- questions they will ask to challenge thinking and encourage critical analysis and deep learning; and
- strategies they will use to encourage students to engage in self-evaluation and reflection.

The following strategies exemplify scaffolding at a macro level. In Chantal's primary classes she assiduously attends to all the above in her planning and the use of varied resources and strategies is a feature. Many visual resources (matrices, pictures, diagrams) are used in conjunction with written and/or verbal explanations. Self-evaluation and reflection is a constant and ongoing process throughout a learning sequence. Similarly, when Eve, a secondary English teacher, is planning a lesson she makes sure she builds on what students already know, based on assessment of the students' classroom learning and their linguistic and cultural knowledge. Knowing students' present achievements and foregrounding this in culturally responsive practices supports each student's schematic knowledge and builds their engagement with the texts they are studying. Eve's macro scaffolding also includes planning ways in which she will demonstrate and model critical analysis through joint construction of texts that will then support students' individual writing.

Micro scaffolding

When implementing their programs with students, teachers tailor the macro scaffolding principles (mentioned above) in ways that are responsive to individual needs by:

- providing clear goals and expectations;
- activating prior knowledge;
- building knowledge of a topic;
- demonstrating;
- joint construction;
- sustained shared conversations;
- reflecting and self-evaluating.

Examples of each of these follow.

'Clear goals and expectations' are vital for all learners, and particularly for bilingual and multilingual learners. The teachers in this study clearly state the purpose of the lesson and foreground related activities and assessment tasks. Nicole believes students should be immediately aware of the purpose because '[it] breaks the secret language of school and assists our students to be successful learners'. Eve uses paraphrasing and recasting to ensure that students are clear about the questions they need to answer when analyzing texts. Students commented that '...she'll come and say "this means...". She re-explains it in different sort of terms...When she gives us quotes for an essay...she doesn't jump straight in...she'll explain the quote...and she'll go slowly over each part of the quote...'

'Activating prior knowledge' is another key scaffolding principle used by the *Fair Go* teachers. New learning is introduced and presented as something curious and exciting but connected to prior knowledge. Teachers remind students about what they have already studied in class that links to the topic, and support students to make links to their family and community funds of knowledge. In the previously discussed example, students in Sue's class brainstorm all the board games that they know and the purpose of the rules of the game in order to construct their own board game. They also create semantic maps of existing knowledge about ancient Egypt prior to planning and conducting their research into Egyptian number systems. Elsewhere, Chantal uses strategies such as 'floor storming' where groups of students identify what they know about a topic and develop questions that they want to investigate in the integrated sequence of learning.

'Building knowledge' occurs when learning sequences are carefully planned and structured to enrich students' technical vocabulary and language structures. The majority of the students in the *Fair Go* schools are learning Australian Standard English as an additional language(s)/dialect(s), and these students particularly need many opportunities to practise the target language, especially within subject specific fields with more decontextualized, abstract and technical language. Nicole very consciously and explicitly models the target language that will be used in a particular learning experience and then provides students with opportunities to use this language. Following a text reading that models the language of personification, students work in small groups to find further examples in the book. Many secondary teachers also use oral and visual strategies to enrich students' vocabulary. Believing that science teachers are also teachers of literacy, Ehab works with the *English as an additional language* teacher in a lesson on dissecting hearts. Provision of word banks of technical language and demonstrations of the language structures necessary for scientific report writing precede students constructing their own reports. This validates that literacy learning within the context of an authentic experience is an important English language learning principle (see also Chapter 9). Matching visual to spoken or written language is important for new English learners because it provides a concrete support. This is a constant feature of Kate's science classroom. She frequently plans lessons to include moving and still images to explain abstract concepts and the associated technical language, and this guided support leads to students' independent construction.

'Clear demonstrations' also scaffold students' learning. Demonstrations can be for a whole class or targeted to particular students in response to their learning needs. Three useful examples follow. Sue demonstrates the structure of a narrative by sharing the narrative she had written the previous evening with students. Elsewhere, Georgia provides demonstrations on the particular features of PowerPoint for a group who want to create a slideshow. Often when teachers provide demonstrations they use metalanguage to scaffold students' understandings, as evidenced when Chantal uses the metalanguage used in scripting to scaffold cine-literacy.

Scaffolding is also effective when students 'learn collaboratively' in small groups and when teachers 'co-construct learning' with students. In a mathematics lesson Georgia encourages small groups of students to negotiate effective designs and 3-D constructions and in the process scaffold each other's understandings. Georgia joins in where appropriate and asks questions or suggests strategies that support students to achieve their goals. These suggestions help to break tasks down into manageable chunks for students: 'If you cut one out first then use that to make the other triangles . . . ' 'You cut out two shapes and then I'll come over'. She asks questions and gives specific directions: 'So how long does each side of the rectangle need to be? You want them shorter? How short? Half? Okay so measure 20 centimetres. Now cut it out and score it and fold it.'

'Sustained conversations', where teachers listen carefully to students' ideas and through comments, paraphrasing and questioning, guide students' learning at the upper end of their zone of proximal development, are significant strategies for extending learning (Gibbons 2009). Many of the teachers do this well. Again, Georgia organizes students to work in small groups and rotates around these groups observing and asking questions that challenge students and extend learning. These are sustained conversations introducing the metalanguage of the subject content. Open-ended questions promote sustained dialogue, and she models problem solving by verbalizing her thinking. Furthermore, Georgia's sustained conversations with students scaffold their understandings. Rather than telling students the answers to the properties of different shapes, she supports them to construct their own understandings through guided conversations. When a group of students are constructing a house she begins by asking, 'How do you know it's a cube? Let me get my shapes. What shape is this? What shape would the sides be if it was a cube?' This learning conversation continues for several minutes. Not only does she deliberately use the terminology of the subject, she also models appropriate grammatical structures.

Students' 'reflections and evaluations' on their own learning focus students' attention on the purposes and goals of the lesson or sequence of learning and their progress towards meeting these. The *Fair Go* teachers use a range of strategies to encourage students to reflect on and self-assess their learning. At the end of maths experiences, students in Jo's class are encouraged to identify what they are confident with and where they need help. They write this in their journals and are reminded to, 'comment on what you know and what you need to know, and who you are going to ask'. Often there is an inextricable link between self-reflection and evaluation and scaffolding, as evidenced when Georgia asks questions like, 'What was one of the hardest things about building this?' and 'How did you make this?' Students are encouraged to reflect on the processes involved as they construct their three dimensional shapes. Likewise, Sue uses prompts from the REAL Framework (Munns and Woodward 2006) and changes these on a regular basis. For example, in one week the prompts were: 'How could you broaden your thinking about what you did today? 'How would you help someone else to learn something that you discovered today?'

Conclusion

This chapter has demonstrated that exemplary teachers in low SES communities use a wide range of pedagogies that are respectful of students' cultural and linguistic diversity, and of the powerful and important funds of knowledge that students bring to the schooling context to support individual learning. Too often the backgrounds of students from low socio-economic areas are seen as a deficit. When this view results in lowered expectations, compromised curriculum and diminished feelings of student self-concept, it is hardly surprising that students disengage from the schooling process. Conversely, this chapter has argued that culturally responsive principles and pedagogies can become powerful ways to engage students in a long-term commitment to learning, and a belief that 'school is for me'.

13 Building community through exploring place and sharing control

Leonie Arthur, Leonie Pares and Les Vozzo

When asked what advice a commencing teacher in his school should receive to make a difference for students, Mark responded:

> Know the kids and know your 'product'... be committed – listen to the kids and the parents... make a contribution to the local community.

These words capture the key ideas of this chapter, namely that communities of practice are created by teachers, parents, community members and students. They occur in places where authentic learning can and does occur. It is through a combination of all contributors' (teachers, students and community members) energy, commitment, vision, compassion and passion that places become communities of practice, and function as valuable learning spaces.

Building community is an essential element in an authentic education. This chapter examines how teachers in the *Fair Go* study build community through a focus on place and shared control. It provides examples of ways in which teachers create strong connections with students, families and communities, where all participants feel a sense of belonging and share in classroom decisions. Many of the *Fair Go* teachers feel a strong sense of belonging in the community where they work. They have positive relationships with families and community members and work to build networks and strengthen social capital within the community. They regularly take students out into the community as well as bringing the community into the classroom, and use a range of strategies to exchange information with families.

Linking to, and building on, knowledge from the students' own lives is a strong thread in the approaches adopted by the *Fair Go* teachers. These connections enable teachers to create classrooms that are powerful learning communities, where students are able to express their voices, make connections with their world outside the school and build positive identities.

The exemplary teachers in this study disrupt traditional power relationships between teachers and students and between teachers and family members to develop more equitable relationships in which all participants have agency and where control is shared. Their relationships are characterised by mutual respect, responsive and reciprocal interactions and democratic participation. The teachers foster positive interactions between students by encouraging consideration of diverse perspectives, shared decision making and respectful interactions. Data from the study illustrate how the teachers' focus on authentic learning experiences and collaborative learning creates high levels of student engagement and student management of their own behaviours. It provides examples of the ways that teachers promote collaborative learning communities with respectful relationships and positive interactions.

Communities of practice and learning communities

The term 'communities of practice' is used in this chapter to emphasize the importance the *Fair Go* teachers place on situated learning where collaboration and the sharing of knowledge is a social, as well as an academic, activity. Communities of practice encompass actual networks and processes in which 'social learning occurs between people with a common interest in a subject or problem (and) who collaborate over long periods of time to share and exchange ideas, find solutions and build knowledge' (Kirschner and Lai 2007: 128). Wenger (1998: 183) describes the action of people who participate in communities of practice as involving 'a combination of engagement, imagination and alignment'. By effectively combining these three modes of belonging, communities of practice contribute to building a learning community (Wenger 1998). When members of a community of practice engage with each other in meaning making, based on mutuality, competence and continuity (Wenger 1998), they shape practice, contribute to the group's shared history, and refine understandings. This engagement supports exploration and reflection and the development of new connections, insights and visions wherein we create 'new images of the world and ourselves' (Wenger 1998:176). Alignment through the establishment of shared visions and the development of procedures for coordinating activities and resources supports the achievement of results within existing structures (Wenger 1998). As evident in Chapter 6, the *Fair Go* teachers belong to a number of communities both within their school and across professional networks. They promote engagement, imagination and alignment amongst these communities. In addition, they create collaborative learning environments where learners co-create meaning and imagine new possibilities.

Each *Fair Go* classroom is established such that students feel a sense of belonging within a community of learners. Teachers and students are viewed as being integral to the learning community, all on a journey of learning together, all connected, all interdependent. Consistent with socio-cultural theory (Vygotsky 1978), there is a focus on interactions and the joint construction of learning. Students generally listen to and respect each other and all ideas are valued. Students and teachers work collaboratively to co-construct knowledge as they predict, investigate, interpret, reflect and evaluate. They enact a 'communities of practice' learning model in which they imagine new possibilities, creatively co-explore and find new patterns and practices, critically reflect on assumptions, and co-construct new meanings (Yukawa 2012). Families and community members are also integral to these learning communities. All contribute to the co-construction of knowledge within and beyond the classroom and students share findings of investigations and projects with the broader community.

A sense of place and feeling of belonging

Many *Fair Go* teachers consistently employ pedagogies that reflect a high level of care for students' wellbeing and these pedagogies support students to develop a sense of place and a feeling of belonging. Begen and Turner-Cobb (2009), in a study of 159 children aged 11–14, found that children's sense of connection to home, school and community impacts on their physical as well as their psychological health. Children who had a stronger sense of belonging experienced higher levels of self-esteem and positive physical and psychological wellbeing.

Being supportive of each other is a commonly identified quality in the *Fair Go* classrooms. The classrooms are described as 'safe places' for students, places where they feel a sense of connection. The children in Jodie's and Sonia's classes, for example, believe the classroom is a place where they can freely share their problems or issues with each other and the teacher. Some of the ways the teachers create this feeling of security is by taking time to listen to students' needs and issues and by encouraging individual respect of others' place in the classroom.

An ethic of care

An unconditional, positive regard for students, their families and communities is demonstrated by the *Fair Go* teachers. This positive attitude and the modelling of care and respect in turn foster a strong learning community within the classroom. Dahlberg (2003: 273) argues that

> Teaching and learning have to start with ethics – with receiving and welcoming – and it is the receiving from the Other beyond the capacity of the I which constructs the discourse of teaching, a teaching that interrupts the philosophical tradition of making ourselves the master over the child.

This ethic of care is enacted by teachers across pre-school to Year 12. Eve, a secondary teacher, creates an atmosphere of security and stimulation and an inclusive feel in her English classrooms where many of the students are learning English as an additional language. Her teaching style involves much individual interaction with students that is respectful of each student's cultural context and prior experiences. She provides a safe environment by modelling language and scaffolding individual students' learning. She breaks tasks down to make the language accessible for students, yet is always extending students to go beyond the security of the scaffolds towards more sophisticated language and synthesis. In the course of achieving unit outcomes Eve includes many micro-lessons and, through questioning, effective listening and responding, she is in constant dialogue with the students. She stimulates interest and caters for individual strengths through the use of a variety of experiences and different modes of representation. Eve's pedagogy encourages student reflection and prior knowledge is constantly activated, as is making emotional connections to texts. She is committed to a rhetorical-critical-ethical model of teaching English (Thomson 2004) and her philosophy is based on a conviction, influenced by Paulo Freire, that every human being is capable of critically engaging the world in a dialogical encounter with others (McLaren and Leonard 1993). Eve is very effective in establishing an authentic sense of a caring learning community. Her students show security in her classes through their level of engagement and the ease with which they ask questions.

A pedagogy of relationships

Like Eve, many of the *Fair Go* teachers' pedagogies include positive relationships with the students in their class, and with family and community members. The term 'pedagogy of relationships' was termed by Carla Rinaldi, a pedagogical director from the Reggio Emilia schools and early childhood centres in Italy, to capture the importance of relationships in teaching and learning. Effective relationships include a 'pedagogy of listening' (Rinaldi 2006) that focuses on openness to, and respect for, difference and active listening and interpretation of meanings. One way that the *Fair Go* teachers enact this pedagogy of relationships is through respect for students as active contributors to the learning community. Georgia, for example, listens with respect to all ideas, engages in collegial discussion with students and provides choices of experiences and resources. Similarly, Andrew's respect for students is evident in a curriculum that is negotiated with the students and that allows for student choice.

The *Fair Go* teachers create learning environments where everyone is treated with respect and dignity. These positive, trusting relationships are essential for students' sense of identity, connections with others, their sense of wellbeing and their confidence in themselves as learners (DEEWR 2009). When students get the message they are valued and respected, they are more likely to explore their environment and to seek out challenges that extend learning and promote feelings of competence and self-efficacy (Alloway *et al.* 2002; Lingard *et al.* 2003). As well as enhancing academic learning, respectful relationships also support social aspects of learning such as collaboration, cooperation, democratic participation, teamwork and active citizenship. In addition, respect for students and their families and communities promotes a sense of connectedness and belonging to the school and facilitates relationships with others.

Partnerships with families and communities

A positive relationship with families enhances a sense of place and voice in the learning community for both families and students. The *Fair Go* teachers have positive attitudes towards families and value their contributions to students' learning. As Haberman (1995:12) has noted, 'Effective teachers continue to believe that most parents care a great deal and, if approached in terms of what they can do, will be active, co-operative partners'. Teachers in the *Fair Go* project take the initiative to find out more about their students' lives and to keep families informed about students' learning. They strive to always keep the lines of communication open, using a range of strategies to build authentic partnerships with families and communities and to engage in respectful two-way communication. Connecting with families is viewed as an important aspect of all teachers' work, not just those working in the early years of school. Across pre-school to Year 12, the *Fair Go* teachers find creative and flexible ways to build respectful relationships with families.

Donna, for example, frequently engages in conversations with family members in order to gain a better understanding of the students' family and community contexts so that she can connect with students and families. To share children's learning with families she uses strategies such as a visual diary or slide show to illustrate what the pre-schoolers have experienced during the day. This creates a focus for families, children and teachers to engage in conversations about learning when families are collecting children in the afternoons.

Many of the teachers are working in areas with substantial Indigenous populations. Donna, Sonia, Danny, and Missy all have strong knowledge and understanding of the local community they are working in – Missy and Danny as insiders and Sonia and Donna as outsiders who have built respectful relationships. As an insider, Missy is able to connect with the families' experiences – 'I put myself in the parents' shoes and I think I know what they want'. Donna has established a pre-school which is a welcoming, safe, secure environment for both children and parents. Over time she has built relationships with Indigenous families which have given her insights into the complexities of the local community. Teachers like Donna and Sonia understand that for many Indigenous families 'yarning' at the school gate or pre-school door is the best way to communicate with teachers. Similarly, Vanessa and Kim, working in highly multilingual urban communities, also emphasize the importance of talking with families about issues in a positive way and of finding ways to work with extended communities in supporting students and families to feel a sense of belonging.

Building social capital

Schools' strong partnerships with families and communities, in which families and community members feel valued and where there are positive relationships and social networks, build networks and social capital (Baum *et al.* 2000). The *Fair Go* teachers resource families in ways that develop their capacity to support children's learning at home. As Vanessa, a teacher in an urban school, notes, many families in low socio-economic areas work long hours, often including shift work, may not have well developed English literacy skills and may not be confident in supporting children's learning. Vanessa and Kim both teach in the early years in schools located in bilingual communities and encourage families to talk to children in their home language in order to develop language proficiency as well as understandings of concepts such as number and measurement. Both Vanessa and Donna provide practical information for families that includes suggestions for how to use everyday experiences such as shopping and cooking as teaching moments. They make this information available informally as well as in publications such as newsletters. In addition, they provide practical workshops for families on topics such as mathematics and talk with families informally about a range of issues including positive social interactions. Families are provided with information from a range of agencies so that the school acts as a hub, connecting families to a range of resource and support services.

Connections with community

As well as positive partnerships with families, the *Fair Go* teachers also have a deep connection with, and commitment to, the local community. These connections enhance the students' sense of place and feeling of belonging in their local community as well as within the school.

Many of the teachers live in the local area and attend community events, showing a genuine validation of, and affection for, the students and the community in which they work. Andrew encourages all teachers to 'get to know your community and get involved'. He states that, 'it is invaluable that I live in the area, walk to school, see kids in the street. It is modelling, communicating.' Sonia believes that the community needs to see teachers beyond their professional role and to have opportunities to interact socially. She says, 'the community need to know you care. It is important to keep in touch with "Pop", the elder. That way you know what is happening in the community'.

Attending weekend sports events enables Sonia to support the students and interact socially with families and community members. When teachers are involved in local events such as these and are able to share their own personal narratives with students, they are able to authentically link students' learning inside the classroom to their real world contexts.

The *Fair Go* teachers work closely with local community groups as well as families to better understand students' cultural contexts and to make connections between the students' everyday experiences and the classroom. Community involvement takes many forms, including linking to cultural knowledge, work-based learning and links to local community organizations and events. The teachers bring the community into the classroom through the use of maps of the local area, local newspapers, photographs of community events, bilingual resources, community elders and local narratives. They take the students out into the local community to investigate local issues, interview community members, visit community resources and participate in local events.

Many *Fair Go* teachers use their partnerships with families and communities, along with their knowledge of the local environment and local issues and events, to help connect students' learning to the wider community outside the school. Classroom experiences are carefully planned to link the students' learning to their out-of-school contexts and knowledge, thereby evoking a sense of excitement in learning and building a sense of ownership and responsibility for the local community. In Andrew's regional school, for example, students are regularly invited to contribute to class, school and local area wellbeing. One project involved working collaboratively with another school to investigate a nearby creek and issues of pollution. Students created a brochure for the wider community and were actively involved in testing the creek's water and monitoring the pollution levels. They began to take an active and respectful environmental role outside of school. This is reflected in the actions of one student who reported that he found a turtle in a creek he knew to be polluted and picked it up and took it to a clean creek near his home. Another student in this class commented that the teacher 'wants us to learn that we can make a difference with smaller things in our lives. ...We are a small school [but] we can do big things'. Projects such as this, that involve the whole school, reinforce the notion of the school as a learning community, as well as the school's connection to the wider community.

Teachers in schools with a significant Indigenous population make connections to local Indigenous cultures by working closely with Indigenous groups in the community to bring culturally relevant resources into the classroom. They integrate local Indigenous knowledge by taking students on excursions and involving local elders in the curriculum. Missy, for example, connects the school curriculum to the students' world and natural environment and extends it, with relevance, to the unknown. Another Indigenous teacher, Danny, shows a strong sense of belonging and commitment to the local community. He uses his links to the local community and his relational knowledge to enhance a sense of kinship and cultural connectedness with his secondary students, which in turn engenders a sense of belonging and place in the learning community within the classroom. These experiences build greater respect for elders, their culture, family and friends. As one student explained, 'We learn about our culture ... because we want to learn about it so it does not get lost, so we can teach the next generation'.

Culturally responsive pedagogies

The research of Moll *et al.* (1992), as well as Haberman (1995) and Thomson (2002), found that effective teachers seek to find out more about their students' out-of-school lives so that they can make their teaching more meaningful to their students and help to 'weave threads between each other's worlds' (Marsh 2000: 129). Hayes *et al.* (2006: 260) advocate that all school systems 'seek to ensure that all students are able to demonstrate connectedness between the classroom and the world beyond it'. As Marsh (2000: 130) notes, 'this metacognitive intertextuality, the awareness that can arise as a result of making such links, is important to children's learning'. Marsh has demonstrated in her work in nursery school and primary classrooms that connected curriculum enables students to integrate home and school knowledge and to create new understandings within a familiar discourse.

Linking to, and building on, knowledge from the students' own lives in order to create a culturally responsive curriculum is a strong thread in all of the *Fair Go* classrooms. The teachers recognize that all students come to school with considerable resources and plan opportunities for them to build on their existing 'funds of knowledge' (Moll *et al.* 1992). In so doing they enact cultural competency by respecting diversity and focusing on equity and social justice (DEEWR 2009). These culturally responsive pedagogies are consistent with findings from other studies (for example Hill *et al.* 2002; Lingard *et al.* 2002) that propose that students' learning is enhanced when schools find out about family and community knowledge and develop local responses to the differences between home and school that move beyond limiting 'deficit' views to positive understandings of students' out-of-school interests and experiential learning.

Building collaborative relationships and positive behaviours

Respectful collaborative relationships are evident in the *Fair Go* classrooms. The teachers in this project have an image of children and young people as competent and capable. They problematize and disrupt the dominant inequitable power relationships between teachers and students that often 'constrain learning outcomes by suppressing students' sense of legitimacy and agency' (Keddie and Churchill 2010: 254). Student–teacher relationships in *Fair Go* classrooms are characterized by mutual respect, responsiveness and reciprocal interactions (Gonzalez-Mena and Widmeyer-Eyers 2009) where students have a sense of agency and there is shared control of decision-making. Mutually respectful relationships and a democratic environment in which teachers know and understand students have been identified as key determinants of a quality teaching and learning environment (Keddie and Churchill 2010). Because *Fair Go* teachers focus on building positive, caring relationships, they are able to 'avoid, deflect, or defuse problems that would inevitably arise if such rapport had not been developed' (Haberman 1995: 5). Instead these teachers negotiate with students.

Focus on intellectual quality

The emphasis in *Fair Go* classrooms is on learning rather than behaviour management. As Andrew states

> The most powerful behaviour management tool we have is curriculum...Teachers need to give students control, negotiate and make curriculum relevant.

Because students in *Fair Go* classrooms are frequently engaged in intellectually rigorous and purposeful learning there are fewer issues of challenging behaviours. Classroom management, according to Gore and Parkes (2007; 2009), is the result, rather than the primary goal, of good teaching. The *Fair Go* teachers do not aim to 'manage' and 'control' students and are not afraid of a classroom that is sometimes messy or appears at first to be chaotic. They resist the dominant construction of a 'good teacher' as one who has a quiet and orderly classroom and instead focus on 'the construction of an intellectually engaging learning environment' (Gore and Parkes 2007). As Gore and Parkes caution, a focus on classroom management can result in students who are quiet and busy, but not intellectually challenged.

That is not to say there are no challenging behaviours in *Fair Go* classrooms, but rather that behaviour management does not dominate the classroom. The teachers use low emotion, inclusive language, high expectations and intellectually challenging and relevant learning experiences to keep students on task and working collaboratively. The teaching style is calm, focused and positive, and humour is used to help refocus students without emotion. (See also Chapter 4.)

While it is true that these exemplary teachers have a propensity not to be overly anxious about students' behaviour, they have a healthy and realistic expectation that having to deal with problems is a necessary and important part of their work. In alignment with Haberman's (2011) 'star teachers', the *Fair Go* teachers use 'distractions, interruptions and misbehaviours as opportunities to redirect student behaviour and push the class ahead without delays' and to focus on learning.

Respectful interactions

The *Fair Go* teachers listen respectfully and negotiate with students. They diffuse and deflect challenges rather than turn them into a power struggle (Martino and Pallotta-Chiarolli 2003). Andrew advises teachers to 'be prepared to negotiate, let students choose work, rather than dictate, butting your head against the wall'. The environment in *Fair Go* classrooms fosters collaborative relationships, where students feel confident to share ideas and engage in meaningful learning. There is 'mutual respect and dignity' (Keddie and Churchill 2010: 265). Teachers negotiate curriculum and focus on positive social interactions. Challenging behaviours are viewed within a broader perspective so, for example, boys' disruptive or disrespectful behaviour may be recognized as playing out dominant masculinities and power relations.

Andrew is one teacher who recognizes these dominant masculinities and works with boys to broaden their 'repertoires of practice' (Alloway *et al.* 2002). He uses modelling and personal narratives to explore the nature of masculinity with students, particularly boys in upper primary, and to encourage positive relationships and respectful interactions. Rather than succumbing to dominant discourses that boys are loud and disruptive and need to be controlled, Andrew moves beyond these to create alternative ways of interacting that support boys to express feelings and establish connections with others. As a result, there is increased respect for teachers and students, cooperative teamwork and improved academic achievement.

Rather than only teachers controlling behaviour, students in *Fair Go* classrooms are encouraged to monitor and regulate their own behaviour. Many students across all contexts from pre-school to secondary school are actively involved in creating the 'rules' of the classroom and so understand why there are rules. They understand both rights and responsibilities and are generally able to regulate their own behaviours and gently remind others of their responsibilities. This is evident from pre-school age. For example, in her classroom, Donna uses inclusive language such as 'we' and 'our' and encourages children to take responsibility for the resources and for their behaviours. The pre-schoolers have input into the rules and responsibilities in the room, including making their own symbols to depict expectations.

Shared control

There is an emphasis in *Fair Go* classrooms on shared ownership and responsibility and students contributing to classroom and school wellbeing. Students have a voice in classroom decisions and control is shared between teachers and students. The importance of space for student voice and shared control has been well established – see for example Newmann and Associates (1996) and Lingard *et al.* (2003) (and examples in Chapter 14). These findings are also supported by the research in the *Fair Go* project. The teachers in this study achieve student choice and autonomy through sharing power with learners and by encouraging discussions, negotiation and collaboration. Learners have a voice in the organization of spaces, experiences, resources and time. They feel comfortable in moving around the classroom to access resources and work collaboratively with their peers in small groups. From a very young age, children have agency in their own learning. Donna encourages the pre-schoolers to have a voice through the children's sense of ownership of their room and their learning. They make choices from a range of available resources and are able to initiate play experiences emerging from their ideas. Donna also discusses and negotiates experiences with children and responds to children's interests and ideas with spontaneous and planned experiences. The *Fair Go* teachers are highly organized and this careful planning enables students to make choices of experiences and resources. An outstanding characteristic of these classrooms is the tangible sense of involvement and engagement resulting from the cooperative sense of ownership of what is being learnt.

In the *Fair Go* classrooms there is a strong focus on responsibilities as well as rights, respect for others, listening to each other and sharing ideas, and the building of relationships. The teachers listen to students' perspectives and interact respectfully with students. This focus on respect, responsibility and relationships begins at an early age. Sonia's classroom, for example, is a place where students know they have a voice in their learning and how their classroom is organized. Students' responses to the question, 'How does the classroom make you feel?' included 'You get to make your own choices about the class, how to arrange the room' and 'We make the decisions', clearly indicating their voices are respected and there is shared control. Georgia also likes to give her students the chance to make decisions in their classroom and encourages them to voice opinions. She says teachers should 'let go of control in the classroom, [it] should be a safe learning environment'. In Andrew's classroom, students also have a high level of choice and control in an environment where their decisions are respected. Andrew facilitates and guides student choices and provides clear and explicit demonstrations and supports for student engagement in learning.

The focus on intellectual quality, respectful interactions and shared control facilitates the development of collaborative relationships and positive behaviours.

Conclusion

There is a strong focus in the *Fair Go* classrooms on student learning and on 'the future in the present' (see Chapter 2). The teachers work hard at instilling in students a sense of ownership of their own learning and affirm and celebrate students' accomplishments. They do this through encouraging student belonging and shared decision-making within a cooperative structure of learning design. A strong sense of ownership is further enhanced through the value put on place, and this is achieved by linking authentic learning tasks with the students' worlds, bringing 'their place' into the classroom and by establishing a sense of pride in classroom space. These democratic learning communities support students' understandings of responsibilities as well as rights and the development of respectful relationships. The *Fair Go* teachers demonstrate respect for students through consciously linking with families and communities, respectful listening, sharing power and control with learners, and negotiating.

14 Student voice(s)

Bronwyn Cole, Mary Mooney and Phil Nanlohy

> She tries to be as fair as possible ... So fair ... very, very fair.
>
> (Student describing Diane, a later years teacher)

As we draw to a close the journeys and stories of the *Fair Go* teachers of early, middle and later years classes, it is the students who have the final word on their learning and the teaching they experience. By referring to student voice(s) we acknowledge 'voice' in three ways. First, encouraging and developing students' voices is an essential requirement in and *of* learning and second it is critical *for* learning and continuing learning. Third, students as the learners are best placed for identifying teacher pedagogies that are responsive to them, relevant for them and respectful of them. In this chapter, we describe how *Fair Go* teachers' pedagogies are framed by giving importance to student voice(s) and how they share control of the learning spaces with the students to jointly construct meaningful learning.

The chapter comprises two sections. The first section explores the significance of student voices in the learning space and, in particular, how students are encouraged by their teachers to talk in order to learn, talk about their own learning, share learning and help others to learn, and participate in the shaping and organization of learning. We describe how teachers structure classroom opportunities for student voice(s) and enable enhanced participation for all learners. There are three sub-sections as we initially focus on early years teachers, Jo, Kim and Harmonie, who facilitate student voice by incorporating deliberate and distinctive strategies to encourage young children to feel confident and competent in engaging in classroom discourse and the shared construction of knowledge. We then view Nicole, Andrew, Chantal and Rebecca, middle years teachers, who implement pedagogies that encourage students to work together, support each other in learning projects and become independent and reflective about their learning and the learning of the class, thereby creating communities of learners. Increasingly, these teachers create spaces for students to negotiate and shape the ways they will learn, the resources they will use and the creative outcomes they will achieve. Finally, we describe later years students taught by Diane, Eve, Kate and Mark and the ways they are included in the control of the learning space and managing learning through systematic collaborative work and extended teacher questioning.

The second section of the chapter represents the students' voices in the study. We provide samples of students' interview data and anecdotal comments that demonstrate that they are aware of the ways their teachers share control of the learning space, enabling them: to construct knowledge; to become aware and confident of their abilities, and to gain a sense of belonging and value through opportunities to express ideas. These 'final words' from students describe how they achieve agency in their learning across the engaging messages of knowledge, ability, control, place and voice. They clearly articulate the differences their teachers make to their learning and the varied opportunities and support structures that their teachers provide to enable them to achieve success in learning.

Student voice(s) in the early years

Young learners commencing school vary immensely in their confidence for talking out and sharing ideas in classroom settings and in their range and use of vocabulary. Such oral language differences are especially great in class-rooms with multilingual learners for whom competence and confidence in both English and home languages can vary. Developing competence with language is a long process and providing opportunities for student voice in all areas of the curriculum is particularly important for young learners. It is essential to becoming an independent and responsible learner. Without opportunities for voice, young learners risk disadvantage throughout their schooling and beyond (Gibbons 2009; Hertzberg 2012).

Pedagogical structures for developing and encouraging voice(s)

The learners in Kim's mixed ability kindergarten class are mostly multilingual learners. Many are compliant, willing to perform well but waiting to be told what to do – an approach to learning that is frequently instilled by the fami-lies of the major cultural group of the class. Kim's challenges are to build the students' proficiency in oral English and encourage them to be more active learners who think, ask questions, discuss ideas and take initiatives and risks – to encourage them as learners who have voice(s). To do this, she inserts highly visual resources in lessons and involves students in whole class conversations, questioning and probing their thinking. 'What do you think? . . . And what about you?' she asks as she introduces, models and recasts vocabulary while exploring the main ideas of a lesson. Kim's lessons continue with kinaesthetic activities such as singing, hand-clapping, role-playing or game playing to repeat and reinforce vocabulary and main ideas. She then switches to provide time for students to think individually, talk and work in pairs or small groups. This pedagogical sequence is deliberately planned and Kim's students practise it well at the beginning of the year. It provides opportunities for students to access and use the English language whilst building shared responsibility for learning. For example, 'You are now going to talk to a friend and tell them what you do to get along', she explains after the class has sung the 'Gabby Getalong' song and discussed the topic of sharing. Kim has high expectations for kindergarten children to work together and talk about their learning and her classroom exemplifies encouragement of students' voices *in* learning and reflection *for* learning.

'Sharing circle' is a structure regularly introduced in Harmonie's kindergarten classroom to encourage full class participation and enhanced intellectual quality in discussions. Students sit in a circle on the floor, allowing everyone to see each other. Sometimes Harmonie sits in the circle, such as at the end of a lesson to consolidate learning, but at other times she sits outside, but close to, the circle. Sharing circle is structured so that students ask questions to clarify, expand or build on information shared by students. It can be introduced at any time in a lesson. For example, following a shared reading of *Alexander and the Very Bad Horrible No Good Very Bad Day* on the interactive whiteboard, the students discuss the story and relate it to their personal experiences of a bad day. They draw two pictures, one of a very bad day and the other of a magnificent, amazing, very great day. Harmonie explains that everyone's drawing should be different. When drawing time finishes, the students come to Sharing circle. Seated in the circle, Harmonie rolls a ball and randomly asks students to share their drawing and story. Students share and respond as other members of the circle question and comment on their story.

Harmonie provides clear structures, timeframes and expectations for working together. The 'sharing circle' strategy and Harmonie's use of a teaching assistant – a student helper selected on a rotational basis to assist with classroom tasks – encourage students to have voice *in* their learning and to talk *about* their learning. As in Kim's classroom, the learners are encouraged to share information with group members, to assist each other if someone is not too sure of what is required for a task and to keep a reflective journal *for* learning, a strategy also used frequently by Joanne with her Year 4 class of eight and nine-year-olds.

Reflection time

At the end of a mathematics lesson in which students explore the addition of fractions by folding pieces of paper, Jo consolidates new learning and challenges students to work with a friend or in a group of three to solve 'challenge problems'. The timeframe is set and all students in the groups are made accountable for resolving the challenges. Jo walks around the room assisting groups, reviewing the task and questioning students as to how they arrived at their answers. To conclude the lesson she asks where students might use equivalent fractions in everyday activities, giving relevance to the learning. She then provides reflection probes for students to discuss and respond to, in their investigations books: 'Could you solve the problem? How did you solve it? Do you need more help? What or who do you think might help you to be able to do this? Do you need more one-to-one work with me, (the teacher)?' As in the classrooms of Kim and Harmonie, these learners are encouraged to talk and self-regulate *in* their learning and to see each other as supports *for* learning.

These early years teachers provide formal pedagogical structures within lessons to encourage students to work together, share language and ideas, solve learning challenges, provide feedback and talk about their learning plans. Middle years teachers incorporate similar pedagogies to encourage classroom sharing and reflective practices but, as the next section describes, they acknowledge students' increasing learning capabilities and plan pedagogies that will assist students to assume greater responsibility for independent learning, supporting each other *in* learning and negotiating and shaping the classroom *for* learning.

Student voice(s) in the middle years

The middle years teachers described in this section hold strong expectations that their classes will operate as communities of learners (as defined in the previous chapter), involved in, and talking about, what they are learning, how they are learning and what will help them learn – building towards greater independence *in* learning. Variations occur in the ways the teachers plan and implement spaces for voice(s) and structures for encouraging independence in learning. Some of the variation is dependent on the previous experiences of the students and some evolves from specific learning goals the teachers may have. Nicole holds to a goal for her class to be more active. Rebecca adopts pedagogy that gradually works towards student independence in learning. Andrew focuses on moving students forward by analyzing what they already know and, like Chantal, initiates community-based learning projects that create contexts in which student initiative and leadership can emerge. Commonly, these teachers commence each year establishing expectations and behaviours that promote student voice(s) *in* learning and *for* learning.

Creating space and expectations for student voice(s)

Nicole creates spaces for student voice(s) in her classroom of Year 3, 4 and 5 students as she holds firmly to her belief that students need to be active in learning and involved with the decisions that are made in the class. Lessons are frequently interspersed with active pedagogical structures such as: think/pair/share, encouraging students to think and talk about learning content and issues; guided reading sequences in which Nicole models reading with expression and gesture, questions and encourages student conversations, involves students in drama activities such as 'questioning in role' to increase understanding of characters, then returns to students reading with (improved) expression; and small group presentation projects. Importantly, Nicole models the importance of voice *in* learning and *for* learning by encouraging students to freely ask questions about their learning in whole class activities and during individual work. She also makes 'student choices' a feature of her programming and planning, as she 'takes direction from the students' about content and interests in learning and creates opportunities for them to make choices about the groups in which they will work, problems they will solve and learning approaches they will take. In these ways, Nicole encourages independence and allows students' voice(s) to influence the curriculum of the classroom. But, this classroom community was not always so. By consistently modelling voice and planning spaces for student voices, Nicole turns around a class of learning resistors, wanting low-order work and free time at the beginning of the school year, to participate as a supportive community, excited about high participation levels and valuing their learning time.

Rebecca similarly works to counter student disruption and resistance in her classrooms of Years 7 and 8 students in a rural secondary school by modelling voice and encouraging students to have greater confidence and participation in learning. Rebecca emphasizes routines and guided learning in which students work at different levels whilst strongly supported with a range of carefully selected digital resources that promote student conversations. Like Nicole, she moves students toward more independence *in* learning as she provides and affirms choices for students about what they will learn and the resources they will use *for* learning.

Creating spaces for students to practice voice, negotiate what they will learn, make choices about the resources they will use and the creative outcomes they will achieve are strongly featured in the daily pedagogies of many of the middle years teachers. In the next section we describe how Chantal and Andrew include integrated, community-based projects to provide enhanced opportunities for improving student voice(s), and promoting student initiative, leadership and advocacy *in* actions.

Projects that encourage student voice(s) and leadership

Andrew competes with a group of students to complete a list of mental arithmetic questions. This task is an enjoyable challenge for the students and a diagnostic tool for Andrew as he uses the results to talk about improved performances, gives praise and assesses what students already know. Andrew believes that 'teaching is explicit, based on data and we don't waste time. Let's teach kids what they need to know.' Like Nicole and Rebecca, he implements pedagogies that use a variety of resources, establishes high expectations *of* learning, and provides spaces for student autonomy and leadership *in* learning. Andrew's mental arithmetic session is followed by a quick succession of small autonomous group-work, larger group-work, and group project work. He intersperses opportunities for students to talk together, such as, 'For 30 seconds talk to those near you about what you think a perimeter is'. At the conclusion of teaching he provides times for reflection to acknowledge students' voices and active role *in* learning. Importantly, Andrew builds a sense of capacity amongst the students in his classes and across the whole school, to use their voices to take initiatives and actions, for example by participating in his school community-based projects.

At the back of Andrew's school is a stormwater drain known as Black Creek, daily seen and smelt by the students. Challenged to make a difference to their local area, students in the school chose to investigate and gather data about their smelly creek – what caused the smells and what could they do to alleviate the smells and improve the local amenity. They collaborated with two nearby schools, involved the local water authority and tested the water in the creek. They held discussions with community members and made choices about actions they should take. Students wrote to the local council and designed a community brochure for the council to distribute. They painted signs on drains that fed into the creek and secured donations from local businesses to plant a garden and paint a mural at the back of the school. Finally, they worked with older students from a local college to construct a video that was aired by the local television station. Projects like the Black Creek project provide opportunities for students to work with community members and use their voice(s) *in* learning and *for* learning about their community as well as *for* actions *in* the community. Students in the project take the initiative in proposing group work. Their teachers support them by fostering discussions, modelling behaviours and procedures, and assisting with responsible decision making and action planning. Collaborating with community members provides students with knowledge that their voices can be heard. As one of Andrew's students comments, 'We are creating a brochure about Black Creek…Everyone at [suburb] will get the message, "Don't pollute the creek!"'

Chantal similarly introduces projects for groups of students across her school. In the Cineliteracy project with 15 gifted and talented students from across Years 3–6, students create a short film called, 'A Step Back in Time, 2009 –1889.' Teams of students work to construct a visual representation of the history of the school. The audience is the school community and the presentation is for the school anniversary. The students have a clear purpose for developing scripts, adopting character roles, exploring voices, investigating camera angles and film direction, and completing the movie. The project is a challenge for students to show initiative, develop and use new skills. Students enjoy 'making a real movie' and reflect, 'You actually get to act. Other people in the future can watch it.' Chantal's teaching, in this project and in the classrooms, gives students a sense of place and prepares them to take responsibility *in* learning and *for* learning. Students voice what they know and what they need to know. They reflect on their own learning and that of their peers. A student comments about Chantal, 'She starts us off, then we start researching. She hands it over to us, then we tell and share.'

By creating spaces, structures and expectations for students' voices, encouraging students to support each other in learning, providing choices for students to negotiate the curriculum, take initiative in lessons and projects and shape the classroom *for* learning, these middle years teachers build students' voice(s), engagement and independence. Later years teachers described in the next section similarly create spaces and expectations that promote students' voice(s) through similar structures and planned, systematic collaborative work. Deliberately, they employ extensive higher level questioning to further expand students' thinking *in* learning, *for* learning and *about* optimizing learning.

Student voice(s) in the later years

Planning spaces and structures for collaborative work

Students in Kate's science classes in an urban secondary school engage with a variety of highly visual resources, interactive experiences and digital materials. They find science learning 'fun'. Kate's pedagogy includes systematic group work in which students adopt distinctive roles and work collaboratively and actively with experiments in the laboratory and in the field. In their groups, students control their learning space by negotiating with each other how they will investigate and reflect on scientific problems, such as the structure of a DNA molecule. Kate's pedagogy targets high affective and operative involvement of students, and provides high support through the structures and expectations of the group members and the range of resources she provides. Students work together successfully because they know their roles, responsibilities and the expected outcomes for the group. They also know they have a voice and can make choices at many levels of their learning.

Creating spaces for extended student discussions

Choices and student-to-student interactions are strong features of classrooms of many of the *Fair Go* teachers in the later years. Diane, an English teacher of later years students in an outer-urban secondary school, asks persistent, probing questions and encourages critically reflective discussions amongst students working in pairs, groups and as a whole class. Students appreciate this form of engagement and the learning community that it creates:

> When you're reading the book and you don't understand something, instead of giving you the answer she asks you questions, and gets you to the answer . . . you pick it up . . . She doesn't throw the answer to you. She turns you around until you get it.

Diane explicitly teaches skills of analyzing and critiquing literary works, models metalanguage and encourages students' higher level thinking through her extensive questioning and challenging of students, reflecting her belief that speaking (that is, 'giving voice') helps clarify thinking. 'What was (Brontë) really trying to say?' she probes her extension English class. Students respond and build on each other's answers as they know Diane will keep probing about particular issues. As a student explains, 'You have to feed off each other... It's good to see what another person thinks; you connect things together. You start like relating things. It opens up your mind.' Diane provides students with choices in what they will do, with whom they will work and how. Students appreciate her encouragement of student voice(s) *in* learning as shown in the student comment that opens this chapter.

Eve's highly diverse outer-urban secondary students also learn through sustained discussions as they ask, and respond to many questions. Discussions in Eve's classrooms embrace, 'Your ideas and my ideas. It's good. I like discussion.' Eve creates a book-club atmosphere where readers share ideas and opinions and feel free to agree or disagree. First, she supports students to talk to each other in groups, but group dialogues often develop into whole class discussions. Eve pauses and waits for students to fill the silences and make connections. When students answer, she defers to another student to respond, interrogate and extend. These extended discussions help clarify and shift students' thinking and act as the precursor to writing. As students note, '(we) get to talk about it before we actually write it down.' After writing, students share and build their knowledge in pairs then peer-mark each other's essay paragraphs. Again students note, 'You get to know other people's ideas and you get to see the way they think.' This pedagogy is a value-added, dual-feedback strategy for students to become more independent and improve their writing of future drafts. As lessons conclude, Eve poses further questions for the students to ask themselves, 'What have I learnt?' 'What was important about the process?' 'How can I organize myself?' She models metacognitive language and reflection *about* learning. Throughout these extended questionings and complex discussions, students in Diane's and Eve's classes use and develop their voice(s) *in* learning and *for* learning at high levels.

Such extended discussions are not just the domain of English classrooms. Conversations about mathematical concepts feature in Mark's later years classrooms in a regional central school. Like the others, Mark uses questioning to build students' understanding and progresses them through levels of questions, posed as a learning barometer: 'What do we know?' 'What if it had been about...?' "How many ways would I...?' He draws on everyday examples to help students find relevance in mathematics problems. Through using such real resources and sustained, probing questions, Mark involves the students in high level mathematical discussions and encourages them to support each other and share in the construction of new mathematical understandings.

Teachers described in this chapter are exemplars for the ways in which many of the *Fair Go* teachers saw student voice(s) as a critical outcome *of* learning and highly salient *in* learning. While pedagogies are described within the stage groupings of our study we do not intend to imply a strict developmental or chronological progression. Rather, across all years in the study, teachers created spaces, held expectations and implemented structures and pedagogies that promoted student voice(s). The ways in which teachers did so varied. Teachers accommodated the experiences of their students and the learning goals they and the students held. In the next section, students give their final words about the teachers and teaching that encouraged their voice(s).

The final word – students talking about their learning and their teachers

An important part of the data gathering for this project involved focus group interviews with students of the *Fair Go* teachers. While these interviews were aimed at triangulating the data gathered through the observations and teacher interviews, they proved a remarkable source of candid comments about teaching, learning and the qualities and pedagogies of teachers who made a difference to students' learning. Students gave responses that affirmed that their teachers stood out, creating learning experiences and spaces that were different and in which they received positive messages about themselves as learners who:

- have and share **knowledge** with their classmates and teacher and construct new and deeper understandings;
- have **ability** to engage in high levels of learning and can shape learning
- can share experiences and insights and contribute to decisions about, and **control** of, learning spaces and resources;
- have a sense of **place**, feeling that they belong to, and value and support members of their classroom learning community in the 'hard fun' of learning; and
- have **voices** and agency as multiliterate, independent and reflective learners.

Knowledge: helps and builds understanding

Amongst the early years, students most frequently comment on how their *Fair Go* teachers 'help us' by providing spaces for students to think and talk during their learning and, most importantly, giving support for completing learning tasks and advancing learning. A student in Harmonie's kindergarten class said, '(Harmonie) puts the story on the interactive whiteboard so we can see it. We have to think about it . . . (then) she gives us more information to help us write the story', and 'she helps us when we don't know something'. Similarly, one of Kim's students described how, '[The teacher] comes and checks our work and (together) we make it better', acknowledging Kim's help in talking about and improving students' learning outputs, rather than just accepting first attempts.

Commonly, young, middle and older learners commented that they want to learn and construct new knowledge. They know and appreciate that effective teachers help them to build their knowledge and skills together. A middle years student in Andrew's class commented that, 'I like it because he does not teach us what we already know. He teaches us new things...we learn a lot'. Likewise, in Kate's later years science class a student responded, 'I like challenging work. If it's easy, you don't improve. You need to go to the next level.'

Ability: creates a sense of capability and achievement

Students in all years express appreciation of the ways teachers endorse their abilities and encourage high levels of achievement. In the early years, students talk about the ways their teachers give them challenging tasks and help them think and achieve, such as in Kim's class in which a student commented, 'I can do work because I think. I think too, much better now', and in Vanessa's Year 1 and 2 class in which students described how they appreciate that '...she gives you reading books in levels and when you start to get better she puts you up a level and she gets hard books...like chapter books and like thick books'.

Rebecca's middle years students similarly reported that they were making progress and acknowledged the growth in their abilities. One student said, 'I used to get frustrated but now I can read.' Another commented, 'The more we write the better our work gets.'

These students know their teachers have a focus on learning and create robust learning experiences that acknowledge and extend their abilities and encourage their achievements, whilst providing support. In Danny's later years woodwork and English classes in a rural central school, students appraised the effectiveness of his teaching by noting that, 'He does good stuff. He doesn't growl. He's one of the best teachers in the school'. Danny ensures students persist in completing their projects and gain a sense of pride and achievement. He guides them to relate this ability and awareness of success to their everyday lives.

Control: encourages a sharing and collaborative classroom

A common feature amongst the early years classrooms in this project is deliberate structuring of pedagogies to encourage students to ask for help, talk with each other, work together and support classroom learning. Students are clearly aware of these structures and of sharing responsibilities in learning. For example, Harmonie's students talked about the sharing circle for sharing stories and ideas, but also about how 'if we need help we put our names on a list and she will talk with us and help us'. Jo's students, who were a little older, reported that 'when we have a maths problem, we get a partner, our investigation books and (we) work it out.'

Middle and later years students are similarly aware of the ways in which their teachers encourage them to support each other. They talked about how their teachers negotiated learning with them and provided choices. Nicole's students, for example, talked about their choices in curriculum content and within activities with comments such as, 'We have choices in problem solving . . . It's important with choice for everyone to get a say'. Similarly, Diane's later years students noted that, 'She gives you the option (to choose) the resources that we have at school . . . she gives us insight into these.'

Students in middle and later years also described ways their teachers encouraged them to assume responsibility and autonomy in their learning and have a role in developing the social culture of their school. Eve's students recognized the way she establishes a democratic, shared learning space in which students demonstrate their voice and agency in learning. 'In group work . . . with your peers . . . you can ask this question to the group and then if you can't decide you can go again to another person . . . There's like multiple ways you can get help.' Students in Andrew's middle years classes commented on the responsibilities and opportunities they had in the school as in, '(Andrew) lets us organize, set up. Take consequences . . . wants us to represent the school well . . . send good messages to the little ones.'

Place: creates challenges that are hard fun

While students in the early years mostly talk about feelings of belonging in their community, such as '(It's) nice because there is nice neighbours' (Vanessa's Year 1 and 2 class), some are very aware of community concerns. Overwhelmingly though, the students perceived and described their schools and classrooms as places that made them 'happy' and 'excited', giving them a sense that learning is 'hard fun' and that their classrooms 'are good – when I come in here I don't feel tired anymore' (Jo's Year 4 class).

Middle and later years students also described their classrooms and schools as places they wanted to be. Comments from Sarah's students included, 'we come to school because we want to, not because we have to'. Kate's students appreciate her unpredictability within the learning environment and explained that '(Miss) tries to make it interesting for us.' These same students expressed that they want to be at school because, 'You learn (and) she always has a smile on her face.'

Two of the middle years teachers planned community-based projects to help students connect with their community. In Chantal's cineliteracy project, students described their enjoyment in 'making a real movie' and commented that, 'we'll get to be remembered in the school.' This sense of belonging and responsibility to the school and the community is evident amongst Andrew's students also who said, 'he (Andrew) wants to learn that we can make a difference with the smaller things in our lives. Just because we are in a small school, we can do big things.' Jen involves her special education students in a range of learning activities that are associated with their lives outside of the classroom, such as community access, shopping and an annual camp. Her students selected visual cards representing the terms 'excited' and 'happy' to respond to how they felt about being in Jen's class and chose picture cards of community involvement to indicate their preferred classroom activities.

Voice: provides multiple ways of learning, including ICT

While learners in the early years report how 'good' they are at paying attention to their teacher, and listening, such as when '(I) fold my arms, cross my legs ... look and listen' (Kim's kindergarten class) they also talk about the ways their teachers encourage them to talk *in* learning and *about* learning, and use a variety of resources, including ICT, to assist their learning. Georgia's students describe how they learn best when they use the computers and talk with each other. They also explained how, if they 'got stuck' then they could 'Borrow Miss for a moment ... I can come in of a morning and I say to Miss "I want to book you" and she helps me and tells us what to do ... (She) doesn't tell us the answers – (she) wants us to find out for ourselves'.

As described earlier in this chapter, learners at all levels appreciate opportunities for developing and using their voice(s), the choices they have in learning and the ways they can support each other and shape their learning. Sue's students use the example of this as, 'Groups – you can choose your own. Everyone shares and combines good ideas. We don't have captains, we are all captains.' Likewise, Rebecca's junior secondary students commented that it was best to 'have fun when you learn, have humour, help each other ... get more ideas.' They talked about respecting the opinions and ideas of their classmates.

Amongst the later years, Josephine's drama students respond to her empathic approach to teaching and reflect that, 'She tries to see things from your point of view.' They reported a strong appreciation for the opportunities to use their voice and talk about their learning at all times, 'Even if she's just writing on the board she's talking to us about it as well and she puts in a couple of jokes here and there and she makes us interested. It's not like you're just writing notes from the board. It's like you're having a conversation with her as you're doing it.' Across all the years, students talked about the focus on learning that their teachers had and the sense of agency students had in shaping learning and accessing resources, including talking with their teacher and with each other.

Conclusion

Across the student interviews, students' comments affirmed the effectiveness of the *Fair Go* teachers and the pedagogies that they implemented. Students commonly described how the classrooms of the *Fair Go* teachers were different, focusing on learning that was new and enabling the voice(s) of the students. The sense of agency that students experienced in the classrooms varied, but the differences in structures and pedagogies were mostly due to students' capacities, previous experiences and the learning goals of the class. Across all the student interviews, *Fair Go* teachers were perceived as:

- wanting their students to build **knowledge**: '[The teacher] wants us to learn. She gives us work where we learn lots, (we) all work in a cooperative team . . . (She) uses different strategies to make hard work easy.'
- helping with the joint construction of **knowledge**: Student: 'Can we do it as a class?' Mark: 'You have a go at doing it by yourself, then we'll do it as a class.'
- endorsing students' **abilities**, achievements and leadership potential: 'She doesn't throw the answer to you. She turns you around until you get it.' (Diane's student)
- listening and talking with students to share **control** of learning and develop communities of practice: 'Learning by myself, I feel relaxed but I feel comfort in groups, moving around . . . by yourself you only have one voice.' (Sarah's student)
- building a sense of excitement about school as a **place** where learning is 'hard fun': 'When I go into the room it is a new day, a fresh day'. (Georgia's student)
- creating spaces and structures for choices, **voice**(s), and reflection on learning processes: 'She gives us several choices of the same thing – we don't just do anything' (Sue's student).

15 A new Monday morning and beyond

Fair Go Team

> Monday morning need not imply an endless succession of the same Monday mornings.
>
> (Willis 1977: 192)

In this concluding chapter of our book we begin by reflecting on Willis's (1977) seminal work about how kids from low SES communities come to believe that school is not for them. Willis had talked about Monday morning in his final chapter as a metaphor for the limited possibilities that classrooms offer for many poor communities. We are hoping that the same metaphor can reflect a sense of optimism for a 'new Monday morning' as captured in the classroom stories of this book. The teachers you have met offer their students a genuine hope that getting up and going to school can be both challenging and engaging in the here and now, as well as giving them a chance for a more successful educational future. We finish this book by suggesting that this chance is manifest through three key themes: measure of a teacher; the call to engage; intellectual challenge. The themes are presented here both as a summary and as a set of provocations for educators to take forward as they open up an educational fair go for students living in poverty.

The measure of a teacher

What then is the measure of a teacher? In times of national teacher accreditation and associated narrowing notions of accountability, how can the profession itself recognize exemplary teaching? How can teachers ensure the best possible social and academic outcomes for the students in their school? The *Teachers for a Fair Go* project focused on a group of individual teachers and examined how they best served the needs of the students from their schools.

The measure of teachers in this book is to do with transforming classrooms with a focus on 'e'ngagement, at high cognitive, affective and operative levels. Such a transformation shapes young lives for success. It occurs amid the competing pressures of limiting policies and agendas such as national standards of teaching quality and accreditation of teachers. On the other hand, these days the Monday morning tension for teachers is often in the balance between external measures and standardized testing versus what they recognize as high intellectual quality and developing creativity. A next question we could ask is about the role of school leaders in supporting the practices of the teachers featured in this book. How can these leaders support and sanction exemplary teaching? We could also ask how, within this tension, can we encourage these kinds of teachers to see themselves as leaders in their schools in designing curriculum, in planning and in mentoring?

Many of these *Fair Go* teachers do not fit into a 'one size fits all' model of what a teacher should be. Need our own world-views of what 'teachers must be' be as formulaic and rigid as media might lead us to believe? The teachers live within national and international agendas driving for 'standardization' while also choosing to embrace diversity, difference and the notion of a 'fair go' for all across each new Monday morning.

Call to engage

The *Fair Go* teachers were not selected because they are the 'best' teachers in their school, state or country. Such selection would be an impossible task with a hotly-debated and ever-shifting list of criteria, as previously discussed above. Rather, these teachers are noticed as making a positive difference to the engagement and achievement of the students they teach. Commonly, the *Fair Go* teachers share an enduring commitment to social justice and view the challenges of teaching in low SES communities as a positive – a call to engage. Before Monday morning arrives, these teachers respond to the call, excited by pedagogical challenges to think creatively about, 'What's the next destination in our learning journeys?' and 'How can I engage the learners in my classroom?'

The stories in previous chapters describe how the *Fair Go* teachers plan. They find out about their students, their families and communities, value their experiences, knowledge and interests and deliberately build on these in their classrooms to provide contextually-responsive, creative, intellectual challenges. They maintain high expectations of themselves and their students. They employ resources that promote active learning, having thought through organizational issues. They continually reflect on the effectiveness of their practices, refining them to better support all students to achieve their learning potential and to see education as a resource of value now and in the future: 'school is for me'. They encourage students to reflect on their learning and to see themselves as able and capable learners, and citizens of their school and community.

Monday mornings, and every other school day, can bring intellectual challenges for the *Fair Go* teachers and their students. Difficult as they are to maintain, these teachers do keep their classrooms as robust curriculum and pedagogical spaces in which students investigate big ideas and engage in critical and creative thinking, and often with the very kinds of students who historically have been turned off by their classrooms and disengaged from school learning.

Intellectual challenge

The *Fair Go* teachers are committed to the learning of their students and their own professional learning. They have a deep knowledge of content and pedagogy and constantly refresh that knowledge. These teachers do not dumb down the curriculum or pacify students with work sheets. They do not take the easy organizational route. Rather, they design rich, robust learning sequences and select resources and teaching strategies that are responsive to students, supporting their learning and enabling them to engage with the intellectual challenge. They practise learning routines and structures with students so students know what to do and how to do it. When confronted by disruptive behaviour, the teachers maintain their focus, teaching through the behaviour, giving positive affirmation and maintaining high expectations in an atmosphere of trust, such that students are expected to accept responsibility for their learning and actions.

On Monday mornings, and every other school day, students in these classes have a familiarity with the repertoires of learning practice, expectations and boundaries that are firmly established at the beginning, and throughout, the school year. They know that somewhere in their day they will engage in experiences that are new and challenging – a new Monday morning. They will be active learners, inside and outside the classroom. They will be involved in a range of groups that are structured to promote substantive conversations. They will work with a variety of current, cognitively and affectively motivating resources and have opportunities to employ their imaginations and be creative.

A recurrent question in folklore is whether the perfect classroom is always one that is full of quiet, compliant students. On the surface, some *Fair Go* classrooms appear noisy and possibly messy. Others look more like the traditional view of a classroom. What unites them is the buzz in the room from students who are able to engage in intellectually challenging encounters that their teachers have 'planned hard'. These classrooms are communities of learners in which students demonstrate high cognitive, high operative and high affective engagement in learning, and in which students value the intellectual challenge.

The teachers' final words

The voices of the *Fair Go* teachers have been interwoven throughout this study. These voices are particularly cogent in this final section where we include the teachers' reflections about their teaching and how it connects with students and leads to successful outcomes. At every stage of schooling, the teachers take time to know the student in order to help each one feel successful as a learner. They express this as 'knowing the children's stories.' As well, they advocate for the community, knowing that 'you want to make a difference for their children.' There is a strong connection with the professional quality of the teachers' commitment to providing messages to students of their knowledge and ability. The authenticity of these messages comes from knowing students and their families and communities.

All of the teachers see the necessity of being learners themselves. One teacher expressed this as 'being an expert learner' who models a love of learning for the students they teach. They 'let go of control of learning', allowing students opportunities to take risks and make choices about their learning. These ideas align with the MeE messages about control and voice.

The teachers reflect on the advantages of creating a stimulating high affective learning environment that minimises negative behaviour. For those who do experience students with disruptive behaviours, their response is, as one teacher put it, 'not to succumb to the negatives.' With these teachers, learning is always the priority and they 'plan hard and teach easy.' Their goals are creating a sense of belonging in the learning environment and co-constructing knowledge with their students.

One strong message from the teachers is that they are not wanting simply to run a 'comfortable' classroom. Collectively they suggest that teachers really should be wanting to make a difference in their classrooms. They also want to affirm that students need to be free to take risks, in order to learn. They are concerned with having high expectations, both of their students and of themselves as teachers.

Our final word

As Chapter 1 argued, we are not romantically naïve about the challenges and difficulties that poverty brings. We are well aware of Bernstein's (1996) caution that education can't compensate for society. However, we have presented in this book the real stories of teachers working in housing estate, urban, multicultural, regional and remote communities who bring high expectations, intellectual quality, careful planning and creativity to their classrooms and to their students. In presenting these stories our intentions are to highlight that within the quite diverse look, feel and sound of these individual classrooms, there is a composite picture of pedagogical approaches that successfully engages students. Encouragingly, this picture works against the media image of the 'heroic' and 'born' teacher, and invites a more careful consideration of what classrooms for low SES students might look like when teachers are engaged in 'teaching for a fair go.'

Bibliography

Alloway, N., Freebody, P., Gilbert, P. and Muspratt (2002) *Boys, Literacy and Schooling: expanding the repertoires of practice*. Canberra: Commonwealth Department of Education, Science and Training.

Alloway, N. and Gilbert, P. (2002) 'Literacy and gender in early childhood contexts: boys on the side?' in L. Makin and C. Jones Diaz (eds), *Literacies in Early Childhood: changing views challenging practices*. Sydney: McLennan and Petty.

Alton-Lee, A. (2003) 'Quality teaching for diverse students in schooling: best evidence synthesis – what role this kind of work can and can't take in building teaching quality', Proceedings of Australian Council for Educational Research (ACER) Conference, *Building Teacher Quality*: 24–27.

Anderman, L. H., Andrzejewski, C. E. and Allen, J. (2011) 'How do teachers support students' motivation and learning in their classrooms?' *Teachers College Record*, 113(5): 969–1003.

Apple, M. W. (2001) *Educating the 'Right' Way: markets, standards, God and inequality*. New York and London: Routledge Falmer.

Au, K. (2006) *Multicultural Issues and Literacy Achievement*. Mahwah, NJ: L. Erlbaum Associates.

Australian Council of Deans of Education (ACDE) (2004) *New Teaching, New Learning: a vision for Australian education*. Canberra: ACDE.

Australian Curriculum, Assessment and Reporting Authority (ACARA) (2011) *The Australian Curriculum: English*. Online: www.australiancurriculum.edu.au/English/Curriculum (accessed 15 December, 2011).

Ayres, P., Sawyer, W. and Dinham, S. (2004) 'Effective teaching in the context of a Grade 12 high stakes external examination in New South Wales, Australia', *British Educational Research Journal*, 30(1) February: 142–165.

Ball, S. (2007) *Education plc: understanding private sector participation in public sector education*. London: Routledge.

Ball, S. J. (2003) 'The teacher's soul and the terrors of performativity', *Journal of Education Policy*, 18(2): 215–228.

Ball, S. (2002) *Class Strategies and the Education Market: the middle classes and social advantage*. London: Routledge Falmer.

Baudot, J. (ed.) (2001) *Building a World Community: globalisation and the common good*. Seattle: Royal Danish Ministry of Foreign Affairs and University of Washington Press.

Baum, F., Palmer, C., Modra, C., Murray, C. and Bush, R. (2000) 'Families, social capital and health', in I. Winter (ed.), *Social Capital and Public Policy in Australia*. Melbourne: Australian Institute of Family Studies.

Begen, F. and Turner-Cobb, J. (2009) 'Feelings of belonging affect school children', paper presented at the British Psychologocial Society's Division of Health Psychology annual conference at Aston University, 19 September.

Berger P., Epp, J. and Møller, H. (2006) 'The predictable influences of colonialism, culture clash, and current practice on punctuality, attendance, and achievement in Nunavut schools', *Canadian Journal of Native Education*, 29(2): 182–205.

Berlant, L. (2011) *Cruel Optimism*. Durham: Duke University Press.

Bernstein, B. (1996) *Pedagogy, Symbolic Control and Identity: theory, research, critique*. London: Taylor and Francis.

Blackmore, J. (2004) 'Restructuring educational leadership in changing contexts: a local/global account of restructuring in Australia', *Journal of Educational Change*, 5: 267–288.

Block, C. C. and Duffy, G. (2008) 'Research on teaching comprehension: where we've been and where we're going', in C.C. Block and S.R. Parris (eds), *Comprehension Instruction: research-based best practices*, 2nd edn. New York: Guilford Press.

Boden, M. (2001) 'Creativity and knowledge', in A. Craft, B. Jeffrey and M. Leibling (eds), *Creativity in Education*. London: Continuum.

Bonnor, C. and Caro, J. (2007) *The Stupid Country: how Australia is dismantling public education*. University of New South Wales: University of New South Wales Press.

Bonzionelos, N. (2004) 'Socio-economic background and computer use: the role of computer anxiety and computer experience in their relationship', *International Journal of Human-Computer Studies*, 61: 725–746.

Bransford, J., Darling-Hammond, L. and Le Page, P. (2007) 'Introduction', in L. Darling-Hammond and J. Bransford (eds), *Preparing Teachers for a Changing World: what teachers should learn and be able to do*. San Francisco: Jossey-Bass.

Bruner, J. (1986) *Actual Minds, Possible Worlds*. Cambridge, MA: Harvard University Press.

Byrne, M. and Munns, G. (2012) 'Getting both pictures right: the importance of the classroom relationship', in Q. Beresford and G. Partington (eds), *Reform and Resistance in Aboriginal Education*. Perth: UWA Publishing.

Callow, J. (1999) 'Reading the visual: an introduction', in J. Callow (ed.), *Image Matters: visual texts in the classroom*. Marrickville, NSW: Primary English Teaching Association.

Castells, M. (1996) *The Rise of the Network Society*. Malden, MA: Blackwell.

Cheyne, J. A. and Tarulli, D. (2005) 'Dialogue, difference and voice in the zone of proximal development', in H. Daniels (ed.), *An Introduction to Vygotsky*. Hove and New York: Routledge.

Christie, F. (2005) *Language Education in the Primary Years*. Sydney: UNSW Press.

Cole, B., Mooney, M., Munns, G., Power, A., Sawyer, W. and Zammit, K. (2010) *Engaging Middle Years Boys in Rural Educational Settings*. Sydney: NSW Department of Education and Training. Online: www.lowsesschools.nsw.edu.au/wcbcontent/uploads/psp/file/myrbreport.pdf (accessed 29 February, 2012).

Collins, P. (1991) 'Learning from the outsider within: the sociological significance of black feminist thought', in M. Fonow and J. Cook (eds), *Beyond Methodology*. Bloomington: Indiana University Press.

Comber, B. (2001) 'Critical literacies and local action: teacher knowledge and a "new" research agenda', in B. Comber and A. Simpson (eds), *Negotiating Critical Literacies in Classrooms*. Mahwah, NJ: Lawrence Erlbaum Associates.

Condron, D. (2011) 'Egalitarianism and educational excellence: compatible goals for affluent societies?' *Educational Researcher*, 40(2): 47–55.

Costa, A. and Kallick, B. (2000) *Describing 16 Habits of Mind*. Online: www.habits-of-mind.net (accessed 13 February, 2010).

Council for the Australian Federation (2007) Federalist Paper No. 2: *The Future of Schooling in Australia*. Online: www.dpc.vic.gov.au/CA256D800027B102/Lookup/FederalistPaper2TheFutureofSchoolinginAustralia/$file/Federalist Paper2TheFutureofSchoolinginAustralia.pdf (accessed 20 March, 2011).

Craft, A. (2010) *Creativity and Education Futures: learning in a digital age*. Stoke-on-Trent: Trentham Books.

Craft, A. (2001) 'Little c creativity', in A. Craft, B. Jeffrey and M. Leibling (eds), *Creativity in Education*. London: Continuum.

Craven, R. G. (ed.) (2011) *Teaching Aboriginal Studies*. Sydney: Allen and Unwin.

Creemers, B. (1996) 'The school effectiveness knowledge base', in D. Reynolds, R. Bollen, B. Creemers, D. Hopkins, L. Stoll and N. Lagerweij (eds), *Making Good Schools*. London: Routledge.

Cummins, J. (2001) *Negotiating Identities: education for empowerment in a diverse society*, 2nd edn. Los Angeles: California Association for Bilingual Education, Ontario.

Cummins, J. (2000) *Language, Power and Pedagogy*. Clevedon: Multilingual Matters.

Cummins, J., Bismilla, V., Chow, P., Cohen, S., Giampapa, F., Leoni, L., Sandhu, P. and Sastri, P. (2006) *ELL Students Speak for Themselves: identity texts and literacy engagement in multilingual classrooms*. Online: www.curriculum.org/secretariat/files/ELLidentityTexts.pdf (accessed 19 November, 2010).

Dahlberg, G. (2003) 'Pedagogy as a loci of an ethics of an encounter', in M. Bloch, K. Holmlund, I. Moqvist and T. Popkewitz (eds), *Governing Children, Families and Education: restructuring the welfare state*. New York: Palgrave MacMillan.

Dahlberg, G. and Moss, P. (2005) *Ethics and Politics in Early Childhood Education*, London: Routledge Falmer.

Dansie, B. (2001) 'Scaffolding oral language: "The Hungry Giant"', in J. Hammond (ed.), *Scaffolding: teaching and learning in language and literacy interaction*. Sydney: Primary English Teaching Association.

Darling-Hammond, L. (2010) *The Flat World and Education: how America's commitment to equity will determine our future*. New York: Teachers College Press.

Darling-Hammond, L. (2000) 'Teacher quality and student achievement', *Education Policy Analysis Archives*, 14(1): 162–183.

de Bono, E. (1985) *Six Thinking Hats: an essential approach to business management*. Boston and New York: Little, Brown and Company.

Delpit, L. (2006) *Other People's Children: cultural conflict in the classroom*, 2nd edn. New York: The New Press.

Department of Education, Employment and Workplace Relations (DEEWR) (2009) *Belonging, Being and Becoming: the early years learning framework for Australia*. Canberra: Australian Government Department of Education, Employment and Workplace Relations.

Department of Education, Science and Training (DEST) (2002) 'Scaffolding learning', *MyRead: strategies for teaching reading in the middle years*. Online: www.myread.org/scaffolding.htm (accessed 15 December, 2011).

Doecke, B., Green, B. Kostogriz, A., Reid, J. and Sawyer, W. (2007) 'Knowing practice in English teaching? Research challenges in representing the professional practice of English teachers', *English Teaching: practice and critique*, 6(3) December: 4–21.

Dreyfus, H. (2001) *On the Internet*. London: Routledge.

Dufficy, P. (2005) *Designing Learning for Diverse Classrooms*. Newtown: NSW Primary English Teaching Association.

Edwards-Groves, C. and Department of Education, Science and Training (DEST) (2003) 'Connecting students to learning through explicit teaching', *MyRead: strategies for teaching reading in the middle years*. Online: www.myread.org/explicit.htm (accessed 15 December, 2011).

Egan, K. (2007) 'Imagination, past and present', in K. Egan, M. Stout and K. Takaya (eds), *Teaching and Learning Outside the Box*. Canada: The Althouse Press.

Eisner, E. (2005) *Reimagining Schools: the selected works of Elliot W. Eisner*. New York: Routledge.

Erebus International (2005) *Review of the Literature on Socio-Economic Status and Learning: report to the NSW Department of Education and Training*. Darlinghurst: NSW Department of Education and Training.

Fair Go Project Team (2006) *School is for Me: pathways to student engagement*. Sydney: Priority Schools Programs, NSW Department of Education and Training.

Fleet, A. and Torr, J. (2007) 'Literacy assessment: understanding and recording meaningful data', in L. Makin, C. Jones Diaz and C. McLachlan (eds), *Literacies in Childhood: changing views, challenging practice*. Sydney: Elsevier.

Fouts, J. (2003) *A Decade of Reform: a summary of research findings on classroom, school, and district effectiveness in Washington State*. Lynnwood, WA: Washington School Research Center.

Fredricks, J. A., Blumenfield, P. C. and Paris, A. H. (2004) 'School engagement: potential of the concept, state of the evidence', *Review of Educational Research*, 76(1): 59–109.

Freebody, P. (2007) *Literacy Education in School: research perspectives from the past, for the future*. Camberwell, Victoria: ACER Press.

Freebody, P. and Luke, A. (1990) '"Literacies" programs: debates and demands in cultural context', *Prospect*, 5: 7–16.

Furlong, V. (1991) 'Disaffected pupils: reconstructing the sociological perspective', *British Journal of Sociology of Education*, 12(3): 293–307.

Furlong, V. (1985) *The Deviant Pupil: sociological perspectives*. Milton Keynes: Open University Press.

Gee, J. P. (2001) 'Reading as situated language: a sociocognitive perspective', *Journal of Adolescent and Adult Literacy*, 44(8): 714–725.

Gee, J. P. (1990) *Social Linguistics and Literacies: ideology in discourse*. London: Falmer Press.

Gibbons, P. (2009). *English Learners' Academic Literacy and Thinking: learning in the challenge zone*. Portsmouth, NH: Heinemann.

Gonzalez, N., Moll, L. and Amanti, C. (2005) 'Introduction: theorizing practices', in N. Gonzalez, L. Moll and C. Amanti (eds), *Funds of Knowledge: theorizing practice in households, communities and classrooms*. Mahway, NJ: Lawrence Erlbaum.

Gonzalez-Mena, J. and Widmeyer-Eyers, D. (2009) *Infants, Toddlers and Caregivers: a curriculum of respectful, responsive caregiving*, 8th edn. New York: McGraw Hill.

Gore, J. and Parkes, P. (2009) 'On mistreatment of management', in A. Phelan and

J. Sumsion (eds.), *Critical Readings in Teacher Education*. Rotterdam: Sense Publishers.

Gore, J. and Parkes, P. (2007) 'On the mistreatment of management', paper presented in the *Provoking Absences: critical readings in teacher education symposium*, at the Annual Meeting of the American Educational Research Association (AERA), Chicago, 9–13 April 2007. Online: http://robertparkes.edublogs.org/files/2007/04/goreparkes.pdf (accessed 10 December, 2011).

Haberman, M. (2011) 'The beliefs and behaviors of star teachers', *Teachers College Record*. Online: www.tcrecord.org ID Number: 16504 (accessed 9 April, 2011).

Haberman, M. (2005) *Star Teachers: the ideology and best practice of effective teachers of diverse children and youth in poverty*. Houston, TX: The Haberman Educational Foundation.

Haberman, M. (1995) *Star Teachers of Children in Poverty*. Indianapolis, IN: Kappa Delta Pi.

Hamston, J. and Murdoch, K. (1996/2004) *Integrating Socially: planning integrated units of work for social education*. Melbourne: Eleanor Curtain.

Hargreaves, A. (2000) 'Four ages of professionalism and professional learning', *Teachers and Teaching: history and practice*, 6(2): 151–182.

Hattie, J. (2009) *Visible Learning*. London: Routledge.

Hattie, J. (2003)'Teachers make a difference: what is the research evidence?', paper presented at the Australian Association for Research in Education Annual Conference. Auckland, New Zealand, November–December 2003.

Hawke, R. (2004) *Soraya the Storyteller*. Melbourne: Thomas C Lothian.

Hayes, D., Mills, M., Christie, P. and Lingard, B. (2006) *Teachers and Schooling: making a difference*. Crows Nest: Allen and Unwin.

Healy, A. and Honan, E. (2004) *Text Next: new resources for literacy learning*. Newtown, NSW: Primary English Teaching Association.

Hedegaard, M. (2005) 'The zone of proximal development as basis for instruction', in H. Daniels (ed.), *An Introduction to Vygotsky*. Hove and New York: Routledge.

Hertzberg, M. (2012) *Teaching English Language Learners in Mainstream Classes*. Newtown, NSW: Primary English Teaching Association Australia.

Hill, P. and Rowe, K. (1996) 'Multilevel modeling in school effectiveness research', *School Effectiveness and School Improvement*, 7(1): 1–34.

Hill, S., Comber, B., Louden, W., Rivalland, J. and Reid, J. (2002) *100 Children Turn 10*, vol. 1. Canberra: Department of Education, Science and Training.

Holliday, M. (2008) *Strategies for Reading Success*. Newtown, NSW: Primary English Teaching Association.

Holmes-Smith, P. (2006) *Socio-economic Density and its Effect on School Performance*. Online: www.mceetya.edu.au/verve/_resources/SES_Report.pdf (accessed 31 May, 2011)

International Reading Association (IRA) (2012) *International Reading Association, Position Statements and Information Guides*. Online: www.reading.org/General/AboutIRA/PositionStatements.aspx (accessed 15 February, 2012).

Jones, P. (1996) *Talking to Learn*. Newtown, NSW: Primary English Teaching Association.

Katz, L. and Chard, S. (1989/2000), *Engaging Children's Minds: the project approach*. Stamford, CT: Ablex.

Katzenmeyer, M. and Moller, G. (2001) *Awakening the Sleeping Giant: helping teachers develop as leaders*, 2nd edn, California: Corwin Press.

Keddie, A. and Churchill, R. (2010) 'Teacher-student relationships', in D. Prendergast and N. Bahr (eds), *Teaching Middle Years*, 2nd edn. Crows Nest, NSW: Allen and Unwin.

Kemmis, S. (2009) 'Understanding professional practice: a synoptic framework', in B. Green (ed.), *Understanding and Researching Professional Practice*, Rotterdam: Sense Publications.

Kemmis, S. (2005) 'Knowing practice; searching for saliences', *Pedagogy, Culture and Society*, 13(3): 391–426.

Kent, N. and Facer, K. (2004) 'Different worlds? A comparison of young people's home and school ICT use', *Journal of Computer-Assisted Learning*, 20: 440–455.

Kirschner, P. and Lai, K. (2007) 'Online communities of practice in education', *Technology, Pedagogy and Education*, 16(2): 127–131.

Kozma, R. (2003) *Technology, Innovation, and Educational Change: a global perspective*. Eugene, OR: International Society for Technology in Education.

Kress, G. (2003) *Literacy in the New Media Age*, London: Routledge.

Kress, G. R. and van Leeuwen, T. (2006) *Reading Images: The grammar of visual design*, London: Routledge.

Lankshear, C. and Knobel, M. (2007) 'Sampling "the New" in New Literacies', in M. Knobel and C. Lanskshear (eds), *A New Literacies Sampler*. New York: Peter Lang.

Lasky, S. (2005) 'A sociocultural approach to understanding teacher identity, agency and professional vulnerability in a context of secondary school reform', *Teaching and Teacher Education*, 21(8): 899–916.

Law, W.-W. (2003) 'Globalization as both threat and opportunity for the Hong Kong teaching profession', *Journal of Educational Change*, 4: 149–179.

Leithwood, K. and Riehl, C. (2003) 'What do we already know about successful school leadership?' Online: www.cepa.gse.rutgers.edu/WhatWeKnow_long_2003.pdf (accessed 8 March, 2012).

Lingard, B. (2011) 'Policy as numbers: ac/counting for educational research', *The Australian Educational Researcher*, 38(4): 355–382.

Lingard, B., Hayes, D., Mills, M. and Christie, P (2003) *Leading Learning: making hope practical in schools*. Maidenhead: Open University Press.

Lingard, B., Martino, W., Mills, M. and Bahr, M. (2002) *Addressing the Educational Needs of Boys*. Canberra: Commonwealth Department of Education, Science and Training.

Lingard, B. and Renshaw, P. (2010) 'Teaching as a research-informed and research-informing profession', in A. Campbell and S. Groundwater-Smith (eds), *Connecting Inquiry and Professional Learning in Education*. London and New York: Routledge.

Loreman, T. (2007) 'Seven pillars of support for inclusive education: moving from why to how', *International Journal of Whole Schooling*, 3(2): 22–38.

Lortie, D. (1975) *Schoolteacher: a sociological study*. Chicago, IL: University of Chicago Press.

Louden, W., Rohl, M., Barratt-Pugh, C., Brown, C., Cairney, T., Elderfield, J., House, H., Meiers, M., Rivalland, J. and Rowe, K. (2005) 'In teachers' hands: effective literacy teaching practices in the early years of schooling', *Australian Journal of Language and Literacy*, 28(3): 181–241.

Lucas, B. (2001) 'Creative teaching, teaching creativity and creative learning', in A. Craft, B. Jeffrey and M. Leibling (eds), *Creativity in Education*. London: Continuum.

Luke, A. (2010) 'Will the Australian national curriculum up the intellectual ante in classrooms?', *Curriculum Perspectives*, 30(3): 59–64.

Luke, A. (2004) 'Teaching after the market: from commodity to cosmopolitan', *Teachers College Record*, 106(7): 1422–1443.

Luke, A. (2003) 'Literacy and the other: a sociological approach to literacy research and policy in multilingual societies', *Reading Research Quarterly*, 38(1): 132–141.

Luke, A. (2000) 'Critical literacy in Australia', *Journal of Adolescent and Adult Literacy*, 43: 448–461.

Luke, A. and Elkins, J. (2002) 'Towards a critical, worldly literacy', *Journal of Adolescent and Adult Literacy*, 45: 668–673.

Luke, A., Freebody, P., Land, R., Booth, S. and Kronk, P. (2000) *Literate Futures: report of the literacy review for Queensland schools*. Brisbane: State of Queensland, Department of Education.

Luke, A. and Luke, C. (2001) 'Adolescence lost/childhood regained: on early intervention and the emergence of the techno-subject', *Journal of Early Childhood Literacy*, 1(1): 91–120.

MacNaughton, G. and Hughes, P. (2003) 'Parents and communities', in G. MacNaughton (ed.), *Shaping Early Childhood: learners, curriculum and contexts*. Maidenhead: Open University Press.

McFadden, M. and Munns, G. (2002) 'Student engagement and the social relations of pedagogy', *British Journal of Sociology of Education*, 23(3): 357–366.

McLaren, P. and Leonard, P. (1993) 'Editor's introduction: absent discourses: Paulo Freire and the dangerous memories of liberation', in P. McLaren and P. Leonard (eds), *Paulo Freire: a critical encounter*. London and New York: Routledge.

McWilliams, E. and Taylor, P. (1998). 'Teacher im/material: challenging the new pedagogies of instructional design', *Educational Researcher*, 27(8): 29–35.

Mariani, L. (1997) 'Teacher support and teacher challenge in promoting learner autonomy', *Perspectives*, 23(2), Fall. Online: www.learningpaths.org/papers/papersupport.htm (accessed 23 March, 2001).

Marsh, J. (2000) 'Teletubby tales: popular culture in the early childhood language and literacy curriculum', *Contemporary Issues in Early Childhood*, 1(2): 119–133.

Martin, A. J. (2009) 'Motivation and engagement across the academic lifespan: a developmental construct validity study of elementary school, high school, and university/college students', *Educational and Psychological Measurement*, 69: 794–824.

Martin, A. J. (2007) 'Examining a multidimensional model of student motivation and engagement using a construct validation approach', *British Journal of Educational Psychology*, 77: 413–440.

Martin, A. J. (2002) 'Motivation and academic resilience: developing a model of student enhancement', *Australian Journal of Education*, 47: 88–106.

Martino, W. and Pallotta-Chiarolli, M. (2003) *So What's a Boy?* Sydney: Allen and Unwin.

Matsuura, K. (2008) *Message from Mr Matsuura, Director-General of UNESCO, on the celebration of 2008, International Year of Languages*, Paris: UNESCO. Online: http://portal.unesco.org/culture/en/ev.php-URL_ID=35559andURL_DO=DO_TOPICandURL_SECTION=201.html (accessed 13 November, 2011).

May, J. J. (2007) 'Language: the gatekeeper of humanity', in P. Chen (ed.), *2007 E-Yearbook of Urban Learning, Teaching, and Research*, AERA Urban Learning, Teaching, and Research Special Interest Group. Online: http://aera-ultr.org/yearbook.html (accessed 13 November, 2011).

Mayer, D. (1999) 'Building teacher identities: implications for pre-service teacher education', paper presented to the Australian Association for Research in Education, Melbourne.

Moll, L., Amanti, C., Neff, D. and Gonzalez, N. (1992) 'Funds of knowledge for teaching: using a qualitative approach to connect homes and classrooms', *Theory into Practice,* 31(2): 132–141.

msn Encarta (2009) Dictionary: Fair Go. Online: http://encarta.msn.com/dictionary_561504422/fair_go.html (accessed 15 March, 2011).

Muir, H. (2010) *Hideously Diverse Britain: the challenge of diversity in schools.* Online: www.guardian.co.uk/uk/2010/jul/14/hideously-diverse-britain-diversity-schools (accessed 8 March, 2012).

Muller, J., Juana, M., Sancho, J., Gil, S., Hernandez, F., Giro, X. and Bosco, A. (2006) 'The socio-economic dimensions of ICT driven educational change', *Computers and Education,* 49: 1175–1181.

Munns, G. (2007) 'A sense of wonder: pedagogies to engage students who live in poverty', *International Journal of Inclusive Education,* 11(3): 301–315.

Munns, G., Arthur, L., Downes, T., Gregson, R., Power, A., Sawyer, W., Singh, M., Thistleton-Martin, J. and Steele, F. (2006) *Motivation and Engagement of Boys evidence-based teaching practices,* Report to the Commonwealth Department of Education, Science and Training (DEST). Canberra: Commonwealth of Australia.

Munns, G., Arthur, L., Hertzberg, M., Sawyer, W. and Zammit, K. (2011) 'A fair go for low SES students', in T. Wrigley, P. Thomson and R. Lingard (eds), *Changing Schools: alternative ways to make a world of difference.* London: Routledge.

Munns, G., Lawson, J., O'Brien, M. and Johnson, K. (2006) 'Student engagement and the "Fair Go" project', in Fair Go Project Team, *School is For Me: pathways to student engagement.* Sydney: Priority Schools Programs, NSW Department of Education and Training.

Munns, G. and McFadden, M. G. (2000) 'First chance, second chance or last chance? Resistance and response to education', *British Journal of Sociology of Education,* 21: 59–76.

Munns, G. and Martin, A. (under review) 'Me, my classroom, my school: a mixed-methods study of the MeE framework of motivation, engagement, and academic development'.

Munns, G. and Woodward, H. (2006) 'The REAL Framework: student engagement and student self assessment', *Primary English Notes,* 155. Marrickville: Primary English Teaching Association.

Munns, G., Zammit, K. and Woodward, H. (2008) 'Reflections from the riot zone: the Fair Go Project and student engagement in a besieged community', *Journal of Children and Poverty,* 14(2): 157–171.

Naples, N. (1996) 'A feminist revisiting of the insider/outsider debate: The outsider phenomenon in rural Iowa', *Qualitative Sociology,* 19(1): 83–106. Online: www.springerlink.com/content/kx0492107n65pt18/ (accessed 27 February, 2011).

National Advisory Committee on Creative and Cultural Education (NACCCE) (1999) *All Our Futures: creativity, culture and education,* London: DfEE.

National Curriculum Board (NCB) (2008) *National English Curriculum: framing paper.* Online: www.ncb.org.au (accessed 30 November, 2011).

New London Group (2000) 'A pedagogy of multiliteracies: designing social futures', in B. Cope and M. Kalanztis (eds), *Multiliteracies: literacy learning and the design of social futures*. South Melbourne: Macmillan.

Newmann, F. and Associates (1996) *Authentic Achievement: restructuring schools for intellectual quality*, San Francisco, CA: Jossey Bass.

OECD (2010a) *PISA 2009 Results: overcoming social background – equity in learning opportunities and outcomes*, Volume II, Paris: OECD Publishing.

OECD (2010b) *PISA 2009 Results: what makes a school successful? resources, policies and practices*, Volume IV, Paris: OECD Publishing.

OECD (2005) *Attracting, Developing and Retaining Effective Teachers – Final Report: teachers matter,* Paris: OECD Publishing.

Pacini-Ketchabaw, V. and Pence, A. (2011) 'The postmodern curriculum: making space for historically and politically situated understandings', *Australasian Journal of Early Childhood*, 36(1): 4–8.

Papert, S. (1996) *The Connected Family: bridging the digital generation gap*. Atlanta: Longstreet Press.

Papert, S. (2002) 'Hard fun', *Bangor Daily News*. Online: www.papert.org/articles/HardFun.html (accessed 18 March, 2012).

Patel Stevens, L. (2011) 'Literacy, capital, and education: a view from immigrant youth', *Theory Into Practice*, 50(2): 133–140.

Perry, L. B. (2008) 'Using PISA to examine educational inequality', *Orbis Scholae*, 2(2): 77–86.

Power, M. (1997) *The Audit Society: rituals of verification*. Oxford: Oxford University Press.

Queensland School Reform Longitudinal Study (QSRLS) (2001) submitted to Education Queensland by the School of Education, University of Queensland, State of Queensland (Department of Education), Brisbane.

Ravitch, D. (2010) *The Death and Life of the Great American School System: how testing and choice are undermining education*. Philadelphia, PA: Basic Books.

Reder, S. (2000) *Literacy proficiency and lifelong learning*, Portland, OR: Portland State University. Online: www2.ed.gov/pubs/HowAdultsLearn/Reder.pdf (accessed 13 November, 2011).

Reynolds, D., Treharne, D. and Tripp, H. (2003) 'ICT – the hopes and reality', *British Journal of Educational Technology*, 34(2): 151–167.

Rinaldi, C. (2006) *In dialogue with Reggio Emilia: listening, researching and learning*. New York: Routledge.

Rivzi, F. and Lingard, B. (2010) *Globalizing Education Policy*. Milton Park: Routledge.

Robinson, K. (2006) 'Do schools kill creativity?' Online: http:www.ted.com/ken_robinson_says_schools_kill_creativity.html (accessed 24 September 2012).

Robinson, K. (2001) *Out of Our Minds: learning to be creative*. Oxford: Capstone.

Rogers, B. (2006) *Behaviour Management: a whole school approach*. London: Sage.

Rowan, B., Camburn, E. and Correnti, R. (2004) 'Using teacher logs to measure the enacted curriculum: a study of literacy teaching in third grade classrooms', *The Elementary School Journal*, 105(1): 75–102.

Rowe, K. (2003) 'The importance of teacher quality as a key determinant of students' experience and outcomes of schooling', Proceedings of Australian Council for Educational Research (ACER) Conference, *Building Teacher Quality*: 15–23.

Safran, L. (2001) 'Creativity as 'mindful' learning: a case from learner-led home-based education', in A. Craft, B. Jeffrey and M. Leibling (eds), *Creativity in Education*, London: Continuum.

Sahlberg, P. (2011) *Finnish Lessons: what can the world learn from educational change in Finland?* New York: Teachers' College Press.

Sarra, C. (2003) 'Young and black and deadly: strategies for improving outcomes for Indigenous students', Paper No. 5 Quality Teaching Series, *Practitioner Perspectives*. ACT: Australian College of Educators.

Sawyer, W. (2006) 'Just add "progressivism" and stir: how we cook up literacy crises in Australia', in B. Doecke, M. Howie and W. Sawyer (eds), *Only Connect: English teaching, schooling and community*. Kent Town, SA: AATE/Wakefield Press.

Sawyer, W., Brock, P. and Baxter, D. (2007) *Exceptional Outcomes in English Education: findings from AESOP*. Teneriffe: Post Pressed.

Schon, D. A. (1983) *The Reflective Practitioner: how professionals think in action*. London: Temple Smith.

Selinger, M. (2009) 'ICT in education: catalyst for development', in T. Unwin (ed.), *ICT4D: Information and Communication Technology for Development*. Cambridge: Cambridge University Press.

Selwyn, N. (2011) *Schools and Schooling in the Digital Age*. London: Routledge.

Shanahan, T. and Shanahan, C. (2008) 'Teaching disciplinary literacy to adolescents: rethinking content-area literacy', *Harvard Educational Review*, 78: 40–59.

Siraj-Blatchford, I. (2009) 'Quality teaching in the early years', in A. Anning, J. Cullen and M. Fleer (eds), *Early Childhood Education: society and culture*, 2nd edn. London: Sage.

Siraj-Blatchford, I. and Sylva, K. (2004) 'Researching pedagogy in English preschools', *British Educational Research Journal*, 30(5): 713–730.

Smith, J. J., Yendol-Hoppey, D. and Milam, R. S. (2009) 'Reflectivity within the teacher research cycle: promoting prospective teachers' progress toward an inquiry stance', in E. G. Pultorak (ed.), *The Purposes, Practices, and Professionalism of Teacher Reflectivity: insights for twenty-first-century teachers and students*. Lanham, MD: Rowan and Littlefield.

Snow, C. E. and Biancarosa, G. (2003) *Adolescent Literacy and the Achievement Gap: what do we know and where do we go from here?* New York: Carnegie Corporation of New York.

Spencer, M. M. (1988) *How Texts Teach What Readers Learn*. South Woodchester, Glos.: The Thimble Press.

Thomas, D. and Brown, J. S. (2011) 'Cultivating the imagination: building learning environments for innovation', *Teachers College Record*. Online: www.tcrecord.org ID Number: 16341, (accessed 2 May, 2011).

Thomson, J. (2004) 'Post-Dartmouth developments in English teaching in Australia', in W. Sawyer and E. Gold (eds), *Reviewing English in the 21st Century*. Putney: Phoenix Education.

Thomson, P. (2002) *Schooling the Rustbelt Kids: making a difference in changing times*. Crows Nest, NSW: Allen and Unwin.

Thomson, S., Bortoli, L. D., Nicholas, M., Hillman, K. and Buckley, S. (2009) *PISA in Brief, Highlights from the full Australian Report: challenges for Australian education: results from PISA 2009*, Melbourne: ACER.

Tosolt, B. (2009) 'Middle school students' perceptions of caring teacher behaviours: differences by minority status', *The Journal of Negro Education*, 78(4): 405–416.

United Kingdom Literacy Association (UKLA) (2012) *United Kingdom Literacy Association Mission Statement*. Online: www.ukla.org/about/mission_statement/ (accessed 17 February, 2012).

UNESCO (2009) 'United Nations literacy decade: international strategic framework for action', *Paris, UNESCO*. Online: www.unesco.org/en/literacy (accessed 13 November, 2011).

van Dijk, J. (2005) *The Deepening Divide: inequality in the information society*. London: Sage.

Vinson, T. (2007) *Dropping off the Edge: the distribution of disadvantage in Australia*. Richmond, Vic and Curtin, ACT: Jesuit Social Services and Catholic Social Services.

Vygotsky, L. (1978) *Mind in Society: the development of higher psychological processes*. Cambridge, MA: Harvard University Press.

Vygotsky, L. S. and Kozulin, A. (1986) *Thought and Language*. Cambridge, MA: MIT Press.

Warschauer, M. and Matuchniak, T. (2010) 'New technology and digital worlds: analyzing evidence of equity in access, use, and outcomes'. *Review of Research in Education*, 34: 179–225.

Warschauer, M. and Matuchniak, T. (2004) *Community Adversity and Resilience*. Online: http://acl.arts.usyd.edu.au/jss/ (accessed 1 May, 2011).

The Washington Times (2011a) *ENLOW: educational freedom, not jail for Ohio parents*. Online: www.washingtontimes.com/news/2011/feb/2/the-new-rosa-parks/ (accessed 26 May, 2011).

The Washington Times (2011b) *Simmons: school vouchers the right option*. Online: http://www.washingtontimes.com/news/2011/jan/27/simmons-school-vouchers-the-right-option (accessed 24 March, 2011).

The Washington Times (2011c) *Topic: Kelley Williams-Bolar*. Online: www.washingtontimes.com/topics/kelley-williams-bolar/ (accessed 24 March, 2011).

Webb, R., Vulliamy, G., Hamalainen, S., Sarja, A., Kimonen, E. and Nevalainen, R. (2004) 'A comparative analysis of primary teacher professionalism in England and Finland', *Comparative Education*, 40(1): 83–107.

Wenger, E. (1998). *Communities of Practice: learning, meaning and identity*. Cambridge: Cambridge University Press.

Wilkinson, R. G. and Pickett, K. (2009) *The Spirit Level: why more equal societies almost always do better*. London: Allen Lane.

Willis, P. (1977) *Learning to Labour*. Farnborough: Saxon House.

Wilson, J. and Murdoch, K. (2008) *Learning for Themselves*. Carlton South: Curriculum Corporation.

Wood, D., Bruner, J. and Ross, G. (1976) 'The role of tutoring in problem solving', *Journal of Child Psychology and Psychiatry*, 17: 89–100.

Yukawa, J. (2012) *Communities of Practice*. Online: www.jyukawa.com/main/cop (accessed 3 March, 2012).

Zammit, K. (2010) 'New learning environments framework: integrating multiliteracies into the curriculum, *Pedagogies: an international journal*, 5(4): 325–337.

Zammit, K., Sinclair, C., Cole, B., Singh, M., Costley, D., Brown a'Court, L. and Rushton, K. (2007) *Teaching and Leading for Quality Australian Schools: a review and synthesis of research-based knowledge*. Canberra: Teaching Australia.

Index